-88

JOHNNY CARSON

ALSO BY RONALD L. SMITH

Cosby
Bedside Book of Celebrity Quizzes
Let Peas Be With You
The Stars of Stand-Up Comedy
Comedy On Record

JOHNNY CARSON

An Unauthorized Biography

Ronald L. Smith

ST. MARTIN'S PRESS
New York

1-88   BT   2200

Photo acknowledgments: Some visuals in this book were provided by the Anthony Stark Collection, Lynn Goldsmith, Inc., Photo Trends, NBC, ABC, Pictorial Parade.

Design by Jaya Dayal

Library of Congress Cataloging in Publication Data

Smith, Ronald L., 1952–
    Johnny Carson.
    1. Carson, Johnny, 1925–   . 2. Tonight show
(Television program) 3. Television personalities—
United States—Biography. I. Title.
PN1992.4.C28S45   1987   791.45′092′4 [B] 67-16262
ISBN 0-312-01051-6

First Edition

10 9 8 7 6 5 4 3 2 1

LIST OF ILLUSTRATIONS

Following page 132

JOHNNY CARSON

PROLOGUE

"Where's Johnny?"

Nobody knew what happened. It was Monday afternoon, the last day of June 1986. Johnny Carson, one of the most famous men in America, was gone. Nobody at his office knew where he was. Even his closest friends didn't know.

But like something out of "The Twilight Zone," Johnny Carson had taken this warm day in June to travel back in time more than fifty years.

He landed, quietly and unannounced, in a place he had known in his boyhood. His first real home on Cherry Street in the town of Avoca, Iowa.

He knocked on the door of what was once his house, his along with his parents, his brother Dick, and his sister Catherine.

Johnny waited. He saw someone inside the house look cautiously through the curtained front windows.

A few moments passed before a man swung open the door.

"Hello," Johnny said, a tentative, shy smile on his face. "My name is Johnny Carson. I used to live here."

He paused.

"Can I come in?"

The owner, a surprised English teacher named Morris Berndt, nodded and brought Johnny in. Johnny's lady friend, a blonde model named Alexis Maas, was with him.

Johnny wanted to see his childhood home—and show it to Alex.

"There wasn't this jokin' around that you'd expect," Berndt says. "This was a pretty serious event. You could tell just by looking at him."

Johnny remembered his old room. He recognized his parents' room right next door. He described the way he'd remembered the old house. He nodded his head wistfully, realizing that the kitchen didn't look much different than it had fifty years ago. The arrangement of the rooms was virtually the same as before.

It was a private time for Johnny. The current owner of the house "faded into the background. I let him alone. Later, he did ask a few questions, and I mentioned a couple of things. In his bedroom there used to be some French doors. When I told him, he stopped for a moment. Then he said, 'Oh, yeah, I remember that now.'"

As much as Johnny was reliving the past, he was sharing it with Alex Maas. "She was interested," Berndt recalls. "She asked me a couple of questions about our family and all, and she did say, 'Gosh, this is a big place,' which seemed kind of strange to me. It is a big, old house, but why anybody'd be coming from that environment and be impressed by this place kind've dumbfounded me a little. Yeah, she was really nice about the whole thing and really interested in what he was sayin'. She took quite a few pictures of the neighborhood and the house when he went outside."

The sense of déjà vu for Johnny Carson intensified when he went outside. There was a swing in the yard.

"You could tell it really struck him. Our swing was right there in the same spot that they had theirs."

The place was still the quiet, warm home it always was. Johnny looked down the street. As Berndt says, "You walk five or six blocks and you're pretty much out in the country."

As the two men stood on the porch, Johnny said, "Boy, I spent a lot of time under that porch."

"On the porch?"

"No, no, I was underneath it, crawling around there, playing in the dirt and all."

This didn't really surprise the house's latest owner.

"Our kids like to crawl under there too. It's just someplace you can go and play and not be seen."

Whatever Johnny wanted to find in this, the first house he remembered, he seemed to find it.

For a few moments, he was really back home. But now, he wasn't little Johnny anymore. Now he was Johnny Carson again. The king of nighttime television, one of America's most famous, most wealthy stars.

People were coming slowly toward the old house. Word had spread fast that Johnny Carson had come to town. The townspeople seemed to wait until Johnny and Mr. Berndt had finished talking before coming over for autographs.

"We live on a corner, and there were I suppose a dozen neighbors or so halfway on the other block, and they waited . . . and when it looked like he was pretty much done lookin' around, they then came over to talk to him. That was kinda nice."

Johnny politely signed autographs and talked with the current residents of Avoca, folks with names like Willie Olesen, Judy Rhamy, and Ellamae Hegna, with Shirley Pattee and Dr. Grulke and Rose Krohn. Jan Niemann made a special little request. After the crowd finished snapping pictures and Carson had signed everything from pieces of paper to baseballs, he drove up to the Niemann house. Jan's mother, Ruth, had just gotten out of the hospital. Johnny stopped by to ask her how she was getting along.

Judy Rhamy noticed the attractive blonde and asked Johnny if she was his wife. Johnny replied, "She's not my wife yet but might be soon."

Johnny and Alex later ate at the Embers Restaurant, and afterward people excitedly asked the waitress, Loretta Hayhurst, if he left a tip. "Yes he did. Five dollars."

Johnny paused at the grade school. As Morris Berndt recalls, "A few people came up to him, and I guess by then he was getting a little tired of it. He got back in the car and went back to Omaha. The fans and all—all he wanted to do was come home. It's unreal to think someone has to live that way."

The people of Avoca imagined what Johnny was going back to: the glittering life of a big television star.

But Johnny was going back to face the greatest challenge of his career. After nearly twenty-five years, the "King of Comedy" was being challenged by a queen of comedy—Joan Rivers. And by a younger version of himself named David Letterman. And by Dick Cavett, Jimmy Breslin, and David Brenner, too.

He was going back to the pressure of being the boss of Carson Productions and the star of "The Tonight Show." He was going back to handle his never-ending legal matters—which had recently included his third divorce, a $50-million lawsuit, and adverse publicity arising from his involvement with the John DeLorean trial.

He was going back to start a new life with a pretty blonde named Alexis.

Was he too old to remain the kind of late-night TV? Too old to have a happy marriage? Was he ready to weather more changes after nearly twenty-five years of change?

He'd come a long way from Avoca, Iowa, in the twenties. In the eighties, he returned briefly. While he was in Iowa, people wondered about the elusive, paradoxical comedian—the man who is so shy and yet so public, so humorous and yet so serious, so easy going and yet so complex.

As one of his three ex-wives said, here is a man who has been on television for decades—"and yet nobody knows what he's really like."

Going back to Avoca is really the place to start.

THE EARLY YEARS

Heeeeere's young Johnny, born in Corning, Iowa, and raised in Avoca. Special guests include: Johnny's first girl friend.

They were still buzzing after Johnny left Avoca in the summer of 1986. Townsfolk were so stunned they weren't sure it was all for real. The editor of the *Journal-Herald* in Avoca, Donald Nielson, shakes his head. "It took me three days to check around and make sure the story was real. At first I thought it was some kind of Johnny Carson imitator. Carson Productions wouldn't confirm it. They didn't know he was here, either. He just took a company Lear jet and came out without telling anybody."

When it was confirmed, Nielson ran two front-page headlines: "Heeerre's Johnny . . . Right Here in Avoca." And underneath, "Carson Company Confirms Carson Was Really Here!"

There wasn't quite as much fanfare when Johnny's father, Homer Carson, first came to Avoca. The *Journal-Herald* did run the following item in 1930:

O.A. Vendeventer, manager of the Iowa–Nebraska
Electric Light and Power Co. here since 1919, will be
transferred to Lincoln, Nebraska. He will be replaced
by H. L. (Kit) Carson, and the Carson family will move
to Avoca, Oct. 1.

When Alex Haley, the author of *Roots*, appeared on "The
Tonight Show" in the sixties, he gave Johnny one of his greatest
thrills in show business. Haley, with the help of the Institute of
Family Research in Salt Lake City, produced a detailed study of
the Carson family's origins.

On his father's side, Johnny's family was traced back to
Thomas Kellogg, born around 1521 in Debdon, England. A century later, Daniel and Bridget Kellogg sailed to America.

On his mother's side, there was Captain James Cook, who
served in the Revolutionary War. His biggest battle was in private: he got into a scuffle with another man who sliced off a piece
of his ear. Enraged, Cook grabbed the man by the head and bit
off a bigger piece.

The family tree twisted through the States, branching out from
the Northeast to the Midwest, where, in the 1860s, Emiline Kellogg married Marshall Carson, Johnny's great-grandfather. The
Kelloggs and the Carsons were farmers. No one has been able to
dig up any evidence of a relation between Johnny and the famous
gunslinging cowboy Kit Carson.

Relatives are at a loss to explain the sudden emergence of
Johnny Carson, the entertainer. There were few members of the
family with any talent. A distant relative, Iowa family member
Samuel Hardy, played the violin. Johnny's father, Homer, was a
string player—in his own way. As Johnny says, he was "a line-
man, a guy who climbed up and down telephone poles" stringing
wire.

John William Carson was born in Corning, Iowa, on October
23, 1925. The family followed Homer, who traveled pretty much
wherever the phone lines took him. Johnny recalls living in towns
like Shenandoah, Clarendon, and Red Oak. The first five years of
Johnny's life were not stable, in the sense that the family was

always on the move, but most people remember Johnny's parents as a very stable, down-to-earth couple.

When the Carsons reached Avoca in 1930, the family was complete: thirty-one-year-old Homer, his wife, Ruth Hook Carson, and three kids: Catherine, Johnny, and Dick.

When Johnny came back from his nostalgic trip to Avoca in 1986, he showed TV viewers a picture of himself, at age seven, fishing with another boy on the banks of the East Nishnabotna River.

The boy in the picture with Johnny, Marion Weinmann, still lives in Avoca today.

He's more than willing to talk about Johnny, but he smiles and admits, "Well, it was a long time ago."

"He was younger than I was. I lived right across the street from him. He came to Avoca around 1930, and I would say I knew him four or five years. His dad worked for the same company my dad did. He was the manager here of the Iowa–Nebraska Light and power. My dad was the accountant."

He remembers Homer Carson as a "very, very nice man." He remembers the town as being "the same as it is now . . . it's just a charming little town. About fifteen hundred people."

Even after more than fifty years, Marion also can recall some of the special pleasures of Avoca living that made such a deep impression on young Johnny.

"We had a big swimming pool at that time here. Of course it's gone now. That was one thing Johnny wanted to go see but it isn't here anymore. It was the second largest pool in Iowa at that time. It had a sand bottom and of course the sides were concrete. They opened it fairly early in the morning and it was open till after dark. I remember I used to go swimming in the morning, go home and eat dinner, go back in the afternoon, go home and eat supper, and come back in the evening."

Marion recalls that he and Johnny had to walk about a mile to get to the pool—and that it seemed like more than a mile to swim it: "It was so big they took a third of it, put a wall in and put in two tennis courts. So it was a good-sized pool."

When the boys weren't swimming, they were fishing. "I don't

believe we caught many fish," Marion recalls with a chuckle,
"but oh, it was a big deal, we thought we were really something,
going fishing. Probably just something my dad thought of to get us
off his back."

The recollections of warm summers fishing and swimming
sound so idyllic that one wonders if the cool, loner image of
Johnny Carson is a myth. A few questions to his childhood friend
seem to confirm this:

"Johnny's often portrayed as a loner, but it doesn't sound like
he was a loner in Avoca. Was he?"

"No, I wouldn't say he was a loner. I wouldn't say he was a
loner in that sense of the word. I would say he wanted to be left
alone. He don't want to be alone himself; he liked to have people
around him."

"So when he moved in he didn't have trouble making friends."

"No. Uh-uh."

"Was Johnny a mischief maker?"

"Oh, he wasn't any worse than any other kid." He laughs.

"You'd describe him as just an average kid?"

"Yep."

"No different than the other kids in school?"

"Not at all. You know how little kids'll tag around with older
ones? Well that's about the way it was. Usually they tag along and
you don't pay any attention to 'em."

Researchers hunting for a sociological reason for Johnny's cold
reputation wonder if his childhood was a bleak one. It was the
Depression. The farm belt was hit hard. Marion Weinmann remembers that times were tough, but it was less so for his family
and Johnny's. Their parents were on salary and working for the
power company; they didn't work on a farm as many in the area
did.

There's no doubt that Johnny saw some of the bleakness, as
Marion did: "You know, corn was ten cents a bushel out here,
and a lot of the farmers had coal-burning stoves and they couldn't
afford to buy the coal, so they burned the corn. I don't know
whether you know that corn will burn, but it will. Burns hot, too.
And, oh, we didn't eat like we eat now. I can remember our

evening meal—we'd have crackers and milk. But we got along all right. Mr. Carson made more money than my dad did, but he had a bigger family, too."

A staffer on "Who Do You Trust?" remembered meeting Johnny's parents in New York once. Asked to describe them, she paused and said, "The American Gothic painting."

Most people agree Mr. and Mrs. Carson were not the warmest people in the world. Nice, but not that outgoing. Marion Weinmann remembers both of them as strict disciplinarians. "Very much so. They were both strict . . . just like parents should be. Mr. Carson wasn't any worse than my dad was."

Johnny can still recall his father's stock phrases for growing up right. "My father used to say, 'Keep your nose clean. Be a good boy.'"

Another neighbor, Mrs. Turner, had a vivid memory of her card-playing partner Mrs. Carson being late every now and then: "She would be late and she'd say she had to whip Johnny, he was in some mischief or other."

Johnny could get into mischief just going to school. As Weinmann remembers, "We were only two blocks from school, if you didn't cut through people's yards. But John would take off across the alley, cutting through the yards. Then it was only a block away."

Johnny even had a "sweetheart" back in Avoca. Her name was Peggy Leach. She has since married English professor Kenneth Eble, but Peggy remembers Johnny, and recalls her surprise when Johnny used to refer to her on TV as his very first girl friend.

"This was something Johnny used on the show for a long time. It goes way back to Skitch Henderson's time. They were talking about their first girl friends and Johnny mentioned my name."

Johnny's nostalgic remembrances of Peggy continued, and each time her name was mentioned, folks would tell her about it. This went on for more than a decade. Finally in 1982 Peggy decided to write to her old boyfriend.

"I wrote him a note, primarily thanking him for what he had done for the town of Avoca. It was wonderful, you know. He always brought Avoca up." She happened to mention that she had been in ill-health for a while, but was becoming a bit stronger.

Johnny did receive the letter from his first girl friend. Learning of her health problems, "he stopped talking about me on the air, and I think that was very considerate of him . . . somebody from his office wrote me a letter back and said he had read the letter, and he certainly extended his best wishes for my health, and hoped that I continued to enjoy 'The Tonight Show.' And that's been the extent of the contact."

Mrs. Eble still treasures a videotape, circa 1966, of a "Tonight Show" featuring guest Barbara Walters. Walters, who had interviewed Professor Eble just the day before, shocked Johnny with a question: "What was your most embarrassing moment . . . was it when you took a young girl to the movies in Avoca, Iowa?"

Johnny smiled in surprise and nostalgia. It was an embarrassing story, this first date with his very first girl friend. Peggy recalls the moment:

"We were in the third grade. It was not too long before he moved away. His mother called my mother and asked if it would be all right if we went to the movies together if Catherine went along. Anyhow, he came, and we went down . . ."

Johnny must have looked cute, arm-in-arm with his girl friend. But on the way to the local movie theater, some of his classmates saw him. "They made fun of him for being with a girl and he ran home!"

It was a long time ago. There are a number of versions of the story. Peggy herself can't remember for sure if she and Johnny ever did get to see the movie. "I have a very vivid recollection of coming downstairs and seeing him in our little entry hallway, waiting. I do remember that. And I have a vivid picture in my mind of the going-away party that our class at school gave him. He had on a black turtleneck sweater and, I believe, knickers. He was a real nice-looking kid."

She laughs lightly. "In fact a lot of young girls had a crush on him. We were all very sad when he moved out of town, even though we were only in third grade."

Peggy doesn't make much of the first date, since she recalls it as hardly even "puppy love." But Johnny still remembers Peggy as his first girl friend. Even if, in his paradoxical way, he talked about her nostalgically on TV but avoided any actual contact.

Does Peggy watch "The Tonight Show" these days? And does the Johnny she sees still remind her of little Johnny in Avoca, Iowa?

"Oh yes. Ohhhh yes, the expression, eyes, the shape of his face, the general demeanor. Well, you'll find out when you get older! People don't change that much." She laughs. "They do, but there's a great similarity in appearance between then and now. Of course, Johnny had very black hair at that time."

Was he a funny kid?

"I think that's why everybody liked him. He must have been an attention-getting young boy. . . . He was good looking, and he must've been forward to call attention to himself, otherwise all of us wouldn't have remembered him so well."

Johnny has admitted that he was a bit of a comic even back in third grade—he once got up to do his impression of Popeye the Sailor.

"We didn't buy a TV really quick, but when we did I watched him on 'Who Do You Trust?' I watched the 'Tonight' show [called "Tonight!"] when Steve Allen was on it, and then Jack Paar [called "The Jack Paar Tonight Show"]. With the kids and all, by this time everything was settled down and this was my time alone. But I thought this was a terrible habit because it was making me go to bed too late. I was extremely glad to hear that Jack Paar was gonna quit. I said this is a good opportunity to break the 'Tonight Show' habit.

"But then they chose Carson!" She laughs. "I had to keep watching it. I don't like to be up that late, but I'd stick with it for the whole hour."

Just seeing Johnny sometimes brings back memories.

Peggy's dad was the catcher on the local softball team. They called it the "Kittenball League." The pitcher on the team was Homer Carson.

"During the Depression in the early thirties Saturday night softball with the men was a way to keep people entertained and

occupied and their minds off their troubles. I do remember going
down there and watching the game. And I may be mistaken but I
really believe that the impetus was for people to survive that hor-
rible period on the farm. This was a farm town and it was pretty
bad. My dad was the veterinarian and he never got paid for about
a third of the work he did for ten years because of the Depression.
We were occasionally paid in produce. . . . I learned to like
sweetbreads, brains, and heart because this is what we got as
payment.

"Tramps would come to town from the nearby railroad tracks
begging for a meal in exchange for a day's chores. They were
harmless, though. It wasn't the kind of place where people locked
their doors.

"The town is really on an island. You don't think about it.
There's the Nishnabotna River. It divides a couple of miles north
of town and goes around on either side, then joins again maybe a
mile south of town. Both rivers are within easy walking distance
of Johnny's old home. The one east of town is not more than eight
or ten city blocks away. And the other one on the west side isn't
much further."

Peggy recalled that aside from the rivers and the giant swimming pool, there were other places around town that all the kids
enjoyed. There was the movie house—admission was only a
dime. Johnny also hiked across the fields. "The lovely, beautiful
rolling green farmland," as Peggy recalls. There was the cemetery
at the north end of town and there was territory around there to
explore. The county fair was always held in Avoca, and Johnny
could have come there to learn firsthand whether pigs were
smarter than horses, as he insists.

They tell the tale in Avoca that when Johnny was seven, he
went to the Avoca County Fair, up to some mischief. A farmer
was giving a demonstration on how to milk a cow when the cow
yelped, "Wow! You've got cold hands!"

According to Johnny, the ventriloquism incident "never happened." But when asked to recall some other childhood anecdote
he simply said, "I don't remember any."

The people his age who remember Avoca don't doubt that

whatever Johnny was seeking when he came back he found. The cornfields and the river haven't changed. Neither has the feeling of home. "He must have felt right at home," Marion Weinmann says.

Morris Berndt, occupying Carson's old home, agrees. "Maybe that's one thing about growing up in a small town in this area. It's still there. You grow up in the city, you go back to your old neighborhood and it might be gone. The buildings all torn down. The people changed."

The old "Fred Holtz Bridge" no longer stretches across the East Nishnabotna River, and the fabled swimming pool is gone, but those are really the only changes Johnny could have missed. They don't have the same wooden desks with the inkwells and bottles of ink, and Mrs. Pickerell isn't teaching there, but even the old schoolhouse where the third and fourth grades were combined remains. When Johnny saw it, he may have remembered the old fire-escape chutes. They were made of metal and bolted together. It was fun to slide down them during a fire drill.

And there's the family house. It holds its memories quietly for Johnny alone, but it continues to hold a fascination for the tourists who come in off Interstate I-80. Morris Berndt sometimes watches as they "stand across the street and take all sorts of pictures."

At first, when Johnny and his girl friend arrived, Berndt thought they might just be tourists, too.

"It was funny," the junior high school English teacher recalls, "I just glanced out the window when the doorbell rang. And here was this really nice-looking girl, and this gray-haired guy. And I almost didn't answer the door. I thought perhaps the Jehovah's Witnesses were out there. Then I figured it might be a salesman trying to train this young girl or something. I thought well, I better at least go answer the bell because they might be able to see me. And lucky for me I did. But I didn't really zero in on the old guy until I opened the door. The girl was the one who caught your immediate attention.

"But you couldn't ask for a nicer man. The guy you see on TV and the one who was in the house here, you know they're the

same one. He was just as nice as could be, it was really enjoyable
. . . none of this silliness that's made him rich. Just your average
fella. When you open the door, there he is, there's no doubt. He
almost acted like he had to introduce himself, like maybe I
wouldn't know who he was. He was just as nice as could be when
he was talking to people, too. Like he belonged here. Everybody
who talked to him said he was just as common as could be.
Which around here I guess is about the biggest compliment you're
gonna get. . . ."

2 THE EARLY YEARS

Johnny is seen in a new location: Norfolk, Nebraska. Featuring the debut of "The Great Carsoni," high school stunts, and an "on location" visit to California.

Johnny Carson, city sophisticate!

From the small town of Avoca, Johnny and his family moved to Norfolk, Nebraska. Population 10,000.

It was a thrill the very first time Johnny hit town.

"I will never forget looking down on Main Street from a fourth-floor hotel window there, thinking how high up I was and marveling at so much traffic down in the street."

The Carsons moved into a house at 306 South 13th Street.

The third-grader from Avoca may have been a little inhibited by the big town and being the new kid, but there were still some old-fashioned good times to be had.

A 1966 *TV Guide* piece waxed nostalgic about what Johnny's childhood had to be like: "The small town of Norfolk, Nebraska, where Carson spent his Huckleberry years, fulfills every specification for an ideal adolescence. Nearby flows the Elkhorn River, delightfully shivering-cold for a naked boy even in midsummer, and alive with fish. The horizon lies many miles from every view; the fertile earth yields corn of impossible height; and beef cattle are sleek and fat. Everywhere is abundance and prosperity."

Johnny's mother added to this painting of tranquillity, describing how she would make peanut butter and jelly sandwiches, enough to "pave a highway" for the adventuresome boy who loved to go out all day hiking and fishing.

Nobody was waxing nostalgic about the inside of the Carson house. That same year, 1966, Dick Carson told *Look* magazine about the Carson family lifestyle: "Put it this way—we're not Italian. Nobody in our family ever says what they really think or feel to anyone else." Friends from the Norfolk era felt that Mr. and Mrs. Carson were just too rigid. Mr. Carson seemed especially paradoxical. He had a well-paying job with the power company, and yet he was always yelling at the family to turn the lights off.

Big changes were happening all at once for Johnny. He was entering a new town, and puberty, at the same time. He was looking for new ways to be noticed, by the strangers in Norfolk and by his own parents.

Johnny was given a BB gun and he used to practice—all around the house. One Christmas he managed to shoot off every decoration on the Christmas tree. Neighbors complained about stray BB shots and it was up to Mrs. Carson to lay on the discipline.

Mrs. Carson might have really given Johnny a tanning if she'd found out about something else he was up to. Johnny and the boys would secretly go to a place they called Black Bridge. It was a railroad trestle spanning the Elkhorn River. They would climb the bridge and daringly swing from one support beam to another with the water rushing below, and the trains chugging overhead.

The family still went on the move—but now for recreation. Sometimes they would spend the summer visiting the cool lake regions of Minnesota. In 1937, the Carson clan trekked out to California. Twelve-year-old Johnny stood in awe as he and the other tourists gaped at the Bel Air mansions of the movie stars. One of the houses belonged to Mervyn LeRoy, who had directed films like *Little Caesar, Gold Diggers of 1933* and, the year before, *Anthony Adverse*.

It was almost beyond a skinny little Nebraska boy's imagination that one day that very mansion would be his.

Johnny's attention was slowly being drawn to show business. From playing a bumblebee in a grade school show to the small part of the boy who bought the turkey for Scrooge in *A Christmas Carol*, Johnny was drawn toward bigger roles in school plays.

He recalled for *Rolling Stone* that he realized in "fifth or sixth grade" that he could "get attention by being different, by getting up in front of an audience or even a group of kids and calling the attention to myself by what I did, or said or how I acted. And I said, 'Hey, I like the feeling.' I think I did that because it was a device to get attention. And to get that reaction . . . is a high that I don't think you can get from drugs . . . from anything else . . . and you walk off and you're just, everything is such a high, and it's a great feeling, and that's why many performers have very big highs and very big lows. Most of them that I know. I know I do. . . ."

At thirteen, he saw an ad for *Hoffman's Book of Magic*. Now he was really in show business. And instead of being a character on stage among other characters, he was the solo star!

Johnny practiced his magic incessantly. It became his driving obsession. It took a tremendous amount of concentration and discipline to stay with his hobby and spend hours slipping a coin over his knuckles or perfecting a sleight-of-hand stunt, but he did it. Whenever he learned a new, impressive trick he ran to his mother to show off.

He told writer Eleanor Harris: "I'd follow Mother all over the house asking her to pick a card." His mother, recalling his look-at-me card antics, thought he was pesty. "He was always at your elbow with a trick."

Actually, he was worse than that. Once Johnny came rushing in demanding that his mother "Pick a card!"—and she was in the bathroom at the time.

When his mom and the other ladies gathered for their bridge games, Johnny would come in and do his little magic act. "They

thought I was great. And I felt great, making my mother so proud,
you know?"

At fourteen, Johnny went pro. He earned three dollars for a
performance at the local Rotary Club. He called himself "The
Great Carsoni" and wore a cape his mother sewed for him.

Johnny did get the attention he craved, but he wanted more. "I
sent to Chicago and New York for magic equipment and in a
year's time when I was fourteen, I was pulling rabbits out of
hats. . . . I even threw in some comedy lines."

Johnny's mom made him a velvet drape to place over his magic
stand, with the words "The Great Carsoni" embroidered in gold.
Carson still has all his "Carsoni" equipment, lovingly preserved.

Amateur psychologists can make much of Johnny's interest in
magic. A magician controls the audience, is superior to the audience, is the center of attention. A magician creates illusions
and enjoys the fantasy—but is realistic, even cynical in his
knowledge of the tricks.

"I started out doing straight tricks, to fool people," Johnny has
admitted. But he added that before long, he practiced magic that
would "entertain rather than fool somebody."

The girls loved Johnny: he was a star in school. None of the other
boys were earning money as entertainers. While some boys
fumbled asking a girl for a date, Johnny did suave card tricks and
got immediate attention. And how many guys had a neat shirt that
was jet-black with a portrait of a white rabbit on it?

The fourteen-year-old was a small sensation. Magician Tom
Prideaux recalls: "Carson has told me that when he was fourteen
he was asked by the Chamber of Commerce of Norfolk to barn-
storm the state in a truck, along with other kid performers, and do
a magic act . . . he was always practicing sleight-of-hand tricks
with cards and coins."

Johnny remembers those days well: "Usually I'd follow something like a demonstration of the fire department's new aerial ladder. A tough act to follow, incidentally."

Johnny went anywhere for a show. Every Christmas he was the
live entertainment for the dozen employees of the Wahoo Hatchery.

Crowds never grew tired of The Great Carsoni, but the Carson
family sometimes did. Mrs. Carson and John's sister, Catherine
(sometimes called by the nickname "Cam"), were going on a three-day
trip and when they went to say good-bye to Johnny, he was standing in
front of the mirror practicing tricks. They called out to him, and
impatiently he answered, "Yeah . . . good-bye." When they came
home, Johnny was standing right where they'd left him. At the mirror.

Johnny reinvested the money he was making into more and more
props. He bought the standard Chinese linking rings, the amazing
dancing cane, and mastered the multiplying billiard ball trick.

Johnny's mom was hoping that the boy would be more inclined
to entertain folks with piano playing. "I remember my folks sending me [to study piano] and it was twenty-five cents a lesson. And
I got through the John L. Williams third book and that was as far
as I could get."

It didn't help that occasionally Johnny pocketed the quarter he
was supposed to give his teacher, Cora Beals, and instead banked
it for magic tricks.

It took a tremendous amount of time and patience to perfect
each new trick. Sometimes, it was even life or death. Johnny
smiled as he told comedian Steve Martin about the time he was
doing a rabbit trick. He related that it looked pretty simple in the
instructions. There's a trick pan. Put the rabbit in, do the dis-
tracting passes and verbal patter and then, voilà, pull the rabbit
out of the seemingly empty pan.

"I put in the lid about a half hour before the show. I'm out
there doing some local Chamber of Commerce show . . . and the
bunny . . . is dead!

"I'm talkin' dead! And I didn't know what to do, but I had to go
on with it. So I grabbed it by the back of the neck and pulled it
out of the pan . . . the thing was even cold."

At Norfolk High School, Johnny flirted with the title of "class
clown." He had his own column in the school paper called "Carson's Corn." He also continued to appear in school plays. He said
he loved "getting up and putting on a costume or make-up, even
in high school, to be in a play where you're actually putting
make-up on your face . . . it made you different. . . . You were

different from other people. You were up on stage and they were
sitting down here, and there's a certain, I don't know if you want
to call it . . . power, but it makes you different."

He told *Rolling Stone:* "I suppose it's the manipulation. I suppose it's the sense of power, the center of attention and the me-
ism. And performers have to have that. . . . That's why a lot of
performers sometimes are good in front of an audience and not
particularly good in a one-to-one relationship."

Though athletic, Johnny had a tough time with team sports. Tack-
led during a football tryout, the skinny 125-pounder was literally
knocked unconscious. So he worked on the school newspaper instead.
In his spare time, he was an usher at the Granada Theatre, worked as
a soda jerk, and was even a laborer. He told Karen Jackovich at the
time that "for twenty-five cents an hour, I hauled dirt in a dump truck"
to help build the runway for the Norfolk airfield.

Of his amateur shows, he recalled to Norfolk graduates years
later: "I was also a member of the Thespians. I joined because I
thought it meant something else. Then I found out it had to do
with acting."

Norfolk classmates don't remember his appearances in school plays
as much as his ad-libbed antics. One day the students were gathered
in the auditorium for assembly, waiting for the arrival of the principal,
Theodore Skillstad. Johnny suddenly ran onto the stage in drag,
wearing a slop mop for a wig and sporting two grapefruit breasts. As
the kids howled, Johnny did some fast dancing. He stopped, looked
off stage for a moment, and made a few more faces. With seconds
remaining before the principal hit the stage, Johnny suddenly popped
the grapefruit breasts out, hurled them into the delighted audience,
and raced away.

The principal had no idea why he was greeted with hysterical
laughter.

Another time, there was a school assembly for no reason at all.
Johnny had forged a note from the principal requesting the classes to
come. After a few minutes of confusion, The Great Carsoni came out
and performed his magic tricks for the captive audience.

Johnny never hesitated trying out a little vaudeville. Miss
Walker, his math teacher, remembers Johnny's little jokes in

class. Once, trying to get the kids interested in geometry, she drew a baseball diamond. She set up the distance from the pitcher's mound to home plate, and the distance of the bases. But Johnny interrupted her: "How can I solve the problem when I don't know what teams are playing?"

Old classmates of Johnny's seemed to recall no end of whizbangers that the budding comedian perpetrated on his teachers. There was the time Johnny was listing the parts of the body, and mentioned "the teeth and the jaw."

The teacher insisted that the teeth and the jaw were not separate parts. "They're together, you can't move them separately."

Johnny shot back, "My father can. He wears dentures."

As a student, Johnny managed decent grades, getting a B in English and algebra, but nobody was sure when the quiet, seemingly respectful young student would suddenly go wild.

Johnny, along with a scientific friend named Robert Reckert, discovered the joys of hydrogen sulfide. They created a rotten-egg bomb with the stuff, set it off, and within minutes had closed the entire school down.

Johnny was called "rascal" by quite a few teachers, but there was always an all-American side to him, too. With the war raging, and Johnny too young to enlist, the sturdy lad organized scrap-metal drives. He was an excellent organizer, and he formed groups of students to search for scrap-metal and knock on doors to ask for donations.

When he didn't get his fair share of donations for his worthy cause, young Johnny was outraged. When a farmer didn't volunteer any metal, Johnny went out under cover of darkness, hitched the man's giant hay-raking apparatus to a tractor and hauled the huge metal appliance away.

Johnny discovered that most of the girls in the fine, upstanding town were fine and upstanding. And he wasn't interested in upstanding girls as much as a few lying-down ones.

His pride and joy was a 1939 green Chrysler Royal. Now he wanted a girl without as much pride to give him far more joy. "As in all small towns," he told reporters on a visit back to Norfolk, "there are certain 'nice' girls, girls that you marry—and girls that you do not. Well, there was this girl, I'll call her Francine. And Francine, well, 'put out . . .' I finally got up enough nerve to ask her out. She said 'Yes' and you can imagine my excitement! Mount Vesuvius!

"But then I had to overcome a problem—protection. I went up to the drugstore counter and the druggist yells, 'Well, John, what can I do for you?' Luckily he then saw that I had Francine waiting in the car and he knowingly handed over the goods. I remember I had, as we used to put it, a swell time."

In the 1943 edition of the Norfolk High School yearbook, *The Milestone*, Johnny tried out his comedy writing.

> "I, John Carson, being of sound mind and body (this statement is likely to be challenged by my draft board and the high school faculty), deem it advisable to give you the lowlights of 1942 and 1943. I can visualize twenty years from now when you sit down by the radio (listening to Roosevelt) with the old 1943 *Milestone* in your trembling hands . . ."

Johnny gave "a month-by-month, drip-by-drip account of Norfolk High School activity during the year." From the fall semester, Johnny recalled: "September . . . football season opened this month and I went out to make the team. I would have, too, if they hadn't found where I hid my brass knuckles. . . . November was the month of blackouts, which the students enjoyed very much. . . . December ended with Bob Jesson waiting at his fireplace for Santa Claus and bag. Bob was interested in the bag, I believe. . . . January ended with the students drooling icicles on the way to school."

School was over. For Johnny and the rest of the guys there was a job to do that was a little tougher than college. World War II was blazing overseas with no end in sight.

The boys gathered around, autographing each other's yearbooks. One student wrote in Johnny's book, "John, if you don't get killed in the war you'll be a hell of an entertainer some day."

THE EARLY YEARS

3

Johnny marches to war. Back home, a TV debut in a drama about brucellosis and stage credits in college follies. Finally Johnny tries to "WOW" 'em on the Nebraska airwaves.

"You folks didn't boo me when I raised the flag on Iwo Jima!"

Johnny Carson's capsulized his war years with that one sentence. It's one of his most famous catchphrases, always uttered in chagrin after a bombed joke. Johnny did do some joking around while he was in the Navy, but the bombs were very real.

After graduating high school, Johnny hoped to become an air cadet but ended up in the Navy's V-12 program instead. Before facing the war, he decided to live it up a little. He hitched to California.

One of the sights he wanted to see most was a blue-eyed "cheapskate" with an enigmatic Mona Lisa grin.

"I was seventeen years old the first time I saw Jack Benny. I hitchhiked to California and went to see one of his radio show tapings at CBS. I was fresh out of high school and about to go into the service. But first, I wanted to see Hollywood—and Jack. I can never forget what a thrill it was actually being in the audience."

A close second in Carson's itinerary was a visit to the exotic Hollywood Stage Door Canteen. At the Canteen big-name stars were doing their part, entertaining the servicemen. There the blue-eyed stars with the Mona Lisa smiles were women.

Now Johnny wasn't in the Navy yet, but he figured, "Why should I be left out?" The skinny kid sauntered into a local Army-Navy store and stepped out in uniform. He got into the Canteen just like any other soldier, and made sure to get his share of the fun. By the end of the evening he was dancing with Marlene Dietrich.

He could've danced all night—except a pair of MP's grabbed him. He was arrested for impersonating a naval cadet. Bail was set at fifty dollars.

Hitching out to San Diego, the fun-loving teen met a star almost as exciting as Marlene Dietrich. Johnny was watching a special magic show performed by Orson Welles. Legend has it that Johnny volunteered to be sawed in half. But that trick requires the assistance of a carefully schooled partner. Orson sawed his partner, Rita Hayworth, in half instead. Johnny was still thrilled to pieces.

The fun ended too soon. Too quickly Johnny was in officers' training school and before he knew it was sent across the world to the explosive South Pacific.

Ensign Carson arrived to discover sailors ripped to pieces by a torpedo. The young officer had his first job: direct the retrieval of the bodies. As Johnny watched, the corpses slowly were brought up from the wreckage where they had lain for more than two weeks.

Ensign Carson was stuck aboard the USS *Pennsylvania* as it lay mired in the middle of nowhere. Finally, the ship headed home and the skinny ensign faced a job even tougher than gathering up the dead. He had to herd the living. Young Carson was put in command of a troop train. The only officer in charge of hundreds of men, Carson was supposed to supervise the sailors as they made their way from the West Coast homeward.

The trek across America was even more uncomfortable than the months in the South Pacific. Johnny and the troop train were stalled in Fargo, North Dakota, in the middle of winter. The restless men watched as a freezing storm pelted them with snow, the drifts rising higher and higher. The grizzled veterans were complaining. The younger ones were furious.

They all wanted to know what nineteen-year-old Ensign Carson was going to do about the situation.

Johnny was no fool. "Give them liberty. It's better than them giving me death!"

The overjoyed servicemen let out a whoop and lit out.

For Ensign Carson, the Stateside assignment was just the beginning. Once again he found himself shipped out, this time to Guam.

Thrown into the company of a thousand strangers, one of the "hated" officers, Johnny went to his tried and true bag of tricks to amaze friends and influence people. His skill with card tricks led to the resurrection of The Great Carsoni.

Whether Johnny was that good, or the sailors that bored, the card tricks went over well. Carson's confidence began to grow. He peppered his tricks with jokes about the officers. The enlisted men ate it up. They didn't have to wait for Bob Hope. They had someone almost as sharp right in their midst.

Johnny wasn't like the other officers. The men liked him. He was nicknamed "Kit" Carson and considered a regular guy. He was the only officer welcomed at the enlisted men's amateur shows, and with his ever bolder cracks about Navy life, he really began to hone the character he would play for most of his adult life: the good guy with the streak of devilish kid in him.

Navy service itself became painfully mundane. Ensign Carson had such exciting assignments as checking water levels and decoding documents.

He was more interested in writing down little jabs and jibes he could use to amuse the sailors. He tried to think up new tricks.

He spent hours and hours simply throwing his voice, talking to himself without moving his lips.

He then branched out from card tricks to ventriloquism, buying a sidekick dummy that he named Eddie. Johnny had a new foil to bounce wisecracks off, but really almost anyone could be a target for him—if he was a figure of authority.

The Secretary of the Navy, James Forrestal, was stationed in the South Pacific and Ensign Carson had to deliver a message to him. The Secretary eyed the young officer for a moment. He asked Johnny if he planned to make the Navy his career.

"Nope," the honest young officer told the surprised Secretary of the Navy. "I'm interested in magic. Back home I'm known as The Great Carsoni."

And within minutes Ensign Carson was making his boss smile with delight with some sleight-of-hand and that slightly mischievous Nebraska grin.

When Johnny came marching home, he attended the University of Nebraska, majoring in journalism. He quickly discovered that the joy of writing wiseguy jokes in the high school newspaper had been dissipated by the thrill of live stand-up performance in the Navy. He switched his major to radio and speech.

Johnny did fairly well in his classes, but, always enterprising, he also found work in his chosen field. He got a job at radio station KFAB, appearing on a morning serial, "Eddie Sosby and the Radio Rangers," at 7:30 in the morning. He had to get special permission—doing the show was making him late for Spanish class. He hung around at the studio studying the disc jockeys, the technicians, absorbing all the information he could. It was an added bonus that they paid him ten dollars a week.

Some of the guys recall one of Johnny's other moneymaking schemes: he rented out his fraternity's car so that students and their dates could have a convenient "necking parlor." The rates were by the hour.

Johnny knew that the most reliable way to earn extra cash was through his magic. The charming young Carsoni was getting the big bucks: sometimes twenty-five dollars a show. Now he could afford a charming young assistant. Filling the bill was one of

Johnny's classmates, Jody Wolcott. She was a local girl from North Platte, Nebraska.

They made quite a duo. They even looked a bit alike, like brother and sister. Jody had high cheekbones, crescent eyes set well apart, apple-cheeks, and a full, white-toothed smile.

Sometimes Johnny and Jody would dream about the big time. Could The Great Carsoni be famous someday? Johnny didn't really think so. He enjoyed performing magic, but he wanted something better for a career. Johnny studied chemistry and calculus and minored in science. He began to think seriously about the idea of becoming a psychiatrist.

Some may have thought he needed a psychiatrist. Among his fellow students, Carson developed the reputation for being stand-offish. He was living with three other students in his Phi Gamma Delta fraternity and they didn't see much of him. He was too busy: He was a full-time student, a part-time magician, and a paid radio performer. When he was being funny, it was on stage. He played Cleopatra in a college farce called *She Was Only a Pharaoh's Daughter But She Never Became a Mummy*.

The other kids couldn't figure out the shy, somewhat driven young man who seemed to always have a cigarette in his mouth and a distracted look in his eyes.

Years later, Johnny remarked to writer Joan Barthel: "The word that's always applied to me is 'aloof,' or 'private,' or any combination of those two. That's me. I didn't invent it. I was that way in high school, although then the word was 'conceited.' It's easy to be popular, but you also become a carrot in the meantime."

Johnny was very serious, especially about comedy. His graduate thesis was "How to Write Comedy Jokes." It was something unusual: a taped lecture by the young student spliced with clips from the radio stars he especially admired. These included three early influences: Jack Benny, Fred Allen, and Bob Hope.

"I think you steal a little from everybody—particularly when you are starting," Johnny has admitted. "You pick it up here and there, and ultimately you have your own style and people start stealing from you."

Benny was the main influence. Jack, above all else, was likable. "If an audience likes a performer," Carson later theorized,
"he can get away with anything. If they don't like you, it doesn't
make any difference how clever or witty you are. It just won't
work. . . . Jack's audience always cared."

Benny's comic style was to let the jokes bounce off him. Carson has admitted: "Basically, I, like him, am a reaction comedian. I play off of the things that are happening around me. That
is what works for me on 'The Tonight Show.' When things happen
around me, I can play off them by reaction, timing, pauses, and
looks . . ."

Bob Hope appealed to Carson's aggressive instincts. Hope was
the wiseguy. Hope could get away with almost any line and still
be the patriotic All-American boy. His tight-lipped delivery was
"no-nonsense" and he was prone to glares and asides when a joke
didn't make it. Like Hope, Johnny can tell jokes about politicians
and get away with it. Johnny is not as tight as Hope, but his
teeth-clenched, throaty delivery has become roundly imitated by
mimics like Rich Little. His glares are softer and his asides less
stridently "show biz," but the influences are still there.

As for Fred Allen, he was radio's greatest wit, the man who
was revered in his time as the master of the ad-lib. When Jack
Benny was devastated by yet another Allen ad-lib during a radio
show, Jack cracked, "You wouldn't have said that if my writers
were here!" Today, Carson is acknowledged as an excellent ad-
libber, a master at both creating spontaneous gags and picking
the spots for coolly switching and inserting a remembered
punchline.

Johnny still practices his college thesis. Today Johnny keeps
people up late at night, nets NBC millions of bucks in ads, and
acknowledges the work his writers do in providing his trademark
monologue. Back then, Johnny said:

"A good comedian can keep you home from bridge parties to
listen to his program, [and] can get you to buy his sponsors' products . . . there are many reasons for a top comedian's success and
one of the most important is in the writing. . . ."

When Johnny graduated from the University of Nebraska in

1949 he was itching to try out all the things he'd learned. He moved to Omaha and got a job on a local radio station. Its call-letters matched his spirits: WOW! The small station was an exciting training ground. For $47.50 a week he was expected to do practically everything: some acting, disk-jockeying, news broadcasting—the works.

Once again, Johnny's dual nature kept people off balance. He was a nice-looking, personable, and professional young man who just didn't seem to mix well. He seemed to be friendly but he kept people at a distance. The only person who was close to him was his magic assistant, Jody Wolcott. She had become his wife.

The radio station thought they'd hired a dedicated young college student—but perversely, once Johnny became comfortable, that wiseguy streak started coming out. The people around him were too surprised to be offended by his impish stunts.

Johnny just couldn't help it. When he had to pause between platters to read a commercial for the Friendly Savings Bank, he made them VERY friendly: "Drop in any time. At two or three in the morning . . . help yourself!"

Since the station didn't exactly have a large staff, Carson decided to become a dozen disc jockeys in one. He enjoyed utilizing bits of high school French. Once he turned the microphone over to a "special guest" announcer from France who began to read a pig feed commercial in an outrageous French accent.

Carson became a favorite "character" on radio, the same lovable rascal he'd been in high school and college.

Johnny was getting bolder and bolder, especially when the targets deserved a good tweaking. Johnny resented the fake "celebrity interviews" he had to do. To promote a star, record companies would send out a trick record. The star would tape a carefully rehearsed interview, then the interviewer's questions would be eliminated and replaced with silence. All the local DJ had to do was read the questions, in order, from the enclosed script, and make it look like the star was in town chatting with him.

This "white lie" radio interview technique is still used today. Over the years everyone from Henry Mancini, the Smothers

Brothers, Julian Lennon, and Genesis have released "open-ended" interview records for disc jockeys to use.

Back then, Johnny dutifully did these celebrity interviews. Only he rearranged the questions. One of the "guests" coming to Omaha was Patti Page.

> JOHNNY: "I understand you're hitting the bottle pretty good, Patti. When did you start?"
> PATTI: "When I was six, I used to get up at church socials and do it."

Today Carson does pretty much the same thing when he takes celebrity photos and adds funny captions to them.

Today Carson makes headlines when he champions a cause on his show, like the time he tried to get Bert Parks back as the "Miss America" MC following his release for the crime of getting a little old-looking.

Back then, Johnny amazed the local citizens by championing the rights of birds. He read in the local paper that the Omaha townsfolk wanted to roust the roosting pigeons in town. Johnny declared over the airwaves that Omaha was being unfair to the birds. He began an "Equal Time for Pigeons" campaign and even imitated a cooing pigeon, translating the bird's side of the story. The stunned citizenry stopped—and cheered. The pigeons were saved. And Johnny's career as a comedy crusader began. Over the years, he's rarely lost a comical case. Unfortunately, his "Save Bert Parks" campaign was one of those rare losses.

From pigeons, Johnny turned his attention to squirrels. As radio began giving way to television at the start of the fifties, Johnny joined WOW-TV and won his own TV show: "The Squirrel's Nest." Johnny had experimented with television briefly in college. He was part of the cast for an experimental closed-circuit broadcast, "The Story of Undulant Fever." He played a milkman concerned over unpasteurized milk.

"The Squirrel's Nest" became an experimental showcase for Johnny's talents as a comic lecturer and quick-skit artist. He couldn't be stopped on-stage or off.

A few years ago, Carson made headlines for growing a beard during a vacation. But during the run of "The Squirrel's Nest," he grew a beard—as a protest when the station was slow in securing enough commercials to replace a departing sponsor.

Bill Wiseman, Jr., the assistant general manager of WOW, saw this side of Carson firsthand. He mentioned to writer Maurice Condon that Johnny was "not exactly a conformist." There was the time when Johnny received a memo from WOW's accounting department: Johnny had used the company phone to make a twenty-cent long-distance call to Council Bluffs.

The company auditor wanted Carson to either explain what that call was for, or pay the twenty cents. As Wiseman recalled, Johnny did neither. "And so it went on, for months, I guess. The auditor was stubborn and Johnny—well—I don't know whether he was stubborn or just having fun. Finally the auditor got tough. You know, pay or else!"

Johnny still wouldn't pay. "The next afternoon an armored car pulled up in front of the station. Two uniformed guards with drawn revolvers got out and stalked into the station with an envelope that could be surrendered only to the auditor, who came a-running! He signed, opened the envelope, and found a check in the amount of twenty cents, signed by John Carson."

To make his point, Johnny had spent twenty-five dollars renting the armored car and the two guards.

Omaha's rising young celebrity was Johnny Carson, star of his own morning radio show and afternoon TV "Squirrel's Nest." Carson was still hungry for more. To pay the seventy-two-dollar monthly rent, The Great Carsoni could still be prevailed upon to perform.

The Great Carsoni was sought after by civic groups. The best of the local magicians, he had little competition. When a teenage magician appeared at the Lions Club in Lincoln, Nebraska, the announcer actually apologized to the crowd: "We have a disappointment for you. We couldn't get Johnny Carson today. But we have a young man who someday is going to be just as good."

And out stepped young Dick Cavett.

Cavett recalled in his autobiography that the two future talk-show stars actually met way back when. Cavett, very much impressed by the older, more successful Carson, went backstage to meet him when he performed at a church affair.

"He looked slightly annoyed. People are always nosing around when a magician is setting up, and the magician rightly would like to catapult them through the nearest window." When Cavett explained that he was a budding magician himself, Carson "became quite friendly." Johnny showed the teenager some card tricks, and Dick felt "aglow" from his "contact with a star."

Johnny was a slick pro even then. During his act, he introduced the celebrity in the audience, the young magician Dick Cavett, and had Dick take a bow. Cavett remembers that Johnny, no matter how slick, had his problems even back then as he tried to entertain the conservative crowd. "Some of the people in the audience were offended by his act, I recall." They didn't think it was right to do cigarette tricks in the church basement. This breach of etiquette didn't matter to Cavett. Cavett and his friends lingered to catch a glimpse of the superstar coming out after the show. "How we envied him as he glamorously pulled out into the night in what looked like a '49 Chevy!"

The restless comedian/magician/radio and TV performer wasn't seeing enough progress, even if he was the biggest fish in the small Nebraska pond. "After a while I was exhausted, so I decided you've got to make your own breaks. I made an audition movie, using WOW's film and WOW's cameraman late one night after the station was closed."

The year was 1951. Carson took his audition film and embarked on a do-or-die trip to California.

4 CARSON'S CELLAR

Johnny's guest is Red Skelton. Or is it? Also on the program: turkey stuffing in drag.

There was nobody saying "Heeeerre's . . . Johnny!" when the skinny Omaha announcer appeared at the door of a San Francisco television station.

When he offered up his tape of comedy, magic, and silly commercials, nobody even wanted to look.

He'd hitched up a U-Haul to his beat-up Oldsmobile, figuring California was ripe for opportunity. But on the Coast, they took to Johnny about as well as they'd taken to Tom Joad in *The Grapes of Wrath*.

Carson's "Earn Your Vacation" vacation to the Coast was a lonely one. He'd left his wife and his young son, Chris, back in Omaha. The journey itself was torturous. An Oklahoma blizzard left him stranded in the bitter cold. He detoured down through Texas, only to encounter the fiercest winter the state had seen in decades. The miles burned holes in his tires till each one had to be patched.

Carson's self-esteem took a beating as he peddled his tape from door to door. It reminded him of years earlier: "I sold vacuum cleaners door to door for about a day and a half. Couldn't take the rejection."

This time he took it. From San Francisco he went down to Los Angeles. He couldn't believe that one station somewhere couldn't use a show like "The Squirrel's Nest."

The year before, NBC had experimented with something called "Broadway Open House" from eleven to midnight. Comedian Jerry Lester hosted the sketches and songs. This initial "Tonight Show" didn't last long. A network for shows after prime time really didn't exist back then. Many local stations weren't looking for anything more adventuresome than old movies or an old test pattern.

Maybe one in ten even bothered to look at Johnny's film audition. All of the had the same answer. They said, No, No, and No.

Johnny came home depressed and humiliated. The only glimmer of hope he had was in meeting Bill Brennan, a fellow Avocan who had come out to Los Angeles years earlier. Brennan had made inroads into the TV world, and would eventually become a CBS vice president. Brennan said he'd keep on the lookout for any job openings for Carson.

After several months, Johnny was once more settled into the routine in Omaha. Then he got a call from Brennan: "There's a staff announcer's position at KNXT-TV."

Johnny grabbed it, even though he quickly learned that "staff announcer" was short for "staff announcer, handyman, messenger, and anything else we can think of." Some staffers made it plain that they didn't think much of a rube from Omaha. Carson bristled but accepted a role he knew by one word: "flunky."

In 1952 Johnny achieved his first moment of glory. The folks back home heard him speak to a nationwide audience. He announced the immortal words, "This is the CBS television network."

This was a painful transition, the small-town star now an anon-

ymous voice in the big city. Slowly, things changed. Johnny managed to get his own radio show, "Carson's Corner," but it was
only on for five minutes a day from 8:55 to 9.

Johnny was making a hundred and thirty-five dollars a week
and living in a small apartment. He had dreams of hope—Bob
Hope. Sometimes he'd squint his eyes and look out through the
light California smog. "I used to say, Bob Hope lives right over
there." All the movie stars' houses were so close.

Now that he was in Hollywood, Johnny once more went to Jack
Benny's show to watch the master at work. Jack and Johnny posed
for a picture together, even though Benny had no idea who he
was. Johnny was forever impressed by Jack's warmth.

Johnny was restless. He was a creative comic in Omaha. He
vowed that he would have a comedy show just like "The Squirrel's
Nest" in the big city. If it didn't happen within a year, he would
quit and fly to New York and see what was happening there.

This was the start of the "Golden Era" of television. Many
local stations were barely making money and many people hadn't
even bought their first TV set. As Johnny solidified his credits in
California, and as the broadcast day lengthened, the break finally
came.

He finally was able to convince KNXT, the local CBS station,
that he could handle a half-hour show for them. He could do it
well, and he could do it cheap.

How well? He'd write the scripts himself and be the star.

How cheap? For twenty-five dollars.

"Carson's Cellar" was the essence of low-budget, but it had the
youthful enthusiasm and schooled comedy smarts of Johnny Carson. Johnny wasn't going to let the tight budget prevent him from
securing big stars and getting big attention. On one show, he had
a member of the stage crew rush past the camera.

"That was Red Skelton," Johnny announced. "Too bad he
didn't have time to stay and say a few words!"

Carson's wiseguy antics surprised the older comics. Some
could even see themselves in him. Fred Allen became the first
star to really appear on the show. Red Skelton came by soon
after, giving Johnny the real thing.

Some samples of 1953's "Carson's Cellar" are still around. They are surprisingly similar to Johnny's "Tonight Show" style: tight, clever monologue followed by loose and laughable sketch material and some songs from the musical guests.

The "Cellar" was just that—the set was a plain room not unlike the home of "Honeymooners" Ralph and Alice Kramden, with boxes and debris in the background, a few barrels in the corner, even a clothesline strung up to one side.

A typical show opens with an announcement: "KNXT cautiously presents . . . 'Carson's Cellar' . . . and here's the guy who has to account for this half-hour, Johnny Carson!"

Johnny comes out. "Thank you very much for coming into the cellar tonight. It's a little bit cold tonight." He presses his fingers together Jack Benny–style. "In fact I think that's why we got one young lady out there. Before the show I said, 'Why did you come to the show?' and she said, 'Because it was cold outside.' But I like to have an honest audience. . . ."

Carson deadpans the line just like Jack Benny. Johnny once admitted to Jack's wife, Mary Livingstone, "I realize now that, in the early days of my career, I was too much like Jack . . . which was wrong. But I idolized Jack . . . I can show you things I did in the early days . . . in which I was so close to his style, it embarrasses me now."

Even this early in his career, Johnny could produce a polished monologue. He was also adept at sketches. Ironically, one of his better ones on the show was a lampoon of the role he would soon have—that of quiz-show MC. He did a sketch in which he shouts, "Aren't we having fun?" every other minute, mimicking a typical brassy MC.

Johnny continues, poking fun at the brainless, hyping quizmasters of the day. Another of Johnny's idols, Stan Laurel, once asked: "Who are these people? What are they stars of? Who made them stars . . . they don't do anything but read some questions from cards. . . . The terrible thing about some of them is that they think they can act or read funny lines well or even ad-lib funny lines, for God's sake. And even worse than that . . . the audience seems to accept them on these terms. These people aren't talents, or even bad talents, they are simply non-talents."

Carson's quizmaster is just such an ad-libber.

"I'm a housewife," the female contestant says.

"Oh! You married a house!" Johnny shouts, rushing center-stage, eyes wide, applauding himself. "How about that! Aren't we having fun? A million laughs on 'Take It or Nothing!' We're all havin' fun, aren't we!"

The contestants have a tough time answering the questions right. But Johnny has a "consolation prize": "Here's something you'll treasure for years to come. You'll get a whole year's supply and you can use them indefinitely."

Aside from this non-prize, Johnny has some real gifts, demonstrating nearly a decade before "The Tonight Show" Johnny's penchant for odd gags:

"First, a beautiful pair of hammered aluminum shower clogs. You also receive a lifesize picture of Buster Crabbe that glows in the dark. And a whole year's supply of marinated Ping-Pong balls for every member of your family. And a beautiful deep-fat fryer that fries deep fat to a golden-brown. If you like fried fat, you'll love the Wilson Deep-Fat Fryer!"

The evening's finale is a rough-and-tumble sketch about a TV cooking show hostess, Emma Steddwider. She's an early variation on Johnny's "Aunt Blabby" character.

Johnny comes out in drag, wearing a tight, flowered skirt and a Minnie Pearl hat with a veil. With his slim body and skinny arms, augmented by falsies, he's pretty convincing.

"Thank you, thank you, television fans out there," he says, his voice a younger Aunt Blabby, sixty and folksy as opposed to ninety and crusty. Today's lesson: How to stuff a turkey.

Predictably but hilariously Johnny goes through the motions, mauling the turkey, dropping it on the floor, blowing on it to clean it. He gets his hand stuck in it, waves it around, and ultimately uses a toilet plunger to push the stuffing deeper and deeper. The women in the audience are screaming as Johnny tries to fit the oversized turkey into a tiny roasting pan—by jumping up and down on it!

As crude as this all may sound, the bit holds up as well as any "Best of Carson" sketch. Even at this early stage of his career, Carson had a great sense of discipline and timing. Milton Berle would have overdone the whole thing with pounds of baking powder and a mishmash of gooey eggs. His foot would've been stuck in it, and he would've hobbled around the stage till the turkey fell apart. Red Skelton might have begun breaking up, laughing at his own corniness. A Jack Benny or Bob Hope wouldn't have done it at all.

This early, Carson was creating a happy medium. Part of it was unintentional: his synthesis of influences. But much of it was his intentional search for his own unique style of comedy. Johnny's ability to take one part Jack Benny and one part Red Skelton and create something unique is like taking one part blue, one part yellow, and creating green. Johnny, like the color green, seems so natural that one assumes it wasn't created at all.

Johnny was still betraying a little of that Jack Benny influence. Coming out for a curtain call in the prop dress, wig and falsies gone, he waves a hand and ad-libs a Benny-like cry of "The bird's so COLD in there!" But then a line that's pure Johnny, "I hope none of you ladies do that for Thanksgiving . . ." The rascal is really a thoughtful lad. Why, he'd probably clean up the stage himself.

Carson's work continued to impress some of Hollywood's greatest comics. Red Skelton loved the silliness of Johnny's sketches, the nice flow of the monologue patter. Red eventually offered Johnny a writing job on his show and Johnny took it. The pleasant-looking young man was also utilized from time to time in sketches.

Johnny began to get some exposure on other network shows, doing monologues and sketch work. He recalls that his first "biggie" was "a guest shot on the old 'Colgate Comedy Hour' in about '53 or '54."

Johnny was leaping for any opportunities to get ahead. On May 23, 1954, he premiered as host of a quiz show called "Earn Your

Vacation." The CBS show included assistants Jackie Loughery and Millie Sinclair. The show's producers had come up with the idea not in a studio think tank, but in an airport bathroom.

This fact made for a lot of jokes, all of them funnier and more interesting than the show, where contestants picked a place they wanted to visit and then had to answer a series of ever-tougher questions to win the prize.

Carson detested the show, but he wasn't alone. It folded four months later.

On the West Coast, ex-Omaha disc jockey Johnny Carson waited for his next big break. At the same time, on the East Coast, an ex-Phoenix disc jockey was preparing for the start of something big. Steve Allen was going to star in a new fall series on late-night TV: "The Tonight Show." Steve had previously hosted his own local comedy-variety program.

Johnny was anxious to get back into real comedy. He enjoyed writing for Skelton and getting a few chances to appear on the show. One thing about Red that impressed John was Red's fearlessness in physical comedy. While Carson has always been too stiff for truly zany slapstick, he did adapt Red's "anything for entertainment" fearlessness in stunts. Over the years Johnny has placed his life in more jeopardy than any comic, Skelton included. On "The Tonight Show" he has bashed his head through a karate board, allowed a tarantula to crawl up his arm, and even let a blindfolded machete-wielding islander slice a watermelon on his stomach.

On August 18, 1954, Red was rehearsing a slapstick sketch. He hurled himself into a prop door. This knockabout bit of slapstick was a knockout. The prop door didn't open, but Red's head nearly did.

With just ninety minutes before air time, the woozy Skelton couldn't do the show. The producers were frantic. In a scene right out of a bad 1930s movie, they wrung their hands wondering, "Who can take Red's place?"

They called Johnny, who was relaxing at home, waiting to see Red deliver some of the jokes he'd written.

Carson raced to his car and began the half-hour drive to the studio. Along the way he occupied himself by thinking up jokes—quick gags to explain to the audience what happened to Red. And who the hell Johnny Carson was.

And just like that bad 1930s movie, the young replacement was a rousing success. The nervous CBS brass were relieved and delighted with the performance of the bright young comic. And almost immediately they began to formulate plans to give Johnny a variety show just like Red's.

The result was like a very bad 1930s horror picture.

5 THE JOHNNY CARSON SHOW

CBS-TV presents a rising new comic, Johnny Carson. When Red Skelton was knocked unconscious, Johnny got his big break. Now watch CBS knock him unconscious.

F ollowing his success on Red Skelton's show, CBS was convinced Johnny had a big future in television. His run with "Carson's Cellar" and his guest spots on variety shows confirmed it. "The Johnny Carson Show," premiering in June of 1955, would be the next step.

"You've finally made it," friends told Johnny. "Your own prime-time TV show! You should be excited!" Johnny was. But he was also depressed and pessimistic.

"There's no place in TV to be bad," he fretted glumly. He remembered the way his idols had gotten started. "In vaudeville there was room to be bad and to learn. Even in radio you had the chance. In his early radio days Fred Allen was canceled but came back. In those days the most expensive show cost five thousand dollars. Today, when ten times that much is considered peanuts, you can't afford to flop."

CBS wanted to give their new star a little bit of added exposure before he went prime time. They brought him to New York to be a substitute host for two weeks on a morning talk show. The host of that show was an ex-stand-up comic from the Midwest by the name of Jack Paar.

Co-workers from that era remember Johnny as extremely quiet. His visit to the big city awed him. His first steps into the clattering "star-making machinery" made him as wary and skittish as a horse the first time at the starting gate. Part of him longed to show his stuff and display his power. But another side resented the confines of the stall and the threat of the whip.

Carson stayed in a New York hotel directly across the street from the Paar show's office. He did his job and came back. All business. No problems. Asked if he was taking in any of the sights in the Big Apple, he answered, "I pretty much stay in my room."

Back in California, the wary young comic insisted "TV has produced few top comedians. Jack Benny, Red Skelton, Bob Hope, Milton Berle are all products of other mediums."

Could Johnny, breaking into TV, become its first homegrown star? The odds were against it. The big comedy stars like Gleason, Berle, Caesar, and Skelton were brilliant top bananas with the charisma to overpower an audience. Johnny leaned toward the styles of Jack Benny and Bob Hope—both nice-looking guys like himself, one warm and the other a wiseguy.

But Hope and Benny had built their audiences over twenty years, and created enduring personalities. Even as Johnny was arriving, several big stars were being towed away from their own wreckage. Sid Caesar was through after four frantic years. Uncle Miltie was dropped by Texaco, barely hanging on alternating weekly with Bob Hope. And Red Buttons, once the nation's hottest comic, was finished.

"I was picked clean and left to die," Buttons recalls now. After making a big splash in 1952 the young comic was bled dry by the demands for fresh and funny scripts. Buttons once collapsed before showtime and couldn't be revived. CBS switched his time spots twice, then dropped him. NBC grabbed him, then tossed him out, too.

Young, inexperienced Johnny was going to take the challenge. The enormous risk and the tension to succeed cut into some of the moment's pleasure. Rather than appearing happy and excited, as onlookers expected, Carson was serious, worried, driven, and withdrawn. People began to describe him as "cold." He just didn't have the time to present a warm façade to everyone.

The odds for failure were high. Casual visitors to Las Vegas might giggle and laugh having fun placing dollar bets. But the big gambler with thousands of dollars riding on bets looks grim, doesn't want to be disturbed, and his pleasure comes only after an excruciating period of tension.

Johnny guessed and second-guessed himself through all the rehearsals, going through the schizoid simultaneous egotism and insecurity that dogs so many who choose to confront an audience of strangers.

He tried not to bring the pressures home with him. Johnny bought a ranch house in Encino. If it couldn't duplicate the comfort and security of a Nebraska home, it did have plenty of trees and grass. John's kids were growing up in an environment similar to Johnny's rural roots. The boys even had their very own "Trac" toy tractor to tool around with on the lawn.

John lived the simple life. He enjoyed carpentry for a hobby, and built things around the house. With his three sons, the doting dad was cornball enough to occasionally dress them up in identical striped shirts and white shorts. And while most stars drove to work in fancy cars, Carson owned a three-year-old Ford and a four-year-old Chevy.

For Johnny and Jody Carson these modest family cars were enough. "Both of us come from very plain Midwestern families, and we know only too well what a buck means. It isn't that a Cadillac convertible is perishable. It's that television comedians are."

In a strange Hollywood twist, Johnny didn't change his name but his kids did. On September 15, 1954, Carson went to court in

Hollywood with two of his boys. They thought their original names were too girlish. So Kim and Barry became Rick and Cory.

There were three brothers in all, aged between two and five. But Chris, Rick, and Cory actually thought they had a fourth brother, Eddie.

Johnny's ventriloquist dummy Eddie, who resembled Jerry Mahoney a bit, was a perfect playmate. Johnny got a kick out of doing ventriloquist bits for his sons. Of course, they couldn't figure out why Eddie would only be around when Johnny was around, and why he didn't seem to mind just sitting in a closet all day. But he was a special friend. Eddie's head could spin around and around or even come off, and he never had to go to school.

Television in 1955 was a fast and furious mix of quiz shows, sitcoms, and dramas, mostly half-hours. Johnny's show was scheduled for Thursday evenings at 10 P.M. On that night viewers could tune in at 7:30 for "The Lone Ranger" or "Sergeant Preston of the Yukon," then watch "Bishop Sheen," "Love That Bob," or Groucho Marx's "You Bet Your Life." At 8:30 there was "The People's Choice" (a sitcom about a talking dog—Cleo) or "Stop the Music." More half-hour quickies followed between 9 and 10, including "Dragnet," "Star Tonight," "Down You Go," "Four Star Playhouse," and "Ford Theater." Restless audiences could spin the dial endlessly while network executives played Russian roulette with the results.

By 10 P.M., Johnny's time, many viewers were already played out. His competition was a travelogue, "Outside the U.S.A." on ABC, and the formidable "Lux Video Theatre" on NBC. NBC had only five shows in the top twenty but three were on Thursday night, with Groucho's quiz the biggest hit.

"The Johnny Carson Show" premiered on CBS Thursday night, 10 P.M., June 30, 1955.

The critics were "amused." Young Johnny is a "nice guy," said Jack Gould. "Nice, pleasant," echoed Jack O'Brien; "agreeable might be the best word." And Sheila Gallagher added "he looks more like a high school valedictorian." Physically, few could find anything distinctive beyond his tall and thin build. Several, Harriet Van Horne among them, did notice he was "snub nosed." So here he was, the pleasant, tall, thin, snub-nosed young comic.

Johnny's show was formatted like most comedy-variety shows of the era. There were sketches and parodies of popular TV shows. The gags were broken up by the weary but traditional spots for the regular boy and girl vocalists (Jack Prince and Jill Corey). The music was handled by The Lud Gluskin Orchestra.

Johnny expanded on the kind of thing he'd done for "Carson's Cellar." He did sketches on everything from a dentist pulling a whale's tooth to a gun-shy daredevil worrying over being shot out of a cannon. Johnny even resorted to celebrity impressions, including a parody of Steve Allen and his "heh heh" laugh.

"Carson's Cellar" had been experimental. In prime time, Johnny tried bucking the network bigshots. He put in some material that was considered not ready for prime time. Johnny's tremendous knowledge of comedy led him to challenge the concepts of what was or wasn't funny.

In recent decades, Steve Martin, Andy Kaufman, and Albert Brooks challenged the standard stand-up techniques. Brooks, in one "Tonight Show" appearance, actually read the phone book. He got laughs, too. But he was just displaying the kind of comic bravado Johnny showed in 1955.

Writer Philip Minoff remembers: "Carson one night bragged to his audience that he could hold its attention simply by executing an elementary tap-dance. He launched into a lumbering 'Tea-for-Two' step, and the people out front didn't take their eyes from their sets for the next three minutes. For there, on a large movie screen behind Carson, flashed a crazy montage of everything from dive-bombers to storm-tossed battleships!"

In some sketches, Johnny demonstrated his flair for silliness, but he knew even then that he couldn't compete with the Berles and Skeltons of comedy. He went for the milder, likable approach. He was such a nice guy he even brought his wife Jody out to sing a song or two one night.

There were a few mild comics out there. Jack Benny was one. George Gobel was another. Still, networks didn't trust this style of comedy. Comics were supposed to be brash. Johnny, to them, was like the pleasant fellow somebody brought along to the party. Who remembered him the morning after?

Oddly, Carson wasn't compared to his mentor Jack Benny. More often critics cited him as another George Gobel. George was a big star then, a wry Midwesterner who always hoped his show "just might keep you from getting sullen."

Jack O'Brien in the *New York Journal American* noted that Carson "has a sudden smile which explodes either in sincerity or in masterful imitation thereof. His manner is restrained. . . . Probably Carson will labor along under the label of 'another Gobel,' for his pleasant, almost aimless appeal has much in common with Gobel . . . charm and imagination and a sense of humor more on the giggle side than guffaws."

In the *New York Times*, Jack Gould added, "CBS apparently intends to use Mr. Carson as its answer to George Gobel . . . the construction of last night's show was disconcertingly similar to the pattern of Mr. Gobel's program . . . such copy-catting is a serious mistake. . . . The young man is no Gobel; he has neither the uncanny timing nor the performing experience . . . what Mr. Carson does have is a singular youthful charm and an impish twinkle in the eye. He seems like the proverbial nice guy down the block."

Johnny's ratings weren't bad, but CBS was panicking. They felt the Gobel trend was ending. They wanted Johnny to be more like Skelton or Gleason.

They felt he needed splashy musical numbers. Johnny, worried about burning out on comedy, reluctantly agreed. He told a reporter his show would have "lots of chorus girls, production numbers, etc. This way the burden isn't on the comedian, as it was on Sid Caesar a few years back . . . he went crazy trying to get new stuff to do each week."

Still young, shy, and inexperienced, Carson was very much the quiet "new kid" and cautiously deferred to his superiors. For the first time in his professional career, Johnny subverted his comedy instincts. He gave in to the pressure from the big men who claimed to know it all.

When Johnny made that first appearance subbing for Red Skelton, he'd faced America with a nervous quip: "The way I feel right now, I think Red's doctor should be doing this show."

Now he could have used Red's doctor to give him some tranquilizers.

Producer Ben Brady huffed that Johnny "is generically not a strong stand-up comedian."

Writers were hired and fired. Sketches veered in all directions, including "home life" husband-and-wife material more suited to Gobel or Carl Betz. There were frantic chorus girls, dancers, guest stars. The dizzy whirl moved faster and faster.

But Johnny's show didn't last the year.

After 39 weeks he was dumped.

Even his manager walked out on him.

Johnny's worst suspicions about friendship and loyalty were confirmed. So was the never-to-be-forgotten chagrin of being powerless to act on his own comedic instincts for what was funny and what wasn't.

After the show ended, Johnny remarked, "I have no great hates, although today I wouldn't want Ben Brady to produce my coffee break." He told writer Bill Slocum about front-office interference. His re-creation of an encounter with one CBS executive went like this:

EXEC: "Johnny, what your show needs is a feeling of importance."
JOHNNY: "What's a feeling of importance?"
EXEC: "A feeling of importance is . . . a feeling of importance."

In retrospect, CBS's mistake was painfully obvious. Unlike Skelton or Gleason, Johnny was and still is a "cool" performer. Put the June Taylor Dancers behind Gleason, he dwarfs them. With Johnny, the singers and dancers made him disappear. Bland-looking and innocuous, he couldn't follow the show's splashy openings. Even today the successful talk show star is almost never seen onstage with a full orchestra behind him or

dancing girls. He's rarely in a sketch with more than a few people—never in a position where he'll be lost in the crowd.

In March 1956, "The Johnny Carson Show" went off the air.

Carson tried to control his bitterness. "Why is it that TV big
shots buy a show because they like it and then proceed to change
it?

"When I was signed everybody told me I was great. Then when
I started the show, everybody had just a few ideas for improving
it. They killed it. I had eight different writers in thirty-nine
weeks. And seven directors. Imagine that. Seven directors. They
couldn't all have been wrong . . . there was interference from the
sponsors. Before long I found myself and my material subjected to
the opinion of businessmen. It was frustrating, believe me."

Johnny never forgot and he never forgave.

"Entertainment is like any other major industry," he said. "It's
a cold, big business. The business end wants to know one thing:
Can you do the job? If you can, you're in, you're made. If you
can't, you're out."

Thursday night changed radically at CBS, and Carson's time
slot was swallowed up by a new show: "Playhouse 90," to begin at
9:30 and get a jump on "Lux Video Theatre."

Johnny was left to lick his wounds. But they never disappeared.

6 THE JOHNNY CARSON SHOW

Johnny switches to daytime. In prime time, CBS canceled him after thirty-nine weeks. Now they drop him in sixteen. Who can he trust?

Humbled and bewildered after his show folded on March 29, 1956, Johnny took CBS's offer of a daytime series. "The Johnny Carson Show" premiered on May 28, replacing Robert Q. Lewis. Regulars included Glenn Turnbull, Betty Holt, Tommy Leonetti, and the New Yorkers.

Carson tried to be optimistic. "After all," he said at the time, "I am getting a daily show of my own. It's not as if I was being dumped into the river."

He looked on the bright side: "Daytime TV has its advantages, don't kid yourself. For one thing, you're not on trial like you are nights, and the pressure is far, far less.

"Boy, on night TV, it's like an opening night every time you do a show. And you're always worried about those ratings the next day, and who thought the show was bad and who thought it was great. You don't get this grinding pressure in the day-time."

The prime-time comedians were all having it tough. Many promising comedians went down with Carson in the frantic fifties. Among those who had their own shows—temporarily—were Herb Shriner, Jean Carroll, Jonathan Winters, and Jack Carson. When Johnny left the air, so did once powerful top bananas like Sid Caesar and Milton Berle. Even low-key George Gobel sputtered away, decimated in the ratings by "Gunsmoke." Carson asked, "What can Gobel do if some people like Westerns?"

"I'm not being unhappy," Carson said, "just facing cold facts. This is no time for comedy, or rather, for comedians. Look, George Gobel is just as funny as he ever was, but people get tired of 'I'll Be a Dirty Bird.' . . . People feel sorry for you when you have an afternoon show. They think you're buried. But you've got ten million people watching and they're more loyal than a night-time audience. . . ."

Johnny convinced himself that the prime-time chance was just too much too soon. "I'd have been wise to start out with an after-noon show . . .," he told reporters. He drew an analogy with baseball: "Put a promising ballplayer in the minor leagues and let him graduate into the majors. I had a long talk about that with Garry Moore, who's a happy and secure man today. It was on daytime TV that viewers learned to like and accept Garry. It should happen to me when I get into the daytime race."

Carson tried to remember one thing: "If you don't keep control, you're going to bomb out, and there's nobody to blame but your-self."

Johnny kept it light for the daytime audience.

TV Guide called it "a take-it-or-leave-it fiddle-de-dee with oc-casional moments of witless banter."

This time, though, they didn't compare him to George Gobel. "Johnny is a junior Steve Allen. His humor is casual; he spoofs commercials; he interviews people in the audience (unlike Steve, he never insults them). Again like Allen, Carson is fond of offbeat guests (sample: A Chinese potbeater) and odd props (sample: the framework of a piano 'uncovered in the desert near Yuma, Arizona'). In one regular sketch Carson wears a mortarboard and answers mock questions."

With reviews like that, CBS was unimpressed. They were losing patience with their rookie phenom.

Johnny tried not to bring his problems home, but the pressure and the insecurity were hard to live with. It was frustrating to be on the verge of success—and failure. He was struggling to stay in big-time show business. Struggling to keep the money coming in. And there was no fame in being on the low rung of the CBS ladder. Johnny was shaken when he realized he was no happier now than he had been in Omaha.

Even at home Johnny was no celebrity: "My kids aren't at all impressed when they see me on television. They just think it's daddy. I remember once I appeared on 'The Red Skelton Show.' After it was over, Red's little girl rushed up to me for my autograph, practically knocking her father down on the way. That's how kids are. They never think of their father as a TV star, everyone else is though, even if they've only done a commercial. But it's a healthy sign, I guess."

Four months after his show began, on September 28, 1956, it was canceled.

"I'd rather be out of work in TV than out of work in insurance or some other field," Carson said.

TV was so much more exciting. So many different ways to fail. The producer or director could take the control. The writers could be lousy. The time-slot could be a killer. The critics could hate it. Or a new show could simply get lost in the newspaper listings and it might take five or six months for viewer momentum to build.

Now the pessimism and regret poured out of him. Johnny repeated his grim complaints about network interference. He questioned the rating system: "They serve a purpose, but it does seem too bad that we have no gauge that takes into account the quality of a show." He chilled in thinking of the viewers themselves: "There is not a show on the air the public cannot remove. All they have to do is write to the sponsor." He even doubted his grass-roots appeal to Middle America: "There are no rubes watching TV," he cautioned. "And comedians are more vulnerable than any other entertainers because people always expect them to do something funny."

Carson was finished in television. Out of desperation more than anything else, he wrote an act for himself and made his club debut at classily named Maison Joussaud in Bakersfield.

He was just another stand-up comedian. "It's the hardest type of entertainment to do—to stand by yourself and make people laugh. And anybody who says anything different is crazy . . . it's lonely; you've only got yourself."

Carson didn't even have an agent to split the $400-a-week fee with.

Desperate and depressed, he met with Al Bruno, an astute manager who specialized in handling game show personalities. "He was at a pretty low ebb," Bruno recalled in a 1962 interview with Eleanor Harris in the *New York Journal-American*. "But it seemed to me he was the only young professional broadcaster capable of staying on camera and saying something to an audience."

To Johnny, returning to the quiz show world had to be humiliating. Even worse, he was so broke he had to borrow two thousand dollars from his father in order to make a trip to New York where the game show action was. He took time off for what was very much an "Earn Your Vacation" proposition.

Groucho Marx was the hot quiz show MC. Nobody could top Groucho for presenting a fast-moving, funny, and entertaining show. Others tried, of course. Among the copies was "Do You Trust Your Wife?" with Edgar Bergen, which arrived in January of 1956. Bergen was a quick wit (he sparred on radio with everyone from Mae West to W. C. Fields on his own "Chase and Sanborn Show"). Still, he wasn't exactly Groucho. "Do You Trust Your Wife?" had anemic ratings. Producer Don Fedderson renamed the show "Who Do You Trust?"

He moved it from California to New York. And he replaced Bergen with young Johnny Carson.

Johnny moved into New York City, but he made sure he could come home each night to the country. The Carsons lived in Har-

rison, New York, just within commuting distance of midtown
Manhattan. Their spacious home was set on 3½ acres, designed
so that the kids would have a nice place to play. The boys were at
that age when they liked to run around: Kit was seven, Ricky was
six, and Cory four.

The towering ivy-covered brick house had two floors and plenty
of places to explore from attic to cellar. Beautiful trees grew right
outside the door, the branches tapping at the windows in the
wind. The area was landscaped with bushes and a well-cared-for
lawn. The driveway in front of the house was huge, a brick patio
area that could accommodate a half-dozen cars comfortably. But
the Carsons were not ones to have that many guests over for partying. Instead, the area remained clear, a place for the kids to ride
their bikes and play baseball.

In 1957, half the Top Ten shows were Westerns. And in 1958,
seven of the ten were Westerns, including the top four:
"Gunsmoke," "Wagon Train," "Have Gun Will Travel," and
"The Rifleman." But there were no cowboys hosting quiz shows.
Johnny was safe. With Groucho Marx's show pointing the way,
Carson was given the freedom to add comedy to the quiz.

Groucho was the big quiz show host of prime time. Soon
Johnny was the big quiz show host of daytime. He was better than
Groucho as far as sponsors were concerned. Housewives loved the
handsome young star, and they did the shopping.

The show was initially telecast live, five days a week, from The
Little Theater on West 44th Street off Broadway. It premiered
July 14, 1957, and kept gaining higher ratings and higher praise
for its star.

Johnny, along with the show's producer Art Stark, were the
ones responsible for the show's success. Stark's smarts and Carson's charm made for an unbeatable combination. Before they
took over, "Do You Trust Your Wife?" was not only a ratings
dud, it was in one way crooked.

A staffer remembers that on the West Coast the show had a
"party staff. A real California attitude. They were giving a party
on any occasion, and things were pretty much in chaos . . . they
had a backlog of undelivered prizes and it turned out that a prom-

inent staff member of the show had been giving them to his show-girl girl friend instead of sending them to the contestants."

They couldn't get the prizes back, but to save the integrity of his show, Art Stark and his staff bought new ones to give to the long-waiting contestants. Years later, when the famous "quiz show scandals" broke, Stark was proud to say that his show could not be faulted: "I remember doing our own in-house check, staying in the office till late calling contestants, asking if they'd ever been offered any answers or anything of the sort. We came off completely clean."

Meanwhile, Johnny listened to good advice from a helpful veteran of the daytime scene, Garry Moore. Johnny remembers Garry saying, "Be acceptable every day. If you get that, you've got it half made." His acceptable, low-key style and his flickering moments of "naughty boy" humor made him a sensation. All Carson had needed was the right setting to grow. It seemed so simple and had taken so long.

"Who Do You Trust?" quickly became a vehicle more for Johnny than the quiz. Carson described the changing format with columnist Sheila Gallagher, a format that just happened to move Johnny even further from the Jack Baileys and Bill Leydens of the quiz world and closer to Groucho: "We made the quiz part of the show secondary. Now the emphasis is back where it belongs, on the contestants. If I get an interesting contestant I'll talk to him for half the program and then just incidentally bring the quiz bit in. . . ."

To Marie Torre he admitted, "I once looked down on quiz giveaways, as I'm sure a lot of comedians do, but it hasn't been a bad life. At least it's not a maudlin-type show. And we don't give away refrigerators. . . ."

Zany guests were favorites, ones that Johnny could sharpen his wits on. He got some mileage from Max and Will Berkowitz, twin undertakers from Cleveland, and even more from Valerie and Leila Croft, blond identical twins. He got double the laughs from a woman who insisted it was possible to breathe through the toes. While the audience giggled and Carson went through a repertoire of faces, she did ten minutes of toe-breathing exercises with him.

Johnny always said he was a "reaction" comic like Jack Benny. With the "Who Do You Trust?" contestants, Johnny found himself getting big laughs being a straight man. His humor worked best in the form of slyly injected ad-libs. Carson learned something many comics never do: to share the laughs.

There was the time a movie heavy named Harold Huber turned up. "How do you feel about having been slain in over 100 films?" Johnny asked.

The answer: "It's a living."

Another time, Johnny's guest was a man from the Bronx who insisted that the most invigorating thing in the world was an air bath. You strip, open the windows up wide, and stand in the path of the wind.

As the tittering died down, Johnny pondered the idea. "But how do you take a shower? Stand in front of a fan?"

Under the surface, Johnny was still an angry comic with a natural inclination for satire. The problems of the world would get a gentle but prickly deflation during his "Tonight Show" monologues. For now, he had to shelve this one part of his personality.

"There are so many things you can't talk about," he admitted, back in 1957. "Will Rogers wouldn't be permitted to make his sharp comments about politics and politicians today. And there are many other matters you can't satirize either. You remember when Marlboro cigarettes had the slogan, 'You can't say no to a Marlboro?' Well, I once said, 'I've had a happy morning. I just said no to a Marlboro.' And you should have heard the calling-down I got." This was still the era when Lucille Ball couldn't say she was "pregnant." Lenny Bruce was still doing Frankie Laine impressions on the radio.

Johnny did some occasional stand-up work on other variety shows. Even though the quiz show was taking off, something was gnawing at Johnny. "Some day," he said, "people will want to laugh again. They'll pull back from their television sets and ask themselves—How long is it since I've had a laugh out of this thing?"

In the meantime, "Who Do You Trust?" became a minor-

56   Ronald L. Smith

league "Tonight Show," complete with stunts and funny, average folks for guests.

Contestants were scripted. As with Groucho's show, they were not furnished with the correct answers to the quiz, but they were pre-interviewed by the talent coordinators to find the most interesting topics of conversation.

A writer, Roy Kammerman, listened to the contestants talk about favorite hobbies and anecdotes, and he sketched out likely gag answers for Johnny. He'd previously written for Groucho.

Groucho and Johnny both relied on pre-written gags. Both are justly famous for their ad-libbing, but having some knowledge of contestants' jobs and personalities, plus ready-made gags, took enough pressure off them to allow them to be natural on the air and let their natural wit show through.

Carson never denied that the show was not ad-libbed. If anyone asked, he told them.

When a contestant was approved, a transcript of the test interview was made. This outlined the usable questions and the contestant's answers. This was submitted to the network for routine approval. The network received a purple-blue rexograph script that included some of the projected gags to be injected during the conversation.

What the network *didn't* get was Johnny's script: which included even more snappy "ad-libs."

Asssociate producer Mary Dodd recalls that the contestants "were interviewed very intensively. As I recall it, actually we had two scripts. One that went to the network and one we kept in-house. You couldn't write the jokes for the network because they all would have been turned down."

With the hidden second script, Johnny could get away with live lines that the network would've fretted over if they had read them. As far as the network knew, these were all ad-libs! And with the audience laughing and applauding, and Carson's "naughty boy" act a hit with housewives, how could they complain? For once, Johnny was getting to play the game his way.

"Who Do You Trust?" seemed more natural than "You Bet Your Life" because the gags were lighter and more conversational. Hector Arce put together an entire book of Groucho's quiz show jokes. Johnny's were less bombastic. Like the majority of jokes he uses in today's "Tonight Show" monologues, the purpose is relaxing laughter, nothing too controversial or quotable.

To a department store manager who divorced her husband Johnny was given this line to work into the conversation: "What did you do, take him to the exchange department?" Interviewing a musician who worked in the musical, *Subways Are for Sleeping*, Johnny was handed a quickie ad-lib: "What do you play, a train whistle?" And in interviewing a woman whose husband worked as a meat smoker in a deli, Johnny was given: "Couldn't he get cigarettes?"

Carson could probably have come up with the same, or better, but he had enough to worry about keeping the show moving.

Before each episode of "Who Do You Trust?" a special script was prepared, one NOT sent to the network. It included all of Johnny's ad-libs.

The script was based on the pre-interview. Johnny was to ask the same questions the pre-show interviewers asked. The contestants didn't read their answers off cue cards, but given Johnny's specific lead questions, practically parroted what they'd said before. Mary Dodd recalls that "when contestants were on the show they said pretty much the same thing they did during the many pre-interviews. Particularly if you're relating an incident. You tend to tell it the same way every time."

In the original script, Johnny and producer Art Stark deleted some of the prepared gags, self-censoring material that was too risqué. This material was red-penciled. Carson's ad-libs were typed in on the side of the script. On one show, for example, he asked a voluptuous model who had been named "Miss Laugh Queen" about her responsibilities.

"I'm supposed to get people to laugh," she responded.

"What do you do the rest of the year?" Johnny asked.

"I mostly pose for cheesecake photography."

"Oh, yes, I thought I recognized you."

"How did they happen to choose you to be 'Miss Laugh Queen'?"

"They saw my picture in one of the cheesecake magazines."

"I guess they admired your funnybone. Is that all they picked you for? Your appearance?"

"No, they tested my laugh. I have a very good laugh."

"From your pictures I guess it would be a belly laugh."

The script continued with questions about her marriage and her ambitions. Obviously, no matter how well-scripted a show like this could be, Carson had to do a good deal of his own fancy footwork. He had to make his scripted answers *seem* ad-libbed. He also had to be prepared should the contestant not answer exactly as during the pre-interview.

Johnny was happy to have a show that let him work somewhat similarly to a comedy-variety show. "The prize doesn't really matter," he insisted. "It's the humor . . . What's entertaining about a closeup of a lawn mower?"

The show was a training ground, giving Carson valuable insight into average people. His comedy was moving away from impersonal gag sketches (like comically stuffing a turkey) or monologue observation. Now he was relating with common people. Without five years of contestant interaction, he might have failed as a talk-show host, as so many pure stand-up comics do. He learned that "almost without exception . . . the best contestants are those you actually have to coax. The more eager they are to be on, the duller they turn out to be."

He got along especially well with housewives. He told Harriet Van Horne: "They're good-natured and quick-witted. And they're not afraid of looking ridiculous. It also might surprise the program directors to know how smart most housewives are. I hate to hear this condescending talk about the twelve-year-old mind of the daytime viewer. A lot of housewives are college graduates. They read books, they travel, they're hep. You probably get more twelve-year-olds at night."

Carson was occasionally annoyed by the restraints of daytime. It was aggravating to continually pull in the reins, to be always smiling, always careful not to offend.

One contestant on the show insisted that the best way to show Russia the real America would be to send Elvis Presley over to entertain. "I don't know about Russia," Johnny said with a smirk, "but it might improve relations here."

Presley fans from all over the country sent in angry letters.

In Carson's office he had a dart board. He used it all the time. "It's a good way to work off the aggressions," he commented. He also had a small drum set—"They're a form of therapy."

Meanwhile "Who Do You Trust?," like "The Tonight Show," became known for unpredictable conversations:

> JOHNNY [to contestants Paul and Maria Mule]: "Maria, how did you and Paul meet?"
> MARIA: "Our parents were friends. We met in our baby carriages. The first time he saw me I was in diapers."
> JOHNNY: "How did she look in diapers, Paul?"
> PAUL: "She looks better in 'em now."
> JOHNNY [take]: "She looks better in 'em now?"
> PAUL: "Much better."

Johnny could ad-lib through problems off-screen. Johnny used to warm up the audience before shows. He didn't mind smoking while he did it, even though this was a violation of the fire laws. Once an official from the fire department caught him at it. Johnny turned him into a stooge: As the baffled man gaped, Johnny effortlessly made the cigarette disappear, reappear, and disappear again.

Johnny had the magic touch. Like a good magician, he polished it into slick brilliance. The show was Johnny—not quiz money. Asked years later to describe the actual mechanics of the show, he shrugged and said, "I don't even know what the hell the point of the game was."

7 WHO DO YOU TRUST?

Johnny loses a wife but gains Ed McMahon. He gets a chance in a Broadway show and gets an offer he wants to refuse: taking over "The Tonight Show."

J ohnny's marriage didn't survive the move to New York and the daily grind of "Who Do You Trust?"

He spent his days pushing hard for his career in the city. Westchester seemed like a world away. Jody rarely came in to watch Johnny work. Johnny's boys were curious about his job, but he kept them away too. "People tend to make too much over them," he said. "It's a phony attention and they can draw the wrong conclusions from it."

One staffer recalls that John's children "were awfully nice kids. They were the typical pug-nosed, freckle-faced, good-looking kids. They weren't around the show that much, but they were all nice. I heard his first wife, Jody, was unhappy, which would make sense, too, if you're stuck up in the suburbs with the kids."

Johnny didn't talk about his home life, but the consensus among the staff was that "there wasn't any real animosity there.

They were very fond of each other, and they just decided to make a change. He may have felt he'd married too young; didn't get a chance to look over the field and see what was out there. And she may have been tired of being alone, being a housewife stuck up in Harrison with the children. . . . I never heard anything bad about her. If I did I probably would've thought she was justified. He was fairly new, he wasn't earning a hell of a lot of money . . . they weren't pinching pennies, but she couldn't leave the kids with a nurse and hang out with Johnny in the city."

Carson was getting five hundred dollars a week to do the show. He would come in around ten o'clock, study the script, meet briefly with the contestants, and break for lunch. After lunch he'd do the show.

Johnny was friendly with the producer of the show, Art Stark, as well as with associate producer Mary Dodd. But as Dodd remembers, "He was uncomfortable socially. What they call his distance and coolness in the days when I knew him I would've categorized as shyness and insecurity." With small groups of people, and those he knew well, things were a bit different. "As long as there were no other people around he would be like anyone else. You don't expect any of your friends to keep you in stitches. He was witty, very pleasant, and a pretty ordinary down-to-earth man."

Some of Carson's insecurities carried on to the show itself. Viewers sometimes wondered, "Why is Johnny always looking out of the corner of his eye?" He was looking for producer Art Stark. Even today, Johnny's encouraging producer stands just out of camera range. Even so, Johnny had some problems. A staffer recalls "one show where one of the interviews ran short. The show was a minute thirty short. Art gave Johnny a 'Stretch' sign and Johnny walked off the stage. He couldn't fill the minute. So they rolled the credits—very slowly."

Carson was not the typical show-biz star. Mary Dodd says: "I had the feeling he was delighted to be on the show and impressed by his good luck. He didn't come on like a brash young comic. After all, he wasn't a New Yorker, he hadn't done the Borscht Belt. He was from Nebraska. He was a nice young Middle West kid. Johnny didn't have any friends here. Any male friends. He had his wife and children."

What Johnny needed was a sidekick.

The original announcer on "Who Do You Trust?" was Bill Nimmo. As producer Art Stark recalled, "He wasn't working out. He was a little too staid."

Stark was looking for an announcer with just a little more style. He found Edward Leo Peter McMahon, Jr.

Born in Detroit on March 6, 1923, Ed's childhood was a bit like Johnny's. He was on the move. McMahon's father was a carnival pitchman. For a time the McMahons lived in Bayonne, New Jersey, for a while in Staten Island. In Avoca, Johnny swam in the big local pool. On Staten Island, Ed loved diving off the pier at the ferry docks—risking the crush of the oncoming ferries to enjoy the foamy spray.

Always the new kid in the neighborhood, Ed never had many friends. He was basically shy and lonely, but by the time he reached high school he'd learned to overcompensate for this by "glad handing," developing an outgoing personality.

His first real home was in Lowell, Massachusetts. It was there that he first got interested in radio. Ed attended Catholic University in Washington, D.C., and graduated the same year as Carson, in 1949. After service in both World War II and the Korean War, Colonel McMahon returned to Lowell to become a radio announcer.

Oddly, there was a "lookalike" already there by the name of Ray Goulding. When Ray left (and with partner Bob Elliott became "Bob and Ray"), McMahon had a free hand and his own show, 6 P.M. to 1 A.M. From there he went to Philadelphia. He had a morning TV show called "Strictly For the Girls" and later starred in a talk and variety show called "McMahon and Company," which aired locally right after Jack Paar's "Tonight Show."

McMahon's skills as an announcer and personality were well known. He lived next door to Philly's other favorite son, Dick Clark. When Clark's producer, Chuck Reeves, heard that Art Stark was looking for an announcer on "Who Do You Trust?" he recommended McMahon. McMahon's number was unlisted, so

Reeves called Dick Clark. And Clark, clad in a bathrobe, went next door to get Ed. But to his surprise, the McMahon family had moved a few weeks earlier. Clever Dick looked in the phone book for the listed number of Claudia, Ed's daughter. He called Ed, and Ed arranged to meet Stark.

Staffers on "Who Do You Trust?" agree that Johnny had no more power on the quiz show than he'd had working for CBS. Producer Art Stark was the man who made the hiring decisions. After deciding on Ed, Art had Ed meet with Johnny.

McMahon probably was not aware that Johnny had little voice in the decision. Otherwise he wouldn't have been so disappointed by Johnny's lack of interest in him. In his autobiography, *Here's Ed*, McMahon recounts this historic moment: "When I walked in, Johnny didn't look as if he were dying to see me. He was standing with his back to the door, staring out the window at the Shubert Theater across the street where a couple of workmen on a scaffold were putting letters up on the marquee. I walked over and stood beside him and helped him watch. It was a good guessing game, like watching someone piece together a jigsaw puzzle. We both stood there fascinated and impatient to see how it would turn out. Finally the two guys finished and we could read: 'JUDY HOLLI- DAY IN BELLS ARE RINGING.'"

Johnny asked a polite, "What have you been doing?" And Ed briefly described his Philly TV ventures. Carson said, "Good to meet you, Ed," the men shook hands, and that was it.

Later, Ed and Johnny did a two-minute test in front of the camera.

As associate producer Mary Dodd points out, "Ed McMahon did not have the same function on the daytime show as he did on 'The Tonight Show.' He wasn't the sidekick, he was an an- nouncer. There was no such thing as 'Heerre's . . . Johnny!'"

Everyone liked Ed, who was just as affable then as he appears on "The Tonight Show" today. He and Johnny would have lunch together, and gradually they became close friends. Ed knew New York, and he was able to show Johnny around. Carson found a companion to help him through the deteriorating stages of his marriage to Jody.

McMahon was the gregarious one. Johnny followed his lead, even though he couldn't hold his liquor as well as Ed. A staffer reports that "Johnny was basically a tourist, the new guy in town who didn't know New York. The bar in Sardi's was next door to where we did the show. That was a favorite spot for Ed and Johnny."

In his book, Ed McMahon admits to the drinking, especially on Fridays: "On Fridays we used to do two shows, a live one at three-thirty in the afternoon and at seven we taped a show for the following Monday. This gave everybody a three-day weekend. Between those two shows Johnny and I got into the habit of strolling next door to Sardi's little bar for a couple of relaxers which we felt we needed before doing the second show. We only had about two hours. How much can you drink in two hours, especially if you're talking business? The trouble was that Johnny, as he's said many times on the air, isn't the world's greatest drinking man. Give him three shots and he gets very frisky. And sometimes when we'd come back to tape the Monday show, tongues got tangled and things got said that had to be bleeped."

According to staffers, the good times between Ed and Johnny mostly involved drinking. Though Carson and his wife Jody separated in 1959, Johnny wasn't conspicuously a ladies' man. He was still very much the shy Midwesterner.

A staffer on "Who Do You Trust?" says that "there weren't that many women coming by the dressing room after the show, you know, admiring fans. When he was on 'Trust' there wasn't much of that. He was a bigger star on 'The Tonight Show.' That's where fans were a little more direct. But everyone wanted Johnny for one reason or another. He and the show were that famous and influential."

As for the drinking, one recalls: "He was young and new in New York, he thought it was a lot of fun. A lot of young people think drinking's fun. And it was probably better than going home to Harrison and helping change diapers or whatever they were doing."

As all offices do, the "Who Do You Trust?" gang threw parties for various minor occasions. At one holiday party, everyone was gathered around celebrating. Johnny excused himself and went into a small office nearby and began making phone calls.

"We pretty much forgot about Johnny," one of the partiers remembers. "I needed to use the phone, and I picked it up. Johnny was on the line—but he wasn't talking to anyone. There was no one on the line. He was sitting by himself with the phone, just making up conversation. He did that because he just couldn't be comfortable at the party."

"Who Do You Trust?" continued to climb in the ratings. Johnny was the hot daytime idol of housewives across America. He wasn't only funny and handsome, he had physical prowess as well. There was the time he had an archery expert on. The man twanged out several shots but never hit the bull's-eye. Johnny calmly picked up a bow and arrow and scored on the very first try.

There was nobody on the air like Johnny and everyone knew it. Associate producer Mary Dodd recalls how far above the other quiz show hosts he was: "He obviously had comedy talent they didn't have, just to deliver the lines. I don't think Jack Bailey could have done those lines. The way Johnny looked, his experience, his talent."

People began recognizing Johnny's talent more and more. In addition to his duties on "Who Do You Trust?" he often turned up as a guest on other quiz programs. He was the mystery guest on "I've Got a Secret" once. Lucille Ball, on the rocks with Desi Arnaz, asked if Johnny was married. Carson paused and shot back: "My situation is the same as yours."

On January 10, 1958, Johnny made a daring move, taking over for Tom Ewell in the Broadway play *Tunnel of Love* at the National Theatre. His co-star was Marsha Hunt. The play was written by Peter DeVries and Joseph Fields. He played the lead, "Augie Poole," in a light-hearted Jack Lemmon–like way.

Marsha Hunt reported that "Johnny played it very close. He meant to make no mistakes and no waves. He was very professional and quiet." On opening night, "we were all braced to catch him and cover for him, in case he forgot a line or became nervous. Of course, he sailed on like a ship, cool as the proverbial cucumber."

The play closed February 23, but the "cucumber" was only cool on the outside. Carson worked so hard doing the show that he lost ten pounds off his already wiry frame. His work impressed some Broadway veterans. Gower Champion hoped to snare Johnny for *Bye Bye Birdie,* but Carson couldn't go out of town and leave "Who Do You Trust?"

Dick Van Dyke rocketed to fame in *Bye Bye Birdie* instead. Strangely, this would not be the last time those two names were bandied together. When Carl Reiner was casting for a new sitcom about a TV writer working in the city and living in the suburbs, the choice came down to the same two men. Of course, the title of the series ended up being "The Dick Van Dyke Show."

Johnny turned down sitcoms regularly. He did take parts in television dramas and comedies. He was seen in *Three Men on a Horse* on "Playhouse 90," and turned up on the "U.S. Steel Hour" in two productions: *Queen of the Orange Bowl* and *Girl in the Gold Bathtub.*

He claimed that doing the same show on Broadway night after night was "very boring," and that he also didn't want to be tied down to one character in a sitcom.

Johnny favored projects closer to his proven talents. He was doing well on both his quiz show and guesting on other quiz shows. He enjoyed variety shows—and talk shows, too. On May 26, 1958, Johnny began a week subbing for Jack Paar.

"Nobody's going to get an ulcer on this show," he said. "I don't expect to 'slay' anybody, but then I never did. My specialty is light satire of the easy, relaxed school, and I've a feeling it's the one form of comedy that'll probably survive on TV . . . on the Paar show, thank heaven, you can't rely on material, not when you have to entertain for an hour and forty-five minutes each night."

Johnny was well aware of the popularity of "The Tonight Show," and his reaction was pessimism. He saw what the show was doing to Jack. "You can't win. Look at the hottest hit on the air right now—the Jack Paar Show. Already *Look* magazine had an article called 'Will Success Spoil Jack Paar? Next they'll start the controversy routine, then the old process of picking the show apart . . . then the high-pressure boys will move in and want certain things done 'their' way, and before you know it, Bingo! Another what-ever-happened-to case . . . and when the show falls apart, look out, brother, all of a sudden there's only one guy holding that great big bag—the performer. Everybody else has crawled back into their martinis."

Johnny approached the show warily, and with a cool, light touch. It worked. His low-key style was a refreshing change of pace. So much so that Earl Wilson wrote, "Johnny is now NBC's secret weapon to succeed Jack Paar in case Jack really quits . . ."

Columnist Ben Gross of the *Daily News* talked to Carson about his foray into nighttime talk TV. He found the "boyish, 5-foot-10½-inch 153-pounder" impatient for a change. Would he like to do a show like Jack Paar's?

"I'd like to do one," Carson admitted cautiously, "but only if the circumstances are right."

"What's the big difference between day and night on TV?"

". . . At night you can do satire and talk about topical things because the audience is in the mood for that type of humor. But not during the day when you're playing to so many housewives."

"You mean that they aren't intelligent?"

"Of course they're intelligent. But satire requires concentrated looking and listening and most women during the day are too busy with children and household chores."

Occasionally people asked Johnny about his own wife at home. Carson replied honestly and directly: "My wife and I are separated and the children live with her. I don't see any disgrace in that. I wish there were more honesty about marriage."

To *The American Weekly* on July 8, 1962, he explained: "My kids seem happy and popular in spite of the fact that their mother and I have been separated for some time. I've seen unhappy couples who claim they can't break up because of the children—and yet their kids are obviously miserable living under the same roof with them."

Kay Gardella was one of the reporters who enjoyed Johnny's fresh honesty: "He's just a bright, straight-forward guy who's not afraid to face a few facts."

It bothered Johnny when he couldn't do honest comedy in stand-up. Looking through the news, Carson found a squib about gangster Mickey Cohen. The mobster's car was stolen, and his dog was in it at the time. On "The Steve Allen Show" Johnny joked: "The car had not been found, but the police recovered the dog—holding up a liquor store."

The following day he got threatening phone calls from a gangster-type who said, "Watch your step—don't make jokes about Mickey Cohen."

When he played it safe, that didn't work either. Johnny opened up a page in the May 17, 1959, *Daily News* and read the following: "What would we ever do without gag writers, and what would gag writers do if they didn't watch other programs on TV? Johnny Carson . . . told the one about the fellow who turned into a one-way street. His pal, terrified, asked him where he was going. 'I don't know,' replied the driver, 'but we're sure late. Everybody is coming back.' A few nights later, Myron Cohen told the same gag on Ed Sullivan's show."

Johnny was also beginning to get some nasty write-ups about his risqué double entendres. Staffers saw his face go white with anger when he read this in the *New York Journal-American:* "The show was constantly dirty. And the dirt was planned, too. There was always some old woman talking about taking her clothes off."

Johnny wanted to inject a little more satire in his stand-up act. He had a line he just couldn't use: "Where are tomorrow's comedians coming from? Based on recent observations, from the Democratic and Republican parties."

To Marie Torre he summed it up sullenly: "It is impossible for a comedian to be all things to all people." He pointed to "The Bob Newhart Show," which was getting solid ratings early in the 1961 season. "Newhart is trying to emphasize his monologues, and already some TV viewers are saying, 'Can he keep it up?' or 'I thought his material started to wear thin by the end of the first show.' That's how people talk . . ."

The idea of being funny about "all things to all people" stayed with him.

The big rage in stand-up at the time was "sick comedy," as personified by Lenny Bruce and Shelley Berman, along with the dark satire of political iconoclast Mort Sahl. Johnny stressed he was not one of those types. Johnny dared them to get out of the nightclubs and onto television: "Mort Sahl and Shelley Berman have about eight or nine routines—enough for about two shows on TV." He also knew that, as far as television was concerned, an act like Lenny's would never get on anyway—"There's no market for it."

Carson was restless. "Sure, I don't want to do this kind of thing all my life," he said at the time. "I may do a straight dramatic film for Columbia. . . . I'm signed up for guest shots with Garry Moore, Dinah Shore, and a few others. You have to keep your hand in the nighttime scene. There are some things you can't do in a daytime show. There's also talk of a night spot for me at ABC, but so far it's still talk."

In 1961 ABC made a tentative offer to Johnny for a talk show opposite Jack Paar. He turned it down, but asked if they'd be interested in "Who Do You Trust?" at that hour. In an interview with Roland Lindbloom for the *Newark Evening News*, Carson contrasted the proposed night version of "Who Do You Trust?" with the celebrity talk of Jack Paar: "I don't have celebrities on my show, I work with people. I've got the greatest staff of gag writers in the world—the people who come on my show . . . the emphasis is on the contestants. Do you know what the people watching us are most intereted in? Other people. The little chats we have with the contestants have more audience appeal than all the gimmicks of the game."

One day Carson's manager came up to him with some news. Instead of going on opposite Jack Paar, how would he like to replace Jack Paar? This time, Johnny was speechless.

8 THE TONIGHT SHOW

Jack Paar is the star, but guest hosts include quizmaster Johnny Carson. Topics for discussion include Johnny's takeover.

When Johnny was approached as a possible new "Tonight Show" host, he shook his head. "I just wasn't sure I could cut it," he said later. He didn't want to leave "Who Do You Trust?," an atmosphere he trusted, a place where he was "solid and secure."

Paar was the era's controversial superstar; his show had top guests the kind that Barbara Walters would have, more liberal empathy than Phil Donahue could ever muster, and a host with a bewildering mix of humanity and ego. Steve Allen's show had been more variety show; Paar made it more a "talk show" with viewer as voyeur.

Jack's style was "intimate" and real. He was humanly erratic, one night all charm and wit, the next night rude and blabbery. He could be the life of the party—or monopolize the show with boring home movies of his wife and kids. His "regulars" were more like kooky neighbors: ditsy women, crabby intellectuals, and non-celebrity "raconteurs" who only had "the gift of gab."

Throwing a conversational party every evening could destroy even the most outgoing host or hostess, and here was Paar, doing it live in front of some eight million people, with big names and high risk. People actually tuned in expecting controversy and chaos as much as comedy and chitchat. Today viewers are used to seeing celebrities yakking candidly and exposing both body and soul. Back in the early sixties, this was a new genre. Before long, Paar was showing stress and strain. It was not unusual to see stuttering "Leaky Jack" on the verge of tears, overcome by a guest's anecdote of sentiment or sadness.

Merv Griffin remembers: "What appealed to me about Jack and 'The Tonight Show' was the spontaneity; you never knew what was going to happen next, and I didn't dare miss the show because if I did that [episode] would be the one everyone was talking about next morning."

Back then, Paar was so well known that his announcer, Hugh Downs, only had to introduce him with two words: "Heeeerre's . . . Jack."

"He really did cry on TV when he felt like it," Earl Wilson notes. "He almost cried the time I called him a few years before and alerted him that NBC wanted him as a successor to Steve Allen. . . ." After Allen left, NBC went through a period of changes, including a show called "Tonight: America After Dark." All were disasters.

Wilson remembered Paar saying "I need that job. I've been so down and so discouraged. I've been about to get out of the business."

Even though Johnny Carson was feeling a little discouraged and restless in his quiz show chores, he wasn't quite ready to make the big step. He'd already been burned with his prime-time variety show, when his low-key presence had been compared negatively to flamboyant stars like Skelton, Berle, and Gleason. How could a hot, emotional Paar be replaced by a cool, impersonal Carson?

Oddly enough, Paar and Carson did have similarities. Just

seven years older than Johnny, Jack was from a small town in
Ohio. He was a radio disc jockey who became a hit when, in the
Army, he did stand-up comedy to entertain soldiers in the South
Pacific. Like Johnny, Paar first came to national TV with a short-
lived CBS variety series. Paar and Carson both had quirks about
people, but handled the situation in slightly different ways. "I'm
unhappy with strangers," Paar once said. "When I walk into a
room where I think people may dislike me, I find myself doing the
very things that would make them dislike me—overstating, being
smart-alecky, letting myself get emotional. All because I'm a terribly shy guy."

Paar did a monologue. He recalled: "Most of the really hard
creative work went into the monologue or opening comments on
the news of the day. I think that Johnny Carson and I were the
only ones really good at that form."

He bantered with bandleader Skitch Henderson and sidekick
Hugh Downs, then introduced the guests. Basically, this was the
format that every other talk show host would follow. Paar modestly notes: "If you are referring to the late-night program that
became the most imitated show in television and that consisted
mainly of conversation and personalities, then I am guilty."

Paar was a pioneer in another way. He was the first talk show
host to conspicuously throw his weight around. Paar knew that he
was hot, and he knew that NBC was making a lot of money from
his show. He was called a prima donna for his contract demands
and his cry for creative freedom and desensitized censorship.

Jack was gutsy and volatile. When he felt slighted by an article
in *TV Guide*, he began attacking the magazine's owner, Moe An-
nenberg, on the show. When NBC president Robert Sarnoff tried
to hush him, he snapped, "I should think that you would be concerned about a story that is harmful to your most successful program."

Paar's greatest controversy was over an allegedly dirty story.
Jack told his audience about an Englishwoman who planned to
travel abroad and wrote to her host asking about the "w.c." (the
polite Briton's term for the almost as euphemistic "water closet").
The host, who was not fluent in British English and thought she

was interested in the "wayside chapel," sent her the following letter, which Jack quoted:

"The w.c. is situated nine miles from the house you occupy, in the center of a beautiful grove of pine trees surrounded by lovely grounds. It is capable of holding 229 people and is open on Sunday and Thursday only. . . . I would suggest that you come early, although there is plenty of standing room as a rule. You will no doubt be glad to hear that a good number of people bring their lunch and make a day of it, while others, who can afford to, go by car and arrive just in time . . . on Thursday . . . there is a musical accompaniment. . . . It may interest you to know that my daughter was married in the w.c., and it was there that she met her husband. I can remember the rush there was for seats. There were ten people to a seat usually occupied by one. . . . I shall be delighted to reserve the best seat for you if you wish, where you will be seen by all . . ."

The humor was obviously mild. Compare it to the toilet humor Johnny was allowed to use in 1986. Describing the possibility of government officials testing urine for drug use, he quipped, "How do we know that the President and members of the cabinet will really take a urine test? Are you gonna believe the CIA? You're never gonna know until *The Washington Post* leaks it . . ."

In another monologue he spoke of a curious ailment: "The Vanna White Flu. It gives you a vowel movement."

Some twenty-five years earlier, Paar's "w. c." joke was considered shocking. It was deleted by the network censors.

Jack went on the air the next evening to explain the problem. Then he announced he was quitting the show. Breaking the show business tradition that the show must go on, Jack walked off. He left a startled Hugh Downs to complete the broadcast, along with scheduled guests Orson Bean and Shelley Berman.

This was national news. It was breathtaking scandal. Emotionally exhausted, Jack flew down to Florida, hiding from the press. The sensitive star was coaxed back weeks later. He told his audience, "When I walked off, I said there must be a better way of making a living. Well, I've looked and there isn't . . ."

Still, it was never the same. Paar wanted out. The job was becoming more wearying and less satisfying.

Backstage, his staff felt the same way. Dick Cavett worked for him as a comedy writer, and remarked "it was a little like living at home with an alcoholic parent." In Cavett's opinion the moody star could be "cagey and suspicious as well as appealing and attractive." It was Cavett's belief that Paar acted like someone with "a low-grade paranoia."

Fame was agony to the sensitive star. In one of his books he reported the misery of trying to use the urinal with fans watching: "Finally you reach the porcelain and find that—with all eyes on your performance—you cannot! What to do? They are all watching! You panic . . . you press the handle of the urinal, you whistle, and you wish you could get the battery-jump starter from the trunk of your auto. You think encouraging thoughts, hoping that it's a mental block, but find that your sphincter muscle has never heard of you . . . I tell you it's very hard being a star in a men's room."

Paar's vacations began to seem like "tryout" times for would-be hosts. Among the many who spelled relief for Paar were two quizmasters: Johnny Carson of "Who Do You Trust?" and Merv Griffin, host of "Play Your Hunch."

Merv was Paar's choice, not Johnny. Johnny was one of the hosts picked by NBC. Paar discovered Merv himself. It wasn't difficult. Griffin was doing "Play Your Hunch" in the same studio that Paar used for the evening's "Tonight Show" broadcasts. One day Paar happened to arrive early. He stopped the show, delighting the audience with his spontaneous appearance. Griffin reacted calmly and with good humor. Paar was impressed. He gave him guest host work and some advice: "Just always remember one thing about talk shows and you'll be fine: YOU always be prepared but let the show unfold. Let it be chaos—planned chaos. Chaos pays off on a talk show. You want an electric undercurrent that keeps the audience from knowing what is going to happen next. You be ready with your next question, but know when to let the show run itself."

Griffin's ratings were good. He figured he was going to take over for Paar. He recalls now, that "the network executives, however, had already signed a replacement, long before I showed up on the scene . . ."

NBC wanted Johnny. Johnny, with his manager imploring him to take the chance, finally agreed to accept.

NBC was happy to have a guy who was, like Allen and Paar, a comedian with a fast wit. He had five years of interview experience. He was nice looking. And, he was a wiseguy. Being a wiseguy seemed essential to having a talked-about talk show. Steve Allen specialized in Groucho-esque asides and deflating silliness. Jack Paar was a wiseguy who out-superstarred the superstars.

Johnny was a rascal, a charmer who could control guests with wit and a smile. There have been a variety of handsome wiseguys since 1962 (Chevy Chase was probably the most successful) but Johnny was the role model.

Before getting "The Tonight Show" assignment, there was plenty of evidence of Johnny's wiseguy abilities. At a dinner for Robert F. Kennedy, Johnny stunned guests on the dais by announcing, "I would have preferred a written invitation to this affair, instead of being rudely awakened at 4 A.M. by the FBI." At Friars' Roasts (these were private functions, in no way similar to the scripted "Dean Martin Roasts" of the seventies) Johnny proved he could duel with the best. He fended off bald insult comic Jack E. Leonard by calling him "The Mean Mr. Clean." Fellow comics doubled over with delight.

When Jan Murray made a long speech eulogizing the late Al Jolson, lamenting that his children would not grow up sharing the joy of Jolie's voice, Carson interrupted: "They grew up while you were talking!"

The Friars, guys like Joe E. Lewis, Buddy Hackett, Joey Adams, and Phil Silvers, enjoyed the young comic who could match them gag for gag. Silvers once said from the dais, "Johnny is the only Gentile on the dais and immediately after his speech we are going to circumcise him!"

Johnny bludgeoned back. Talking about Friar Alan King, he said, "All I've been reading about in the papers is Alan King and I'm tired of it! Alan King has guest shots. Alan King's producing

four shows. Alan King has a Rolls-Royce. Just once I'd like to
pick up the paper and see 'Alan King Has Gonorrhea.'"

When Jack Paar stepped aside, he chose to try a less strenuous
weekly prime-time series as a compromise. Even though he was
really not going off the air then, his farewell show was a major
event. For fifteen minutes Jack remained in his dressing room
while Hugh Downs read tributes to the "towering personality" and
celebrities filled the stage. On tape, everyone from Billy Graham,
Richard M. Nixon, and Robert F. Kennedy to Bob Hope and Jack
Benny paid him a final good-bye.

Just to show that bygones were not bygones, he took one last
opportunity to attack Dorothy Kilgallen, who was going to India
"to fight a mongoose." Then he called Walter Winchell a phony
who wore his patriotism "like a bathrobe."

At the end, a tearful Paar was serenaded by Robert Merrill
singing "Pagliacci." A "Tonight Show" title card was flashed on
the screen: "No More to Come."

It was no more, all right. March 29, 1962, was Jack's farewell.
On March 30, Johnny Carson didn't take over.

Not on March 31. Not on April Fool's Day.

Johnny's big break was being held up by ABC. When Paar
left, Johnny's contract had a half year still to go. When ABC
refused to let Johnny leave, he called them "the network with a
heart" on the air. They still wouldn't let him leave.

Frustrated and tense, Johnny was sentenced to six months of
waiting. Sometimes he could hardly wait to go in and show his
stuff. Other times he was like a prisoner on death row waiting for
the execution everyone predicted.

On March 28, the day before Paar's departure, Bob Williams
of the *New York Post* asked Johnny about "The Tonight Show."
Carson said: "What can I say? That I'm worried? How would that
look in print?"

While he waited, NBC went with guest hosts, including some
of the most famous names in show business. Any one of them
could catch fire and become a candidate to replace Carson the
moment his ratings dipped.

The nervous young quiz show host had to sit and anticipate

what he was going to do. Waiting with him, like chatty relatives accompanying him to the dentist's office, were the reporters. They took his mind off the agonizing wait with irritating questions: "Johnny, what are you going to do? How can you replace Paar? What will your show be like?"

He found no peace. Acquaintances were shaking their heads saying, "Gee, how can you possibly do better than Paar? We sympathize with you, pal." Co-workers offered a dizzying array of advice. "Grab big guests." "Go back to sketches." "Use regulars." "Go it alone."

New York Herald-Tribune reporter Richard K. Doan remembered interviewing Carson once he was announced as the new "Tonight Show" host. Carson lit a cigarette and began to answer one of Doan's questions. Then he looked down and saw a cigarette already burning in his ashtray. "Who's nervous?" Johnny said.

Columnist Kay Gardella witnessed Carson nervously reciting all the pitfalls of the job: "The job primarily, on a nightly show, is to be a catalyst. . . . The trick is to keep things going. . . . I know it's a tremendous strain doing a nightly show. You could dig a ditch for twelve hours a day and not be as tired. It's the hottest spot on television." But there was that paradox to Carson. He wanted it. "It's also the only place left where you can experiment. . . . It's a comedy laboratory. Sure, I could remain secure by staying in daytime TV and not running the risk of failure . . . but there's something more to show business than security. I suppose it's ego. . . ."

He knew he was no Jack Paar. Carson told Gardella: "It would be difficult to continue that kind of rapport with the people. I'm going to try to make it an entertaining show."

As the months passed, Carson's feelings seesawed, sometimes coming to rest in the numb middle-ground of ambivalence. To Margaret McManus he shrugged and said, "I guess I'm glad to be leaving ["Who Do You Trust?"] after so long a haul, although you develop an affinity for something you've done this long. I can't tell how I'll feel on the last day. After a few weeks of 'Tonight,' it might look darn good to me." Of the impending show, he allowed,

"You cannot be brilliant on every show. There will be nights when you won't be funny and times when you can think of nothing to say. There will be times when the show just hangs there and you must sense this quickly, and do something, anything, to change the pace."

He wasn't quite sure what he was going to do, though. Even the monologue, Carson's strong point, was in doubt. "It can be a trap," he told one reporter. "We'll probably vary the opening."

Ed McMahon was coming along as Johnny's sidekick. He asked Johnny, "How do you see my role in this show? What's my stance? How do I fit in?"

Johnny answered, "Ed, if you mean, what are you going to do, let me put it to you this way. I don't even know what I'm going to do. So let's just play it by ear and see what happens."

Carson ended "Who Do You Trust?" on September 7, and had barely three weeks to pull together the premiere of "The Tonight Show."

Johnny doubted his bold and brash decision to leap for the top. He had very few close friends to lean on. The fall could kill him professionally. All he was doing was taking over the most prestigious, pressure-filled five-times-a-week job in show business. All he had to do was be funny and effortlessly charming, score big ratings, and make everyone forget about Jack Paar.

One day at the office Johnny opened a copy of the *New York World-Telegram* and was greeted with a headline in inch-high type: "Will Carson Be Up to Paar?"

The first sentence: "Several hours before air time on the night of Oct. 1, Johnny Carson will step out before a studio audience in Rockefeller Center and run a risk few performers care to undertake: laying a big, fat egg."

THE TONIGHT SHOW

9

Starring Johnny Carson. Greeting Johnny:
a hoard of reporters, surprise guests, and
feuding Jack Paar.

hile Johnny waited to take over "The Tonight Show," the
ratings began to dip. The guest hosts included everyone
from Groucho Marx to Jerry Lewis, from Mort Sahl to Soupy
Sales. Merv Griffin was given a good look when he guest-hosted,
as was Joey Bishop. Comedian/quiz show host Jan Murray was
auditioned along with veteran Art Linkletter.

Without Paar, relying on an uncertain collection of guest hosts,
NBC lost a million dollars as sponsors slowly began to defect.

On April 6, 1962, while NBC was struggling with "The
Tonight Show," Johnny kept up appearances. He was booked on
"The Timex All-Star Comedy Show." Johnny was still very much
the low-key comedian, and anyone looking at him as the new star
of "The Tonight Show" couldn't see much.

The show starred powerhouse comedians like Buddy Hackett
and the team of Carl Reiner and Mel Brooks. It opened with the

stars confused over who would host the show, which featured a
variety of novelty acts and singers in addition to the comedy. "Get
outta here!" Hackett shouted, "Me a host?" Brooks said, "No. I'd
be perfect but I'm a bit of a nut." Hackett said, "You gotta get
the right type. A fella who won't offend anybody, a colorless personality . . . he should be neat and not too bright. A real loser!"

Buddy and the rest of the cast turned to stare at Johnny.
Johnny looked into the camera uncomfortably and said in dead-
pan chagrin, "Hi there. This is your host: Johnny 'colorless, neutral, neat, and not too bright, a real loser' Carson."

Johnny had little to do as he shyly introduced the acts. He
appeared in a few blackout sketches that had the look of "Carson's Cellar." In one quickie, he was a tough-looking cowboy—
only when he holstered his guns his pants fell down. In another
quickie, he was a construction worker who, when interviewed,
spoke in a high effeminate voice. In another quickie, a commercial parody, he was a doctor with sound advice: Drink booze. He
pulled a bottle out of his desk and started guzzling. Fade to
black.

This was not very impressive stuff. Some at NBC were very
worried. In a now-famous move, executive Mort Werner called a
meeting. He unveiled a photo of Steve Allen—an unknown who
nobody had thought would be a success. Then he brought out a
picture of Jack Paar—also an unknown whom everyone had
thought would bomb. Then he explained that Johnny Carson was
just like them—so relax—this dull guy could turn out to be the
most expplosive host of them all.

Johnny was the co-host of the 1962 Emmy Awards in May, and
he was far more in control, displaying much more of his true self
than on the odd, deprecating "Timex" special.

Everyone awaited the arrival of Johnny Carson. *TV Guide* announced he was "Johnny on the Spot." The newspapers were
buzzing with the report that Carson was getting $100,000 a year,
the magic number reserved for a handful of public heroes like
Mickey Mantle and Willie Mays. "The term is for a firm twenty-
six weeks," Carson said. "It can be extended to two, three, four,

or five years, but like any contract written for new talent, if the show doesn't go, the contract doesn't mean much."

The show premiered on October 1, 1962. October 1 was the day that Johnny had moved to his first real home in Avoca, Iowa. And it was on another October 1 that Johnny had married his first real sweetheart, Jody Wolcott.

Before the show Johnny received two gifts. He received a pair of cuff links in gold that depicted St. Genesius, the patron saint of actors. And from his new girl friend, Joanne Copeland, he received another pair of cuff links. These were custom-made, with NBC cameras on them. Johnny wore one of each, hoping this would double his luck.

CBS and ABC hadn't come up with anything to stop "The Tonight Show." Both networks were still allowing their affiliates to pick their own programming. On the night of Johnny's splashy debut with Joan Crawford, Tony Bennett, Rudy Vallee, and Mel Brooks, CBS's New York affiliate ran a 1935 George Raft movie called *Rumba* and ABC offered *Father Was a Fullback*, a 1949 Fred MacMurray comedy. The competition really was coming from the syndicated Steve Allen show.

One of the greatest comedians of all time came out on that October night to face the expectant audience. It was Groucho Marx. He introduced Johnny, who had been expectant for about six months. Johnny said, "Now I'm aware of what you ladies must go through in a pregnancy. The difference is I didn't get sick. But I'm the only performer ever held up and spanked by General Sarnoff."

Johnny was off and running.

Like an important Broadway show, the debut of the new "Tonight Show" was hot entertainment news. *New York Times* critic Jack Gould delivered the big verdict: "The permanent replacement for Jack Paar is off to an attractive start," he pronounced. "The format of 'Tonight' remains unchanged, but Mr. Carson's style is his own. He has the proverbial engaging smile and the quick mind essential to sustaining and seasoning a marathon of banter."

The critic was impressed with Carson's fiesty honesty: "At the outset he said he was not going to describe every guest as an old and dear friend, an indication of a refreshing attitude against prevalent show-business hokum. A healthy independence without overtones of neuroses could wear very well."

And, establishing what would be a common critical complaint over the years, Gould found less fault with Carson than with the guests. Gould wondered why the guest he liked didn't get as much time as a guest he didn't like: "It was a particular pity that Miss Crawford had to sit mute and out of camera range while Mel Brooks went his strained way."

In Chicago, Johnny racked up phenomenal numbers, grabbing 58 percent of the viewing audience. Reports were high all over the country. *Variety* reported that "The Johnny Carson version of the 'Tonight' show is heady stuff . . ."

Johnny kept wearing his mismatched cuff links and the good luck continued.

Checking back on the show a few months later, Jack Gould reported that "Mr. Carson . . . has worked out a style much his own. Chiefly the program is a showcase for one of the quickest minds on the air. When a colloquy gets going he can come up with an inverted quip that is often hilarious. He leans to an imp-ish quality and admittedly savors the double entendre, occasion-ally to his own disadvantage. But for light laughter his batting average night after night is extraordinarily good."

On an emotional level, Jack Paar could not have been happy about Carson's success. He could not have been pleased that a fickle public loved John as they'd loved Jack. Paar was "The King" of late-night TV, and Johnny had modestly told reporters "Just call me 'The Prince.'" But the ratings anointed Carson as the new royalty.

Paar was reminded of this every day, and to make matters worse, for several awkward weeks he taped his new prime-time series right across from "The Tonight Show" studio.

Johnny had won the biggest battle of his career: succeeding on "The Tonight Show." But he had yet to face that show biz stress test—the personality feud. It was Jack Paar vs. Johnny Carson, man-to-man.

Johnny tried to avoid it. Interviewed by Herbert Kamm, Carson admitted that he and Paar were not close. "When I was signed as his permanent replacement early this year, he didn't write or call, and I didn't feel it was my place to do it. I've never seen Jack Paar socially any place and I was never a guest on the show when he was presiding. He might be an interesting guy to know. I just don't know. I really don't have the slightest idea what he's like."

Johnny said, "Paar works emotionally. I work intellectually."

Johnny also said, "I don't think Jack is an easy man to get to know." He added, "I think I am very easy to get to know."

He told the press that Paar was irreplaceable: "It would be foolhardy to try and top Jack Paar." Then he said: "The only way it could be done is to walk on stage and drop an atom bomb."

Somehow Carson's compliments sounded a little left-handed. "He [Paar] took a show that was absolutely nothing . . . and he made it the most talked about show in television history," Carson said. And: "Whether you liked him personally or not had nothing to do with it. He did one hell of a job."

"I've always had respect for Jack," Carson told John P. Shanley in the *New York Times*. "Disregarding the emotional aspects of the show, it was seldom dull."

Daily News columnist Ben Gross was among the many who came in search of controversy: "Isn't it true that it was Paar who suggested you as his successor?" Gross asked.

"I've heard reports to that effect but really don't know," Johnny replied. Actually, it was well known that NBC's Mort Werner was the man responsible. Carson was asked how he got along with Paar.

"Well, on my opening night he sent me a nice wire and since then I've run into him at the NBC studios. He's been most cordial. We get along well, but we've never really had a social relationship."

Jack Paar had a different story.

To Jack Iams in *The Saturday Evening Post*, he insisted that

Carson was so unsure of himself he went to Jack for help. "It used to be embarrassing," Paar complained. "Johnny would be hanging around the studio where we were taping, and he'd say, 'Well, what do you think Jack? How's it going?' And all I could say was, 'Johnny, I hear it's great . . .'

Paar inferred that Johnny's show was past helping. "Frankly it isn't my cup of tea," he said. He added that he couldn't even sit through a show. "I don't mean to sound condescending, it's just that I can't stay awake that late."

Cool Johnny blazed white-hot. After *The Saturday Evening Post* hit, Carson fired back.

"Controversy is something that must come naturally and honestly," he said. "I don't deliberately start arguments and never shall."

Then, in front of his "Tonight Show" audience, Johnny showed his disgust for Paar's comments. "I didn't 'hang around' his studio like a cocker spaniel, any more than Goldwater goes swimming at Hyannis Port." He denied even talking to Jack about "The Tonight Show," insisting that the longest conversation they had was when he wished Jack well with his first season in prime time.

Carson couldn't understand what could've made Paar so sensitive. Then he said that if anything embarrassed Jack, it might've been the time they happened to meet in the men's room. "Maybe that's what embarrassed him," Johnny said. After hitting low, he cried foul. "Paar says he's honest," Johnny deadpanned. "But how could someone as childish as Paar know right from wrong? I don't want to get into an argument," he added, "it's like getting into an argument with my children. They get petulant and the truth gets all mixed up."

Paar fired back: "Other than recommending to NBC that he replace me, I have never done or said an unkind thing publicly or privately about Johnny Carson. Further, I have ignored or chosen to disregard snide references to me by Carson. If Johnny needs a feud to help his ratings he will find this like tickling. He can't do it himself. I don't need it, as my last national rating was 48 percent of the audience, our highest of the year."

On Paar's prime-time show in February 1963, guest Oscar Le-

vant described Johnny: "He's quite amiable about being dull."
Carson took pity on Levant, the renowned hypochondriac, and
refused to "pick on a man who has emotional problems."

The feud sputtered on. By April 1963 Carson had no praise for
Paar at all: "When it comes right down to it, Paar didn't do anything different from Steve Allen."

In June 1965, Paar's prime-time show faded away and Jack
reclusively bought WMTW-TV in Poland Springs, Maine, for
three and a half million dollars. Johnny was amused to think of
Jack "off somewhere communing with a moose."

Paar made a very determined effort to be forgotten, rarely
granting interviews. When he did, somehow Carson's name came
up. In 1967 he told *TV Guide* that Carson was no Merv Griffin:
"He started with 180 stations and followed the most successful
commercial show in television. . . . Merv Griffin had to begin
from zero. Griffin has, in my view, the best-booked show and he
obviously has read a book."

Paar told Tom Shales that his show "was a more literate show
than it is now." And in the *New York Times* he asked, "Can you
prove to me that Carson has ever read a book?"

Jack mellowed slightly. In 1983 the ex-star wrote a memoir.
Often caustic and nasty, he skewered everyone from Steve Allen
to Groucho Marx. But Paar wrote: "I have enormous respect for
Johnny Carson." Then he insisted that even if it really was NBC
who chose Carson, he supported him: "I can take no credit in
recommending Johnny. I wanted to get away so badly that I would
have accepted, if I was asked, to be replaced by . . . Yogi Berra.
It's just that Johnny was my choice, and being stubborn, I like to
be right!"

Paar's opinion of Carson flickered the other way within a
month. He wanted to promote his book on Carson's show, and
when producer Fred DeCordova was slow in getting back to him,
Paar got spooked. "He has a thing about me," Paar moaned to
reporters. "I invented that kind of television.————them, I'm
not going on at all."

In May 1986, Jack was coaxed into appearing on an NBC special honoring the network's thirty stellar years of broadcasting.

All "The Tonight Show" hosts were reunited. Surprisingly, they all got along. In a charming bit of mutual revisionist history, the story went out that Paar and Carson had "never even met." Johnny was quoted in the paper as walking up to Paar with a handshake, a smile and a "Hi, we've never been properly introduced. I'm Johnny Carson."

"He couldn't have been nicer," Paar told everyone.

In November 1986 Jack came back for a special to show kinescopes of his shows with the Kennedys, Judy Garland, Richard Nixon, and "discovery" Bill Cosby, who actually made his "Tonight Show" debut during Carson's reign. In a tense publicity move, he agreed to go on "The Tonight Show" to promote it. This would be a historic "first-time" for Jack on Johnny's show.

Johnny gave Jack a nice introduction, and when Paar came through the curtains, he stayed there. Moved and emotional, Paar stayed in the spotlights acknowledging the applause until Johnny came out from behind his desk, embraced him, and brought him over to the couch.

"Dr. Livingstone, I presume?" Jack asked. Then he turned to "Doc" Severinsen, asking, "Who are you?"

"I'm a friend of José Melis," Doc shot back.

"We should lay a couple of things to rest," Carson said. "Jack and I are not what you'd call close friends . . . the longest conversation we had was maybe five or ten minutes, some years ago when we first met, and that was about it."

And that was about all Johnny could say. Jack took over, glossing over questions, hardly letting Johnny ask any. Instead it was a Paar monologue, featuring anecdotal story after story.

"I'm sorry to go so long . . .," Paar said during one tale, but it was obvious that he was too nervous to sit still for any serious questions.

"Why do I feel I'm guesting on your show?" Johnny asked with a smile. Paar smiled, and asked to tell another story. Johnny, eyeing Jack more with curiosity than anything else, politely listened, his hands in front of him on his desk like a schoolboy.

"Why'd you give up 'The Tonight Show'?" Johnny finally asked. "You could've been here today . . ."

"Well," Jack answered quickly, "you needed the work . . ."

The audience laughed at the neat deflection, and Jack carefully added, "Nobody will ever ever equal what you have done on this show."

Paar was, as usual, compelling with his conversation. The great "meeting," the subject of great expectation for those who remembered Paar, turned out to be an anticlimax. No fond stories about "The Tonight Show," no one-upmanship, nothing but a slightly edgy and attentive Carson holding the steering wheel while Jack drifted off with stories and turned away from any potential disaster.

When Jack bid farewell, choking back a self-deprecating, "I talk too much," Johnny seemed relieved. His face pinkened, an improbable smile twisted over his lips, and he started breaking up as he said, "That's the longest conversation I've had with Jack Paar in thirty-two years!" And it was nothing much at all.

The next night he couldn't resist getting in a few lines about the anticlimactic meeting. "I was almost late tonight," he said. "Jack Paar is still backstage. He was talking about his trip to Guam with Randy . . ." He did a light impression of Paar's small, sincere little voice: "Jack does like to talk, you know . . ."

A week later Jack told the *New York Times* that Johnny was "a great, great clown," and then admitted "I go to bed early. I've seen Johnny Carson maybe five times in my life." He refused to comment on the new talk show hosts, the Kleins, Brenners, etc., etc., though he sided with Johnny over Joan Rivers: "I don't care for her or for that kind of aggressive tastelessness." Then he added, "I'm better than any of them alone, if I have something to talk about."

But it was too late now, and it was too late then. In 1963, the hot star was now Johnny Carson.

The same as twenty-five years ago, fans were still trying to figure out who was the real Johnny Carson. Johnny offered a few glimpses back then. He did more interviews. He even allowed for some self-analysis.

In an issue of *Esquire*, a month after his premiere on "The

Tonight Show," he drew his own self-portrait and answered a kind
of questionnaire about himself.

Carson's cartoon-doodle of himself looked like a drawing of a
twelve-year-old, not an adult. The hair was mashed forward "pud-
ding bowl" style, the ears were large, and the nose crooked. The
eyes were enigmatic. The mouth was a goofy half-smile. The head
sat on a bare, squared outline of a neck and shoulders.

Rather than answer *Esquire*'s questions with the kind of glib
and evasive wisecracks he uses during "questions from the audience" today, Carson was remarkably serious and truthful:

"What would you really rather do?"

"I once thought of being a doctor . . ."

"What's your most paradoxical quality?"

"The outward relaxed appearance often does not match the inner feelings. Sometimes after a program someone will comment on
how relaxed I seemed to be . . . when in truth, I felt like I was
coming unglued."

"What are the chinks in your armor?"

"A certain restlessness . . . the inability at times to finish one
project before taking on another one."

"What's your boiling point?"

"I can get pretty angry at myself at times . . . perhaps because
I let petty things annoy me. Other than that: strangers who want
to tell me a dirty joke."

"What's your personal panacea?"

"To be by myself for a while . . . and try to bring my problems
down to their perspective."

He mentioned that he had the fear that his good fortune, health
and luck would run out. And when asked for his "secret satisfaction," he responded with a golden rule drilled into him from
childhood: "I believe the only real satisfaction anyone can have is
by doing something for someone else. If you can do it anony-
mously, so much the better."

Johnny's first months on the air were a success, but he wasn't
comfortable. "I'm too close to it," he told Jack O'Brien.

Johnny was still very self-conscious. He had to live with the
insecurity that at any point, something said in the course of con-

versation could turn out wrong. It could be libelous. Or it could just be dumb.

One night Robert Merrill came on the show and sang an operatic piece. Johnny was impressed. "Is this guy still writing operas?" he asked. Merrill replied, "He's been dead seventy-five years."

When Art Stark, his producer on "Who Do You Trust?" became available, Johnny eagerly brought him on board. Many believed Stark was responsible for calming Johnny down, tailoring the show to his needs, assuming some of the pressures.

"After six months I had become comfortable," Carson later remarked—coincidentally the time of Stark's arrival.

Stark reinstituted the scripting policy used on "Who Do You Trust?" where staff writers Alen Robin, Jim McGee, and Herb Sargent blocked out good questions and funny ad-libs for Johnny to use with the guests. Pre-interviews were crucial, especially now that Johnny was handling big names in prime time. He couldn't afford to look foolish. Johnny could bluff through talk with a couple on "Who Do You Trust?" but he had to ask Art Stark and Skitch Henderson who Simon and Garfunkel were when they were booked on the show.

With Stark, commercial breaks weren't as rigid. Johnny could keep going if he was hot, or be rescued when things got cold. Stark was a tough producer with definite ideas on how the show should be run.

Coincidentally, without Art Stark "Who Do You Trust?" died out completely. New host Woody Woodbury refused to follow Stark's formula, and on December 23 the show was history.

And, coincidentally, another show premiered on October 1, 1962, along with "The Tonight Show." It was a talk show hosted by Merv Griffin. Griffin was given his own daytime show by NBC, perhaps to groom him as a possible successor should Carson fail. The idea of "daytime talk" to "nighttime talk" had been used when Paar was promoted from the morning to "Tonight." It would be used repeatedly with morning tryouts for everyone from Dick Cavett to David Letterman.

Merv recalls: "Since Johnny Carson's version of 'The Tonight

Show' had debuted on the same day as 'The Merv Griffin Show,' a natural rivalry existed between the two shows. . . ." This produced some minor skirmishes at first. On Johnny's show one night, comedian/actor Mickey Shaughnessy happened to mention "The Merv Griffin Show." Then "Tonight Show" producer Perry Ross bleeped the plug. Merv was furious, and said so on his show. There wasn't enough time to start a rivalry, though. Merv's original show folded after six months.

Johnny's show was a powerhouse, sold out months in advance. Advertisers couldn't wait to get in on the action, though viewers, and even guests, felt there were more than enough ads. Lauren Bacall, interrupted by Johnny for yet another commercial break, said, "I can't complete a thought!"

Carson defended the breaks: "On the BBC they don't have any commercials—and not too many good shows, either."

The *New York Times* monitored Carson's show and counted every commercial, every introduction to a commercial, every second wasted by a placard saying "Back in a Moment." In ten minutes (11:51 to 12:01) "there were seven commercials totaling five minutes and fifteen seconds while redundant title cards and promotion material consumed another twenty seconds. Carson, the star, finished second to the clutter. He was allotted four minutes, nineteen seconds. Profits, anyone?"

The difference between Johnny's "Tonight Show" and Jack Paar's version was now even more pronounced. The agile, younger Carson did more and more "stunts," with the approval of Art Stark, who had encouraged him on "Who Do You Trust?" From playing baseball with Mickey Mantle and Roger Maris, Johnny went on to wrestle Antonino Rocca and become a human canvas for painter Walter Gaudnek.

He did a free-fall 10,000 feet from a plane. It was his very first parachute jump. "NBC thought it was a little hairy, my doing it that is, but what could they do about it? I hadn't told them in advance what I was planning!"

NBC was equally worried when naughty Johnny did stunts with lovely ladies. He practiced a snake dance with the exotic Margo, took hula lessons from the new Miss U.S.A. from Hawaii, and exercised with fitness buff Debbie Drake. When they were stretched out on a mat together, he cracked, "Do you want to leave a call?"

Carson, getting into the swing of city living off-camera, radiated the pleasures of city living on his show. He was super hip, he frolicked with guest stars like Mamie Van Doren and Jayne Mansfield, and he traded quips with hot shots like Buddy Hackett. One night while the camera was on Ed McMahon during an Alpo commercial, Buddy began taking his clothes off just out of camera range. The audience roared. And Buddy went all the way.

Johnny's scripts were definitely to the left of "The Red Skelton Hour." Here's a portion of a script he was handed for a sketch with guest Mamie Van Doren. Johnny is playing "Kit" Carson, Western hero. He's describing an encounter with a bear. He says he tried to shoot the bear in the leg. Mamie feels his leg. Then Johnny explains, "I figure I missed his leg so I aimed for his chest." [Johnny looks at Mamie and she grabs him around the chest and back and feels all over.]

> ED: "Did you finally shoot him?"
> JOHNNY: "Yep."
> ED: "Where?"
> JOHNNY: "You gotta be kidding . . ."

Middle America ate it up. Because Johnny was one of them— and he was living a lifestyle they longed for. The vicarious thrills just kept on coming, and Johnny often did slicker-type gags poking fun at the "Timmies" who were too hokey to dig guests like Buddy Rich and Sammy Davis, Jr.

Many cited Art Stark for stacking the deck with the stacked starlets and oddball guests who would become a Carson "Tonight Show" standard. When called on the carpet for the double entendres, Carson huffed, "If you can't say a few sophisticated things at twelve o'clock at night without being called dirty, we're in trouble."

Johnny knew the audience was behind him. Even now, he asks

their approval on a questionable joke. At his desk, shuffling
through the gag cards during a specialty bit, he'll go "Nope . . .
That one's too sexy" or "I can't get away with this!" The audience
cheers, cries out, and goads him on. He shrugs and gives in to
"popular demand."

Back then, he really pioneered risqué humor on TV. He had
the censors cringing over every line. There were flare-ups, like
the time he described how his path to work was a minefield because dog owners weren't cleaning up after their pets: "And that's
how The Twist started!"

Yet for every double entendre scored, viewers seemed to cheer
for the next one.

"The Tonight Show" was a hot ticket—and an "R-rated" one at
that. No one under eighteen was allowed in. One reason was that
the expletives were heard live but deleted on the tape delay. But
sometimes even the show looked risqué! Johnny would run around
with his pants off! Ed McMahon says, "Sometimes when he has to
make a quick change for a Mighty Carson Art Players sketch or
something else that calls for costuming, he'll just wear his shirt
and jacket because it takes too long to drag off a pair of trousers."
This is hidden by the desk—but the studio audience is laughing
at the secret.

There was the time the studio audience saw even more of
Johnny. He was doing a bit as Shirley Temple. The camera was
focused straight ahead. But the front rows, looking up, could see
he had forgotten to wear anything under his skirt!

Watching "The Tonight Show" with Paar was like being in
someone's living room. Now it was like being in a flashy New
York City nightclub. It was glamorous. But, for the host, it was
also hard work and a lot of drudgery.

Johnny described his workday this way: "I get up between nine
and ten in the morning. I don't believe in jumping out of bed and
shouting 'Hey, hey, another day.' I just grumble and sulk for a
while. I don't really start to function until noon or afterwards."

Breakfast was always simple. A few glasses of juice were
enough, maybe some scrambled eggs if he was really hungry. At
two in the afternoon he would be up at the studio.

Studio 6B at 30 Rockefeller Plaza first opened its doors in 1941. Radio shows like "Manhattan Merry-Go-Round" were broadcast there. The studio was renovated in 1948 and was used for Milton Berle's TV show and the very first "Tonight"-type program, "Broadway Open House," starring Jerry Lester.

Carson recalled his afternoon would involve sitting down with Art Stark and going over the show. "And it takes a couple of hours to lay out the night's show." After checking the questions mapped out for each guest, Johnny would tackle the hardest part: the monologue. The show had to open with a hook and he was the center of attention.

He hated the routine just as much as any office worker, grumbling, "I just wish I could find some way so I don't have to spend four or five hours in the office, because I would be fresher when I went on the show."

He wasn't spending all his time working on the show, though. Staffers noticed a petite brunette hanging around him. Her name was Joanne Copeland.

"When I was divorced from my first wife," Johnny Carson once told Alex Haley, "that's the lowest I've ever felt, the worst personal experience of my life. We'd been married ten years . . . children were involved . . . that's the worst guilt hangup you can have, when children are involved. But divorce sometimes is the only answer. I think it's almost immoral to keep on with a marriage that's really bad."

With Joanne, things were looking really, really good.

10 THE TONIGHT SHOW

Johnny's very special lady is brunette Joanne Copeland.

In October 1963, a year after his premiere on "The Tonight Show," Johnny was such a hot property he was signed by MGM for a movie, *Looking for Love*, co-starring Connie Francis, Jim Hutton, and Joby Baker. Johnny recalls: "Technicians in the colorization lab are going back to electronically remove the color by computer—and I asked them if they could remove me by computer!" He basically played himself (a TV personality) in a guest-starring role. The film was a bomb, but he wasn't in it long enough to be singled out for abuse.

In real life Johnny had been looking for love for some time. He and Jody were long separated, and divorce was only a matter of time. Johnny and "Tonight Show" producer Art Stark were out in California for a week and had dinner with Mary Tyler Moore. Johnny told Art: "That's the kind of wife I should have."

Some time later he was squiring a brunette named Joanne

Copeland. She seemed pretty close to the bright, sexy, happy-housewife-type Mary Tyler Moore played on "The Dick Van Dyke Show." Joanne didn't exactly resemble Mary physically, but from a distance they looked alike. Both were conspicuous in the early sixties for favoring slacks over dresses. Joanne's wardrobe would eventually contain over forty pairs.

Born on October 20, she was going to be the balancing Libra to the October 23 Scorpio Johnny.

Joanne Bee Copeland had three sisters, Barbara Glee and Carole Lee and Shirlee Mee. The girls' childhood wasn't as cute as their names. Born in San Francisco, Joanne's parents separated when she was a year old. She was disposed of in Catholic convents. Different interviewers reported that she attended different colleges. Kay Gardella reported she majored in psychology at Stanford University. Susan Rogers reported she majored in decorating at San Mateo College. Most remember that at San Mateo she was a very popular cheerleader.

Out on her own, she first worked as a stewardess and then came to New York as a model. She graduated to "elbow grabber" on the quiz show "Video Village," the hostess escorting contestants up onto the stage. The host was Monty Hall. The host of "Who Do You Trust?" was cuter.

She claims her first meeting with Johnny was arranged by her father, George.

"I have a young man I want you to meet," he told her.

Mr. Copeland took his daughter down to Eddie Condon's restaurant for dinner with Johnny. After an evidently uneventful meal, the trio went back to Joanne's apartment. Joanne's father wanted Johnny to listen to an audition tape of Joanne's sister playing the violin.

Johnny politely listened for a while.

"What's your professional advice?" Mr. Copeland asked.

"I advise she quit as soon as possible."

Joanne was impressed. She told Gael Greene later: "Anyone who can be that honest when he's trying to impress a girl's father . . . I said to myself, I have to marry this man."

Later she and Johnny went out by themselves. Johnny sug-

gested something simple—hamburgers at P. J. Clarke's. As they
were leaving, Joanne noticed that heads were turning. The pretty
petite model turned to Johnny and said, "People are staring at
me!"

Johnny began to blush.

"I think it's me they're staring at."

Someone close to Johnny at the time believes that the story of
their meeting, told often by Joanne in the press, might be just a
story: "My guess is he probably picked her up at the neighborhood bar. She lived in the same building on York Avenue;
there was a restaurant downstairs in that building. My guess is
that's where they met."

Joanne's bright and bouncy style seemed to impress Johnny.
She seemed to be the model of the "Total Woman," and there
wasn't even a term for that yet. The ex-cheerleader just wanted a
chance to impress Johnny even more. She started by decorating
Johnny's bachelor apartment at 1161 York Avenue.

With a bruising separation from his first wife, a pressure-
packed television show, and a lot of worries, Joanne was just what
Johnny needed.

At work Johnny was sitting in the hot seat, calmly enduring the
electric volts zapped at him every day as he interviewed guests,
entertained the nation, and dealt with business problems. After
work, he'd been extinguishing the electric fire by dousing alcohol
on it. As Ed McMahon recalled: "With his first marriage . . . like
most men in that situation, he dreaded going home. We got into
the habit of stopping next door at Sardi's for a drink after the
show. I'd miss my train to Philadelphia . . ." Johnny couldn't
handle the liquor as well as Ed, and soon he developed a reputation for being a "mean drunk."

One night at a celebrity gathering Johnny had one too many
and was making salty jokes. Jacqueline Susann finally turned to
him and said, "You are unbearably rude. Please leave." Johnny
ignored her. Jackie was drinking a Black Russian—until she
threw it right in his face.

Sometimes the battles were a little more even. In the company
of other comics, it was impossible to get too drunk or too obnox-

ious. Several insiders, including Ed McMahon, can recall the comedy war between Johnny and Jonathan Winters. It took place in Philadelphia. It was a freezing cold day and a large group, including Johnny and Jonathan, went to a football game. Afterward they went back to Carson's hotel and began drinking "to warm up."

As one person there remembers, the two funnymen "got into almost a duel. They could easily have come to blows. It got meaner and nastier. It was Winters and Carson, each topping the other with ad-libs, and they were so funny it was frightening. Johnny was a very mean drunk, and it was turning very nasty. They were still in the persona of performers, insulting each other—they were both unbelievable."

In front of a half-dozen people they continued to fence and parry. The gags were fast but the competitors were furious. Fortunately, the effects of the alcohol served to dampen the fire and they one-upped each other till five in the morning, when neither could keep his eyes open.

Carson's problems with alcohol and aggression reached a peak one night in Las Vegas. Some "Tonight Show" staffers still shake their heads remembering it. After one drink too many, Johnny got into a dispute with a showgirl. Just what happened no one cares to recall on the record. But whatever happened, the girl wasn't too pleased. She told her "pals."

When Johnny came up to his room the next night, a few goons were waiting in the hallway. When they left, the comedian was so badly beaten he couldn't perform for a week.

"That was probably the worst," one insider remembers. "But there were other times. Once he was drunk and accidentally cut himself pretty badly. The story went out that he hurt his hand in a cab door."

Johnny admitted on "60 Minutes" years later, "When I did drink, rather than a lot of people who become fun-loving and gregarious, and love everybody, I would go the opposite. And it would happen just like that. I just found out that I did not drink well. That's one reason I found that it was probably best for me not to tangle with it."

Aside from the tension of doing the show, Johnny could have been forgiven a dozen drinks when, for several heart-stopping days, he was subjected to insane death threats from a deranged man with a German accent. The man claimed to have a Luger pistol. As far as staffers could see, Johnny was his usual stoic self. But during a monologue that was bombing, he made a strange remark. Something like, "Now's a good time to kill me, I'm dying out here anyway!"

Into this pressure cooker came Joanne Copeland, the sprightly, attractive "cheerleader." Supportive, unthreatening, she barely reached five feet two inches and weighed 95 pounds. She was so petite Johnny once remarked, "She looks like she would wear Donald Ducks on her underpants."

Although some around Johnny at the time were slightly put off by this sugary girl who was "almost too good to be true," they all agreed she was about as "total" a "Total Woman" as her tiny frame would allow. "There's so much of me to give," she once said.

A friend of Johnny and Joanne at the time recalls that Joanne "made herself one hundred percent totally available to him. He was married; most women wouldn't do that. She knew what she wanted and I think she wore him down." Joanne was, without question, Johnny's greatest fan.

Carson co-workers speculate that the shy Nebraskan was simply overwhelmed. One recalls, "He was not a very experienced person. He married very young, right out of college." A staffer during those early days adds, "He was a straight arrow. I do think when he was running around in New York it seemed he was more into drinking than he was seeing how many beds he could hop into."

One New Year's Eve, Johnny and Joanne were at the apartment of two friends. Joanne asked to talk to the hostess alone. "And Joanne was complaining to me, 'I'm thirty-two years old and not married.' How could she make him marry her? I had no idea. I suggested to her that she dump him and go on about her life." Joanne was not about to listen to that kind of advice.

Johnny and Jody were divorced in 1963. In August of that

year, Johnny married Joanne. The Reverend Donald Hoffman conducted the ceremony at the Marble Collegiate Church. Aside from the happy couple, only three people were there: Dick Carson, producer Art Stark, and manager Al Bruno.

Johnny and Joanne set up housekeeping at 450 East 63rd Street. In 1967 they moved to the thirty-fifth floor of UN Plaza with a spectacular view of the East River. When a next-door apartment became available, they simply knocked through the walls and expanded, ending up with an extremely odd ten-room, three-kitchen condo.

The Carsons didn't go out much. Johnny was seeing so many famous people every night, he hardly wanted to conduct another "Tonight Show" for a Saturday-night party. As for Joanne, she only needed one famous person around the house.

Every now and then Johnny and Joanne would try a social function just to keep from being considered complete clams. If it was a small gathering, and Johnny was feeling good, there was the chance he'd entertain with his magic tricks. He'd be talkative if the subject was right and it was one-to-one with someone he trusted or respected. But more often the big, stuffy party atmosphere would be misery for him.

Explaining the paradox of the genial host on TV and the withdrawn figure offstage, he once said, "On the show, I'm in control. Socially, I'm not in control." He would grow suspicious, then angry, being bombarded by both famous and ordinary people auditioning for him either boldly or by sly ingratiation.

More powerful than any two people, everyone knew he was not only an important person to be seen with as a star, he could make someone a star just by putting them on his show.

Quiet, shy, and cautious by nature, Carson resented being used for an easy break when he himself had been working since age thirteen perfecting his craft. With so many wanting something from him, it wasn't hard for the protective shell to harden.

Johnny admired Joanne for her ability to react with a more outgoing show of warmth. Johnny bristled when it came to tolerating the boors and hustlers. Joanne took the fakery in stride and smiled. Not that she enjoyed the parties much either. She hated it when women flirted with Johnny and dullards told her jokes. "I thought my face would crack from smiling whenever anybody said, 'Your husband goes to bed with me' or 'Oh, Johnny, you're the man who keeps me awake nights.' As if we had never heard the lines before."

For fans and people desperate to get on the show, it didn't take a party setting for them to buddy up to Johnny. Johnny was asked for autographs while he was using the urinal. He was begged to sit still for a quick audition while eating in a restaurant. "I can't even take my boys ice skating," he said. "In twenty minutes they have us backed against the wall . . . 'Hey, come here and take a picture with my idiot cousin . . .' "

Johnny's tensions showed but people weren't seeing it. For instance, it was considered just an interesting "quirk" that Carson had almost no appetite. Sometimes dinner was just a snack— popcorn and some milk. He didn't seem able to sit down to a real dinner, but kept his energy up with endless nibbling on Sara Lee chocolate cake.

He had the habit of humming to himself. He couldn't break the smoking habit. He had pencils on his desk that he could nervously drum with. They had erasers at both ends.

At the office he was called aloof. But by whom? By people who wanted something from him. All he wanted was time to concentrate, and some peaceful moments in the midst of chaos.

Those who saw him as the smiling comedian and affable conversationalist were shocked when they saw him looking grim and turning away from idle chatter. He simply had his fill of it. He had enough trouble making lively conversation on the air—he didn't need to answer every "Hi Johnny!" from every stranger. In a way, he was like many another office worker who did his job, kept to himself, and had no answer when the chit-chatters came up to say on a rainy day, "Nice weather for ducks!" or on a hot day, "Hot enough for you?"

Few could understand that if someone could be a hundred times wittier than they, he might also be a hundred times as sensitive, or a hundred times as pressured. Members of the staff could take time for a break. They could afford to "lighten up."

But Carson had no time for breaks. The pressure was always there.

It was easier to ignore all and be aloof. It was less painful to ignore uncomfortable situations than to open up and be vulnerable. Part of being a star—and being able to face millions every night—was to wear the cloak of invulnerability.

Another nervous eccentricity was Johnny's inability to spend time on the phone. Though there were sixteen phones in the apartment, Joanne would mention to reporters, "I've yet to hear him talk to anyone for more than five minutes."

Johnny filled the place with his favorite toys: a drum set, telescope, video tape recorder, barbells, archery equipment, scuba gear, fencing foils, guitar. There were eight color TVs and a sauna.

For company, the couple had two terriers, Fluffy and Muffin— each a gift from the other.

Johnny's pleasure was to spend hours away from everything with his collection of hobbies. Joanne spent her time in the apartment decorating it.

The Carson apartment had some interesting innovations. A friend at the time recalls: "Books were coming into 'The Tonight Show'—it seemed like every book ever published would come in and Johnny brought back shopping bags full. The first time I was in the apartment, decorated by Joanne, I was shocked to see all the books arranged according to color."

The walls were all brown—John's favorite color. The furniture was brown too, pieces of stained oak and walnut wood. "It's a masculine apartment," Joanne was quick to say. The floors were bare wood with fur rugs. A foyer carpet was made out of baby cheetah. Johnny's sons, who stayed over on weekends or on vacations from school, had rooms like Dad. Sturdy furniture, leopard-skin rugs, and zebra-striped sheets.

Johnny once mentioned on "The Tonight Show" his experiment with that ultimate of masculine bedroom furnishings, sensuous bedsheets: "I sent away for those black satin sheets advertised in the back of the men's magazines. Don't send away for them. You slide right out! The top sheet never stays on. If you get in quick you just hydroplane right out!"

Joanne could probably have weaved the silk for those sheets herself. Reporters from women's magazines came for interviews, jaws dropping at all of her handiwork. She displayed the antique wood closets she'd had built and confided that she had aged the wood herself, having gone to the Metropolitan Museum to check the archives on "wood-rotting technique."

Johnny could not have asked for more. "If I ask him if there's anything I can do to improve, he says, 'Joanne, you're perfect.'"

Joanne, the model wife, continued to model. She was a hit at the National Society of Interior Designers fashion show in 1969. She deflected the compliments and instead praised Johnny's wardrobe: "He has perfect taste and knows exactly what he can wear. He has good, broad shoulders and no hips and he looks well in anything."

In addition to providing Johnny with the ultimate in house-wives, Joanne had time for monumental self-improvement. Joanne's regime would begin with a morning exercise program that was topped off with fifty sit-ups. She took courses at Hunter College. She was active in charity work, everything from the Bonds for Israel fashion show to teaching classes in make-up to wayward eighteen-year-olds at the Lenox Hill Settlement House. With her pony tail, Joanne almost looked the same age. She was dedicated, too. She didn't abandon her girls after the course was over.

She held weekly meetings every Tuesday night at the apart-ment to make sure the girls were getting along. "We talk about politics and morality. I got them to subscribe to *Time* magazine and introduced them to ballet. I showed them how to shop at Saks Fifth Avenue on a budget—that it's better to buy one $50 dress than five $10 dresses. . . ."

She was such a total woman that many around her were totaled just watching. One friend remembers, "She even made her own candles. Every Christmas she would send out the candles she made as gifts. For a while she took painting lessons, too."

Like many affluent couples in New York City, the Carsons

spent their summers out on Long Island. Johnny and Joanne had a boat, *The Deductible*. He told writer John Patrick: "I've been interested in boats ever since I was in the Navy during the war. And planes have fascinated me since I was a kid. I finally got around to learning how to fly a couple of years ago. Both boating and flying appeal to me even more these days because about the only places a fellow can get away from everybody are either out on the water or up in the sky."

Joanne understood the shy, quiet side of Johnny and tried to explain it to reporters. To the *Ladies' Home Journal* she said: "It takes him a long time to know people. He's been betrayed and burned by too many people . . . but he has me. He has Art Stark, his producer. He has Jeanne, his secretary. Johnny's life is so full he doesn't have time to get to know someone. The show is his life."

She added: "He's under so much pressure. Everybody is after him for something."

Everybody wanted a piece of Johnny, the star. But for Joanne, Johnny was the sun. "I orbit around him," she told Eugenia Sheppard. This became the most quoted of Joanne's cheerleading remarks, though sometimes she came up with more down-to-earth metaphors, like "He's my rock."

She admitted, "I would have been a very unhappy person if he hadn't [married me]. I would have waited around for him outside stage doors and followed him and written fan letters. He made me alive and opened a whole new world for me."

The whole new world threatened to shut again; there would be some fighting moments in that paradise in the UN Plaza.

THE TONIGHT SHOW

Johnny's killer pace is taking its toll. Changes have to be made—and Ed McMahon is about to be fired.

Johnny was TV's late-night king. His nearest competition was coming from Steve Allen's syndicated show for Westinghouse, netting a third of Johnny's numbers. He began seeking out other avenues of show business to conquer. On July 7, 1964, he headlined in Las Vegas for the first time.

His half-hour show at the Sahara Hotel won raves. *Variety* wrote: "The boyish charm and quick wit of Johnny Carson make a graceful transition from the TV screen to the nightly stage . . . he demonstrates what led him to video success—smooth stand-up comedy, expert ad-libbing, accurate impreshes [sic] and hilarious visual situation humor.

"He lampoons TV and TV commercials, also puts in a whack at the airlines. In a very funny takeoff, he has Edward R. Murrow reading 'The Three Little Pigs'; he gets laughs with swift answers to questions submitted on cards from members of his audience

. . . if Carson could spare the time, he'd be a blockbuster addition to the nightly circuit."

They weren't kidding. Johnny broke Judy Garland's attendance records. The Sahara awarded him a three-year contract.

Johnny became a top act in Vegas, telling jokes that would never make it to "The Tonight Show." On TV commercials, he quipped: "I'd like to see somebody run up to the Jolly Green Giant and say, 'Ho-ho-ho yourself, you big queer!'" An ultimate big breast joke: "Women don't like topless shows. They say to their husbands, 'You'd get sick if you had to look at that all day.' But Carlo Ponto hasn't had a sick day in his life." And a Q&A with the audience: "Johnny, why don't you put your damn show on earlier so my wife will come to bed with me?" "Have you ever thought of putting on a better show than I do?"

Johnny saw that a few weeks in Vegas yielded big, big money. Talking dollars and sense, he explained, "I'm interested in money for one reason. I like the freedom to say, 'Yes, I will do that show; no, I will not do that show.'" Could the Vegas bucks influence him to quit "The Tonight Show"? He left that open. He seemed to enjoy the workaholic grind. "I never want to stop working . . . after two weeks' vacation, I get edgy and very restless," he admitted.

"I don't do on TV what I do in clubs," he said. "I wrote the material for my act and very, very little of it will ever appear on television. I don't believe in giving away for free what people are paying $50 a night for in a club . . . a good club act or portions of it can be used profitably for years. On television, it's burned out in one night."

Johnny branched out from Vegas westward. He turned up with his idol, Jack Benny, on Jack's show. Benny and Carson had a great rapport—and Jack gave Johnny a rare opportunity to display all his talents.

Jack unveiled a duplicate of "The Tonight Show" set, so shy Johnny would "feel more comfortable." Then, in the guise of a concerned friend, Jack asked Johnny to show off his skills. On the show. "You just talk," Jack said. "How long can you last?"

Johnny demonstrated his card tricks, fanning the cards out and

making them disappear. Then he went to the drums and casually
bashed out a thirty-second solo. And finally, in what would be an
extreme rarity, he sang and danced! In a pleasant, Sinatra-influ-
enced baritone, he made his way through "Ballin' the Jack,"
hoofing the "eagle rock" with style and grace. He finished up with
a few Curly Howard backward skips.

"If you're so versatile," an exasperated Jack asked, "why don't
you do that stuff on your own show?"

"I'm too busy acting," Carson deadpanned. He explained that
paying attention to guests and acting interested was hard work.
They did a little sketch where, using a voice-over, Johnny told
the audience what he was really thinking during the show. For
instance, after he introduced Jack, and waited for the studio audience applause to stop, the camera zoomed in and in voice-over
Johnny groused, "Look at him milk that applause! He's doing
everything but curtsy!"

In ten minutes Johnny had effectively told America that he was
a talented magician/singer/drummer/dancer/comedian who was
restless with the phoniness and fake smiles that go along with
talking to strangers and stars. When Jack asked, "How long can
you last?" no one, Carson included, could have believed it would
be longer than the TV careers of Benny, Skelton, Ed Sullivan, or
any of the other television greats.

As early as February 1964 "The Tonight Show" was restlessly
winging westward, for special week-long visits to Hollywood.

Then, as now, many of Hollywood's greatest names shunned
the show, unable to face America as themselves. Sometimes they
gave strange excuses. Talent coordinator Sheldon Schultz's note
to Bing Crosby: "Johnny Carson has asked that I write you regarding your interest in appearing as his guest on 'The Tonight Show'
during our Hollywood series . . . if you are able to join us we
would be most appreciative . . ."

Der Bingle wrote back, "I'm afraid it would be impossible for
me to consider an appearance on the Johnny Carson Show. It
would be unlikely that I would be coherent at that hour of the
night, as I am generally asleep two hours before. With very best
good wishes, As ever, Bing Crosby."

With or without big stars, there was no topping Johnny.

Steve Allen's show sputtered and Regis Philbin replaced him. For his premiere, October 26, 1964, Philbin unveiled a new talk show strategy, the "guest star of the week." The first week it was Ann Sothern. By the second week his days were numbered.

On December 6, Johnny Carson unveiled his own new talk show plan. It was his "Monday nights off" idea. The grind was too much. An NBC executive, anxious to keep Johnny, thought up the plan. It worked well, but Johnny still was thinking of leaving. Jack Paar had moved on to a prime-time series. Johnny had an idea for a show called "Friars' Roast," a weekly show where he could ad-lib with other comics and do one good, solid hour of comedy.

Johnny was enjoying his appearances on the dais with the Friars, even though he was taking his lumps. During a 1965 Roast, Buddy Hackett told him: "The first time we ever worked together, many years ago, you were just a snotty guy. It's nice to know you haven't changed! One thing about your show, talent is all that counts. That's why you hired your brother as director!"

Johnny really thought the "Friars' Roast" concept could work—but he was talked out of it. NBC wanted him on "Tonight," even if it meant Monday nights off.

Johnny didn't follow Jack into prime time, but at least he followed Jack into the bookstores. Paar had come up with a pair of best-seller memoirs. Johnny came up with a pair of top selling novelty books, *Happiness Is a Dry Martini* and *Misery Is a Blind Date*.

Carson's style in his early days is preserved in these books, which were co-written by "Tonight Show" staff writers. Johnny believed:

"Happiness is discovering the prune juice your doctor ordered you to drink has fermented.

"Happiness is discovering the giant plant you gave your mother-in-law for her bedside table is a meat eater.

"Happiness is going to the opera and finding out your balcony seat is directly over Sophia Loren."

Johnny had the formula down pat. Still, he was never given

credit for his mastery of the formula. He had the jokes work with his personality and his delivery.

Ed McMahon also helped make it look easy. Quite often what sounded spontaneous was actually completely rehearsed. When Johnny does a "desk" routine with Ed, it seems as if Ed is react- ing instinctively to Johnny's lines. Actually it's often completely scripted.

On a 1966 broadcast, Johnny talked about some "popular quotes" he'd read. "Why don't I read them and see whether Ed can guess who they belong to?"

Then he launches into the routine. "This is our latest bomb, Mr. President," says Johnny. Ed pauses for a moment. He says, "That must be Secretary McNamara talking to President Johnson." Carson shakes his head. "No, that was the head of NBC's creative department talking to the president of NBC!"

Naturally, it's expected that Johnny's comic zinger is scripted. But so was his opening line, and Ed's rejoinder.

The script for the next joke reads like this:

> JOHNNY: "Most of my plays this year were more of a comedy than a farce."
>
> ED: "I can only think of the famous playwright, Neil Simon, saying that."
>
> JOHNNY: "No. That was Coach Allie Sherman talking to the owner of The New York Giants football team."

The two men worked so well with the material that few realized that the entire thing was so cut and dried.

Often Johnny's guests would be supplied with gags. One of the best-known examples of the "scripted ad-lib" was when Johnny played host to Barry Goldwater, who had recently been defeated by Lyndon Johnson in the presidential elections.

Johnny was asking a question when he stumbled over a word. Flustered, he said to Goldwater, "Did that ever happen to you? When you just can't get out what you mean?"

Goldwater answered, "Yes. For three and a half months two years ago!"

It got a big laugh. Goldwater seemed pretty witty. But actually, Johnny's "stumble" was rehearsed and so was the Goldwater answer.

Some critics complained that Johnny was not the master ad-libber he was given credit for, but as Johnny once told fellow comic Larry Wilde, an ad-lib isn't always a "new, completely original line . . . very often it's memory . . . it's switching something . . . it's something you have used before. The trick is to have it at the right time . . . the ability to take the situation and create something or to make a comment on what is happening."

Staffers noticed how easily Johnny could not only make a staged remark seem fresh, but how he could deliberately make something easy seem comically difficult. When he did his monologue, he rarely muffed a line as he scanned the cue cards. But often, when he was doing promos or commercials, he would deliberately blow a line or two, as if he couldn't read the cue cards. It got a laugh—and was just his way of lightening up the whorish chore of doing commercials.

Johnny was becoming such a big star he was getting offers even Bob Hope envied. No mere quiz show personality now, Johnny performed at the inaugural for Lyndon Johnson. But the honor was ruined for him when one of his jokes was blasted as low-class by columnist Dorothy Kilgallen.

Carson did a joke about being on late at night: "I've done more for birth control than Enovid." Kilgallen sneered at the tasteless comic in a front-page column.

Cool Carson erupted. At a dinner for the White House Photographers Association, he said, "For Dorothy Kilgallen to criticize me for bad taste is like having your clothes criticized by Emmett Kelly. I don't know why Dorothy should take offense at a joke I made. I didn't when her parents made one!"

He was quoted as saying, "I don't see why she would object to a joke about birth control. She's such a living example for it. She's the only woman you wouldn't mind being with if your wife walked in."

The feud might have blazed as brightly as Paar's battle with Dorothy but she died a few months later.

"The Tonight Show" itself continued its risqué ways. By now the audience was anticipating Johnny, and loving it. One night Zsa Zsa Gabor talked about wearing a skirt so skimpy "you could see all the way to Honolulu." The audience was already roaring as Johnny shook his head, saying "I'm not going to touch that line."

Another time Carson had the president of the American Heart Association on the show. The flustered spokesman began to talk facing away from the camera. Carson said, "Doctor, it's National Heart Month—we have the wrong part of the anatomy!"

And then there was the time a Mr. America was interviewed. "Remember, Johnny, your body is the only home you'll ever have."

Johnny shot back, "Yes, my home is pretty messy, but I have a woman come in once a week to clean it out."

Audiences loved Johnny's brand of risqué comedy. They were in on it; co-conspirators. When Tony Randall mentioned that he resented canned laughter, Johnny asked what was wrong with a few "titters." It was Johnny and the audience laughing at Randall, who became so exasperated he shouted, "Oh, you guys! Any kind of shit goes, doesn't it!" The word was bleeped for the home audience—who knew exactly what word it was and probably chuckled louder than the studio audience.

"Once they get to know you better, once they like you, it's amazing what you can get away with," Johnny said.

Though Johnny's been accused of imitating many past comics, he was certainly an original at playing the audience. They were with him when jokes bombed, they were in on his "show biz" terms like "I'm the prince of blends" or "watch this segue," and they were even straightmen for him:

"It was really wet today."

"HOW . . . WET . . . WAS IT!"

"All I know is twice on my way to work I was photographed by Jacques Cousteau!"

The old-time columnists like Kilgallen, who feuded with Paar, were toothless trying to bite Carson. Johnny satirized a Kilgallen-type of columnist when he went on the air as "Hedda Carsons."

Wearing a wig and a crazy hat, he did a monologue very typical of the breezy, early "Tonight Show" style. In part, it went like this:

"Adolph Kleig wins my nomination for the most embarrassed producer in Hollywood. Last week in his office he was giving a young starlet a screen test and the screen fell down!

"After so many years of trying, I'm glad Jayne Mansfield finally got the perfect part. You'll next see Jayne Mansfield in *Two for the Seesaw. . . .*"

Considering that only a few years earlier Jack Paar had his "w.c." joke axed, Johnny was considered almost X-rated by some people.

Backstage, Johnny was considered tense and distrustful. When *TV Guide*'s Edith Efron came to interview Johnny, she was struck by his mood.

Acknowledging that Johnny on the show was all "sweetness and calm, interspersed with quiet chuckles," she believed that in reality "what you find is a slender, tense young man . . . very, very angry . . . a wary, aloof human being who seems to be on guard against some invisible danger . . . Johnny Carson isn't holding the lid on himself to safeguard his private life. It's to safeguard his anger."

Efron discovered a long list of Carson peeves ranging from irritation over public apathy in politics to the mistreatment of the American Indians. He was frustrated over having to remain "neutral" on TV, unable to talk about racial unrest or drug abuse on his "entertainment-oriented" show. But to interviewers, he sometimes couldn't help speaking out.

"What people say and what they do are two different things. Take racial integration. Everybody's for it, so long as it doesn't touch THEM. Everybody for doing something about dope addiction—but don't put up a hospital near THEIR house."

When Edith Efron asked Johnny if he had a favorite book, he

shook his head. She asked about the people he admired. "I have no heroes," he answered.

He reiterated his anger over his "loner" tag. If people were suspicious of his enjoyment of solitary pursuits, he was even more suspicious and cynical of people who needed to gather in large groups: "I don't like clubs or organizations. This will be misinterpreted: Johnny Carson is anti-Rotary Club, he's anti the Conference of Christians and Jews. I'm not a joiner. I think most groups are hypocritical, restrictive, and undemocratic."

At the same time, interviewer Betty Rollin said: "Carson, off camera, is testy, defensive, preoccupied, withdrawn and wondrously inept and uncomfortable with people . . . each short sentence is punctuated with a smile that goes on and off like cold tap water."

Carson confronted his accuser: "I'm friendly, aren't I? I'm polite, aren't I? I'm honest. All right, my bugging point is low. I'm not gregarious. I'm a loner. I've always been that way."

Others interviewed about Johnny gave a similar picture. Ed McMahon commented that Johnny "packs a tight suitcase" and that he was a perfectionist: "Johnny gets angry at the ineffectual, inefficient people who don't do their job properly. It bugs him when people don't pull their own oars."

Johnny soon learned that it was better to say nothing to the press. Honesty was not the best policy when shyness was jeered as coldness, and when his workday tensions and nervous preoccupation were labeled "hostility" and "aloofness."

Instead of accepting interviews, he began handing out a gag-sheet of all-purpose answers:

1. Yes, I did.
2. Not a bit of truth in that rumor.
3. Only twice in my life, both times on Saturday.
4. I can do either, but I prefer the first.
5. No. Kumquats.
6. I can't answer that question.
7. Toads and tarantulas.

8. Turkestan, Denmark, Chile, and the Komandorskie Islands.
9. As often as possible, but I'm not very good at it yet. I need much more practice.
10. It happened to some old friends of mine, and it's a story I'll never forget.

People still wanted Johnny to be the same funny, smiling, carefree entertainer off screen as on. And Johnny asked rhetorically, "People are unhappy more often than not, aren't they?"

Sometimes interviewers went back to Johnny's parents for a quote or two. They barely got a sentence or two. "I don't know where the boys get their love for show business." His mother shrugged. "My husband and I are both retiring and conservative."

Viewers continued to watch "The Tonight Show" before retiring for bed. By 1965 ten million viewers were hooked. Folks needed a good laugh back in the turbulent sixties—so badly NBC began rerunning shows on the weekends! Starting in January 1965, "The Best of Carson" turned up on Saturday nights. Johnny was uneasy about the overkill. Prophetically he said, "They should turn that time over to some young comedians, or an experiment."

Carson insists that the show was "TV as it really ought to be. The rest is all film, situation comedy, and such. 'Tonight' is live, spontaneous, and intimate. It's the kind of thing that got people looking at TV."

The other networks began to agree. ABC brought competition: Les Crane. An ancient ancestor of Phil Donahue and Tom Snyder, Crane attempted controversy but, to *Newsweek*, came off as "a combination of egotism and logorrhea . . . an oppressively strong personality." One minute he was bludgeoning a guest, the next fawning outrageously.

By contrast, Westinghouse now had Merv Griffin. *Newsweek* found him "at best, mildly funny." He'd "not yet proved himself able to carry the show alone." Only Carson had the magic: "He is a sharp, original wit."

Johnny's show was sharp all right. So were his guests. One memorable night Ed Ames came on. He was playing Mingo in the

Fess Parker series "Daniel Boone" and demonstrated his sharp Indian hatchet throwing skill. As millions have seen on "Great Moments" reruns, Ames took aim at a cowboy drawn on a huge wooden board. Accidentally he sank the hatchet right into the cowboy's crotch.

As the crowd howled, Ames tried to retrieve his hatchet. Johnny held him back, waited for the crowd to quiet down, and said, "I didn't even know you were Jewish!"

The laughter exploded louder than ever. Johnny was all set for another line, just waiting for the shocked giggles to subside. "Welcome to Frontier Bris!" Johnny added.

Now a familiar, perhaps too often seen moment, it still remains vintage Carson and vintage "Tonight Show"—a moment of spontaneity and cheerful sexiness.

Carson was extremely frisky in the early sixties, an era brimming with the signals of change, everything from Beatle haircuts to miniskirts. Johnny was doing his part, night after night stretching the boundaries of what was considered adult entertainment.

The FCC and NBC fought him at every turn.

One night Ray Milland told an anecdote about movie making. The man who was always "wide-eyed in Babylon" was amused that movie "romance" wasn't always reality. He described the time he was making *Jungle Princess*, doing a romantic love scene in a swimming pool with Dorothy Lamour.

As Ray recalled, "I had to go to the bathroom. I thought, 'Oh God, not now! Not now.'" But the call of nature had to be obeyed. "As she put her arms around my neck and started kissing me, the cold water of the pool did its work and I let go . . ." And he kept going all during that steamy necking scene.

The audience laughed good-naturedly.

Carson ended up in hot water.

Robert E. Lee, the commissioner of the FCC, complained "There have been four or five incidents on his show over the past year which would raise some eyebrows . . . I don't want the industry to degenerate into indecency." The Milland incident was the last straw.

"I'm not a prude," said Lee. "I haven't been offended and

maybe nobody has. After all, Carson has a sophisticated show at an hour when the kids are in bed . . . but I do feel that late-night shows are getting pretty close to the line of indecency."

"I don't know what to say," Carson remarked coolly. "I'm baffled by Mr. Lee's terminology. I don't know what he means. Lee himself said that he could not define what indecency was. I can't define it either. So what are we talking about?"

Johnny was courteous toward the FCC commissioner: "Mr. Lee says he wasn't offended, so who was?" He added, "He sounded like a hell of a nice guy to me."

Later, the Carson anger began to smoulder. He told Kay Gardella, "On one hand we rush to an art movie to see a film dealing with rape and incest, and the next day we're screaming censorship because somebody used 'damn' or 'hell' on television. . . . Everybody wants to protect everybody else's morals but their own. They showed *Divorce Italian Style* on TV at 7:30 last week and nobody complained."

An NBC executive, Robert Kasmire, confirmed that there were "no phone calls and no letters" after Milland's appearance on the show. Johnny went on the air: "Welcome to NBC's rendezvous in the bedroom. I'm Johnny Carson. I say that because the FCC has been mixing me up lately with Lenny Bruce."

He did a joke about Flipper being named in a paternity suit by a Christmas seal. He paused during the laughter and added, "Sorry about that, Commissioner Lee."

Johnny was on a roll. He took on Paar and won. He took on the FCC and won. His bosses at NBC treated him like a loser—he didn't have their respect. Now he was waiting to take them on, too.

Johnny was NBC's new hot superstar, yet he felt snubbed. His budget wasn't what it should be. The network didn't throw their publicity and support behind him. One year they threw a party for their star—and embarrassed him by holding it in a dowdy conference room and using plastic cups and paper plates. Carson's offices were so lame, he groused, "I have to go to the Port Authority Bus Depot to pee!"

During the summer's Republican and Democratic primaries in

1964 NBC constantly interrupted Johnny's show for news reports.
Johnny uttered a desultory remark about the unfunny comedy
team of Huntley and Brinkley and a feud erupted between the
news division of NBC and "The Tonight Show"—with the bosses
siding more with the classy news than their clowning Carson.
During a question-and-answer segment with the audience, someone asked if Johnny was planning to stay with the show for a long
time. Carson said he hoped to, "if I don't make any more cracks
about NBC News."

There were more miseries. Back in the sixties, most local late-
night news shows lasted fifteen minutes. "The Tonight Show" ran
105 minutes, beginning at 11:15 and ending at 1 A.M. As TV
grew up and the news stretched to a half hour, many stations
simply tuned into the show 15 minutes late at 11:30.

In February 1965, NBC's San Francisco affiliate joined the
other big cities in expanding the news and dumping the first fifteen minutes of "Tonight"—Johnny's monologue.

Nobody bothered to tell Johnny. When he heard about it, on a
Friday afternoon, he acted passive. As in passive/aggressive. He
stayed in his dressing room and refused to come out.

Ed McMahon and bandleader Skitch Henderson filled in. Ed,
who "warmed-up" the audience with a quick monologue before
each show, wasn't bad telling a few gags.

At 11:30 Johnny arrived. He explained to the viewers that the
only people who watched at 11:15 were "four Navajos in Gallup,
New Mexico, and the Armed Forces Radio on Guam." Carson
said with scheduling like that, "If there's a bulletin on World War
III during the show, it will have to wait."

Once off the air, he gathered reporters around and let NBC
have it: "It isn't worth it, working to prepare material if the network isn't going to put it on the air in New York, where the show
originates, or a major city like San Francisco." He called his
monologue "an integral part of the show, a commentary on the
day's events. It's not going to be put in a time capsule . . . but a
lot of effort goes into it."

Johnny left with a warning: "Maybe somebody will listen to me
now. They'll have all weekend to think about it."

Asked what he had been doing in his dressing room for fifteen minutes, he said, "Sulking."

Johnny won the battle, but he didn't like the way some of his people were fighting the war.

Ed McMahon had been pretty funny—he didn't have to be THAT funny, did he? Johnny wasn't thrilled with Skitch Henderson's antics, either. Like the time Skitch told a reporter, "Johnny is very easy to work with if you don't get in his way."

Ed McMahon and Johnny enjoyed an on-screen relationship that was a bit like the one Johnny's idol Jack Benny had with portly Don Wilson. Wilson was a good straight man and stooge. But McMahon, who was once the host of his own Philadelphia talk show, liked to ad-lib a line, too. After years of watching Carson up close, he knew many of the formulas.

One night Johnny was talking about a new science report. He deadpanned to the audience that, according to scientists, mosquitoes don't just bite anyone. They go for those warm-blooded "passionate people" first.

Instinctively, Ed McMahon slapped himself on the arm.

"It killed his punchline," McMahon recalled with remorse. "I had to apologize to him during the next break . . . I stepped out of line." Johnny wanted him to step out of the nearest window. Several times Carson warned Ed about upstaging him. And several times, Ed's head was close to the chopping block.

Johnny came to producer Art Stark with a demand to get rid of the obstreperous stooge.

Art Stark shook his head.

"Why would you want to do that?" he asked. He reasoned with his sullen star. "How is it going to make you look if you fire Ed?" Stark felt it would give Carson the same nasty image Arthur Godfrey got for canning sidekick Julius LaRosa.

Johnny allowed Stark to talk him out of firing Ed. But now there was a new resentment. Johnny was getting a little sick and tired of Art Stark.

While McMahon found release for his "second banana" misery by hosting TV game shows like "Snap Judgment" and taking over for Alan King during the 1965 Broadway run of *The Impossible Years*, the friction mounted between Carson and Stark.

Stark was a very strong producer with a determined sense of what worked and what didn't. Described by co-worker Sy Kassoff as "volatile, but honest, straight and fair," Stark was choosing guests, making decisions, and daring to talk back to the star.

But as Johnny's star burned brighter, the star didn't like to hear "No." In 1966, director Dick Carson knew that his brother was fuming. "Johnny's trouble is that he isn't the kind of person who fights back . . . even now he can't throw his weight around."

Dick never got in Johnny's way. Dick had to knock before entering Johnny's dressing room, just like everybody else.

Only Art Stark seemed to have some control in dealing with Johnny. Stark devoted himself to the show—almost as much as Johnny himself. Stark had a two-pack-a-day cigarette habit to prove it, and a trial separation in his marriage.

Stark confided to a reporter: "It's taking a toll, a heavy toll. Even as I'm being interviewed here or talking to a friend on the phone I'm thinking about five or six things at the same time, for tonight's show and for what's coming up three nights from now. It never lets up. Even at the hospital, where I recently went after a back injury, I receive forty or fifty calls. . . . There is no such thing as a calm day. [The show] always demands my being on top of it."

The taping schedule wrecked the home life of every member of "The Tonight Show" crew. When most people were coming back from work, these workers were just going on duty. Taping was from 7:30 to 9. Most workers didn't get home till 10. Dinner was ruined, theater impossible, the kids missed a parent and not a few marriages broke up.

There would be tense times ahead for Johnny, his wife, and many people on his show.

12 THE TONIGHT SHOW

Johnny goes out on strike. And he begins to strike back. And another marriage starts striking out.

The year 1967 was a crazy one for Johnny and it started with a conflict every month. First came a skirmish between him and ex-wife Jody. It reached the courts on February 16. The court fight, behind closed doors and with papers sealed, took eight hours. Johnny missed the show because he couldn't get back to New York on time.

The problem was Johnny's thirteen-year-old son Cory. He'd been attending Nyack Prep in Southampton, like older brothers Chris (sixteen) and Ricky (fifteen). Then Jody transferred him to Wamago Regional High School in Litchfield, Connecticut, near her home in Warren. It took a long time to finally iron out exactly where the kids should be and for how long.

The following month, Johnny made headlines again. New York's Governor Nelson Rockefeller appeared on "The Tonight Show" and shocked the nation by announcing his displeasure with

New York Senator Robert F. Kennedy—and his choice for a replacement: John W. Carson.

"You've got very good ratings," Rockefeller told the surprised host. "You'd have to let your hair grow. But you wouldn't have to worry about residency."

The Governor was alluding to Senator Kennedy's long hair and short stay as a native New Yorker, having spent most of his life in Massachusetts.

The studio audience buzzed with excitement, but Carson resented being put on the spot. "I'm flattered . . . but I'm not sure I'd be very good in politics," he said.

Backstage, Carson gave reporters his appraisal of Rockefeller and his idea: "I thought he was just being a cutie pie," he said.

But Rockefeller said he was serious: "I think it's a tremendous idea. . . . There's a great potential there, believe me. I'd like to get his reaction and then we'd discuss it later."

Robert F. Kennedy vs. Johnny Carson for the U.S. Senate. An astounding race! It would be a night-and-day battle, too, since both men lived in the same building, the UN Plaza. But Johnny insisted: "Who am I to be a pundit? I have opinions like anybody else, and I might even be better informed than the average person because this is my business, to keep up on what's happening. But who am I to foist my opinions on the public? Why should they care?"

And why make the kind of enemies politicians did?

"Besides," Johnny finally said, "you can't win. I say something like I'm for easing the divorce laws and a good part of the people listening will always think, 'Ah, he's for loose morals.'"

Carson was enough of a public figure to warrant a biography—Nora Ephron had written a series of articles on Carson for the *New York Post*. These were expanded into a paperback original.

The following month would be one of the most tumultuous in Johnny's twenty-five-year reign on "The Tonight Show."

Staffers and friends had noticed the gradual change in Johnny. As he became more confident, as "The Tonight Show" continued to dominate the competition, he demanded the respect that was rightfully his. NBC was still dictating policy to him, and so was his long-time producer, Art Stark.

Johnny had plenty of ammunition to fuel his feelings of being used. All he needed was something to ignite all that built-up gunpowder. He found it when his union, AFTRA, called a strike. It was mostly about a raise for TV newsmen and a revision of the mandatory retirement rule. Newsmen walked the picket lines. Some of their replacements were complete amateurs, including secretaries grabbed from the office pool.

In support of the strike, Johnny walked off the show. NBC went to reruns of old shows. On April 4, viewers were treated to a December 20 "Tonight Show." They laughed—at the ludicrous winter jokes Johnny was making in the spring!

Johnny was looking like a fool—for the last time.

He charged that NBC had breached his contract by rerunning the unauthorized show. It was a loophole, all right, but a good one. Johnny vowed not to return to the show, even if the strike was settled.

After five years, the Carson habit was an addiction. Could viewers do without Johnny? Could NBC do without the money he was generating? *Newsweek,* in their April 24 issue, called "The Tonight Show" a "90-minute verbal tranquilizer," letting millions of Americans "slowly find their way into uncluttered sleep . . ."

Carson was chided for using the rerun issue. Today, the ploy seems all the more transparent, since "Best of Carson" reruns always seem to be out of season. A show during Christmas of 1986 was a rerun of a show two years earlier—with Johnny joking about Labor Day, Pete Rose's base hits, and (strange considering what had transpired earlier in the year) a joke about "The Joan Rivers Doll . . . wind it up and it ridicules people."

Still, Johnny steadfastly insisted that it was the rerun issue that disturbed him most.

Ben Gross, in the *Daily News,* gave the general point of view of the reporters. He wrote that Johnny really "wants more money." Headlining his piece "Success Changes Carson and All Other TV Stars," Gross insisted that it was impossible for Johnny to have "risen from comparative obscurity to the status of a millionaire national celebrity" without changing. "Such a lack of change would be against all human nature . . . it would be a miracle if Carson weren't affected by such success . . . any way you look at it, he is not the same fellow he was when he first appeared on 'Tonight' in 1962."

Reporters uncovered another twist to the story. NBC President Julian Goodman, during a routine meeting, was asked to okay a publicity stunt to take the steam out of the premiere "Joey Bishop Show" on ABC. How about having Johnny imitate Jack Paar—by storming off the show for some reason or other, only to come back the night Bishop premieres?

NBC execs had dismissed the idea but reporters weren't so sure. After all, Bishop's show was now only weeks away. Not only that, Bill Dana and his "Fourth Network" talk show was hitting syndicated stations on May 1.

Carson stuck to his story: "What is the price that should be paid for a rerun when it is used while your union is on strike? That's the main point . . . I was required to join AFTRA in order to work for the network. I know of no business except the broadcasting industry in which a performer becomes a scab to himself and his union because of videotape."

He raged over the stalled talks with NBC: "They're trying to make me look like an ungrateful wretch."

Newsweek scoffed at Johnny the union man: ". . . while second banana Ed McMahon loyally walked the picket line in Manhattan, Carson . . . took off for Fort Lauderdale, Florida . . ." In Florida, CBS News caught up with him. Asked about his status, Johnny quietly said: "I'm an unemployed prince."

Behind the scenes, the negotiations centered on a raise in salary, more control, less network interference, and something else: "Some changes in personnel on the program."

Al Salerno of the *New York World Journal Tribune* speculated in a headline piece that "Carson Wants Someone Out." He noted that "Carson would not have to negotiate with NBC . . . to change most of the people on the show." Most already belonged to his own Stage C production company.

Producer Art Stark had an uneasy feeling. He went to Johnny, and Johnny said: "You're one of my best friends. If I had anything on my mind regarding your job, I'd tell you."

Stark, one of only three guests at Johnny's wedding to Joanne, and one of the few to see Johnny socially after work, felt relieved. He began making plans for Johnny's upcoming battle against Bishop.

The strike was settled—but Johnny was still out. He wasn't about to come back just because NBC needed help. "The whole thing would look like a gigantic hoax if I marched back as he opened," Johnny remarked.

Now Joey Bishop could jump in and get a big lead in the ratings. The NBC Peacock pushed her head into the sand and braced for the attack.

Joey opened with Danny Thomas, Debbie Reynolds, and Governor Ronald Reagan. Bishop was so humbled by Reagan's appearance, the Governor quipped: "Another ten seconds of this and I'll go back to 'Death Valley Days.'"

From exile, Johnny waited for the ratings and the reviews. Columnist Harriet Van Horne spoke for most reviewers when she panned Bishop: "Though he's a quick wit and an able performer, he lacks the poise, the what-the-hell assurance that has distinguished all the successful night-owl hosts. . . . Johnny Carson has nothing to worry about."

NBC was still worried. Overnight in New York, Bishop's ratings were better than the Jimmy Dean–hosted "Tonight Show" and the syndicated Griffin show combined.

NBC announced that Bob Newhart was their choice for new (and perhaps permanent) guest host. They intimated that they were going to keep Johnny on ice for the two remaining years of his contract. Let him face a two-year blacklist and be another forgotten man, like Jack Paar!

Paar, insisting he'd never return to the show, did take the opportunity to question Carson's morality. After all, Jack didn't want cash when he walked away from NBC, he wanted respect for his water-closet joke.

"I can't believe that it's money," Jack told writer Al Salerno.

"But if it is, it's wrong . . . it eventually will get him in a jam with the public."

Carson claimed he was ready to dump TV entirely. He was planning a stand-up tour, with a booking for April 29 in Baltimore. He was ready to spend July performing in Vegas.

Jack Gould in the *New York Times* pointed out exactly how important Johnny Carson was to NBC. Carson and his show was "almost indispensable. Economically, the program fills up 7½ hours a week, less repeats, and in being presented between 11:30 and 1 A.M. conveniently falls outside the bounds of any stringent codes on the number of commecials that can be inserted . . . in cold cash at the moment the show represents a gross of upward of $25 million yearly for NBC."

Johnny stuck to his guns. He even brought in another hired hand, lawyer Louis Nizer, to help in the negotiations. NBC held up their hands and surrendered, renegotiating his contract. From $15,000 a week for thirty-nine weeks and $7,500 for the thirteen weeks of his vacation, Carson got a raise to $20,000 a week plus a million-dollar life-insurance policy.

Carson gave out a prepared statement: "I return with new enthusiasm to 'The Tonight Show.' I am grateful for the many many people who have been kind enough to say they missed me. Television makes friendships possible with a host of unknown persons. I hope to repay their generosity with the very best that is in me."

Johnny asked Art Stark to come to the UN Plaza apartment. The minute Art was in the door Carson told him he was through.

"When do you want me to leave?"

"Right now."

One of the most important men in Johnny's life for the past decade had become a non-person to him.

Stark, months earlier, had made a prophetic statement: "If I were in trouble here, as good friends as we are, he'd never fight for me. He doesn't like to be dependent on anyone."

Now that he was out of his $150,000-a-year job, he could only add: "I honestly don't know what prompted it." He could have blasted Johnny—but two things prevented him. He had too much class, and he probably had too much of "The Tonight Show" anyway. "I think I did just about all I can do in those idiot hours."

"Stark is a close friend of mine," Carson told the *New York Post*. "He has done many things for the show." He hoped Art would find work somewhere else.

Ironically, one of the few to dare be seen publicly with Stark and his wife was Joan Rivers and her husband, Edgar. Stark continued his career as a producer, working with David Susskind. He was soon making as much if not more money than ever before.

Al Bruno, the manager Carson had known even longer than Art Stark, lasted just a little bit longer. He too was fired. With Stark, there was little doubt that there was no room for two strong, controlling personalities. With Bruno, several reasons were whispered by staffers and friends.

One story was that Bruno, not the "super manager" some of Carson's pals thought, was out of his depth. Carson was infuriated when Bruno booked Johnny into a club where the sound system was so amateurish Carson bombed, struggling to be heard. Another story was that Carson became enraged when his manager turned down a lucrative commercial deal with Budweiser. It involved big bucks plus a distributorship. Frank Sinatra took the offer and made a small fortune.

The worst of Bruno's alleged misdeeds was the time he and NBC met during one of the periodic tiffs between Johnny and the network. Bruno, instead of sticking up for Carson, supposedly pitched another client, Mike Douglas, as his replacement.

Whether the story was true or not, Johnny was so angry he even contacted Douglas to get a legal deposition. Douglas was willing to help, but perhaps the ultimate removal of Bruno was punishment enough. And once more, Johnny's suspicions about his co-workers and friends seemed justified.

In his autobiography, Dick Cavett mentioned Johnny and his problems: "I have heard that he has been manipulated and screwed more than once by trusted associates, to the point where he is defensively wary to what some find an excessive degree. I see this as a perfectly reasonable response. . . ." Backstage, he knew that Johnny was having to manage his own company, maintain a quiet private life and a splashy public TV show, handle big money and big fame. It was tough to deal with "hangers-on, well-wishers and ill-wishers" and "sort out conflicting advice, distinguish between the treacherous and the faithful or the competent and the merely aggressive . . . when you have to kick some people's fannies and kiss others in order to get to the point where you won't need to do either anymore . . ."

Cavett believed "if you don't change . . . you don't survive." But on "The Tonight Show," some staffers were demoralized by the tough, frosty atmosphere. Johnny's brother, Dick, would leave soon, too. He moved on to direct a prime-time series starring Don Rickles. When Dick told Johnny the news, all Carson could say was, "Do you think we can get Bobby Quinn?"

Quinn had been on the staff of Steve Allen and Jack Paar's shows as a stage manager and assistant director. Carson got Quinn, staffers just got nervous.

Bob Lardine in the *Sunday Daily News* interviewed several "Tonight Show" employees who, as usual, requested anonymity. Even today, long retired, they are fearful of talking on the record. One staffer complained about the show as run under the complete control of Carson. "In all the years that I've been on the show he has never once said hello. He maintains that attitude with most of the other fellas, too. . . . Carson is the most uptight, nervous guy you'll ever want to meet. His short temper creates tension backstage. Everyone is sniping at everyone else."

Another confirmed: "After the show Carson is often enraged. 'Don't ever put that——on the show again,' he'll scream. And then Carson will rant about how inept some of the other guests were. If those celebrities could only hear what Carson thinks about them, there would be some dandy street fights around town."

Johnny was in an awkward position as both star of the show and the boss. The boss needed respect. Besides, given his nature, the office games of small talk and false cheer were not for him. Why make a big deal of greeting people you see every morning?

"The Tonight Show" offices weren't completely demoralizing.

When Gael Greene visited the place, she noticed that many staffers were females, "nubile with calendar-girl-shelves-of-bosom making a point out of the elasticity of knit dresses." As for Johnny's secretary, Jeanne Prior, she was "all glamour and efficiency, bouncing between floors like a grown-up drum majorette with layers of sooty false lashes and white Courrèges boots." Jeanne wasn't grousing about her boss: "How can I say it without sounding icky poo . . . we have psychological rapport."

The staffers had to be rooting for Johnny—especially when upstarts like Joey Bishop were threatening their jobs.

On April 25, having given Bishop a week's head start, Johnny returned. Bishop anticipated him—and on the first night of the head-to-head competition, his guest was none other than Jack Paar.

The gunfight around midnight was the talk of the town.

Johnny chose to ignore the competition. In his opening monologue he talked, not about Paar or Bishop, but his negotiations with NBC. He mentioned the Passover holiday and said, even though it was a time for eating unleavened bread, he'd wanted "more dough."

On ABC, Paar happily took over to tell his stories. The *New York Times* noticed that Paar "inadvertently drew further attention to Mr. Bishop's mounting plight as a host who is ill at ease in the presence of guests." Johnny, along with Buddy Hackett and Peter Paul and Mary, easily outpointed his present and his former rival.

The overnight ratings gave Carson 41 percent of the audience, Bishop 12 percent. CBS, running movies, got 22 percent. Merv Griffin, in syndication, even topped Bishop with his 16 percent. A few weeks later, Bill Dana's talk show premiered—and quickly the syndicated "Fourth Network" crumbled like old halvah.

Johnny was paying a price. His hair was slowly going gray. He was becoming more isolated, hiring "yes men." After work, there was only Joanne, and his private room filled with solitary toys. Joanne knew how to handle him. When he wasn't in the mood to talk, she didn't press him. If he wanted to be alone, she let him. At the office only the sternest demeanor kept the back-slappers and glad-handers at bay. He desperately needed his privacy, not parties: "They bore me. My threshold of boredom is very low. I think it's insane to walk into a room made for a capacity of 12 and find 104 people there, and you sit down to eat something and somebody steps on your food."

He couldn't go out to movies: "Not when everybody else in line sees you in their bedrooms every night . . . people grab you by the arm and haul you over to meet their idiot cousins who'd be 'great on "The Tonight Show."'" He wouldn't accept the alternative of being ushered into the theater in privacy, and sitting in a "star" seat: "I don't like that idea, the special treatment bit."

Like so many comics, his humor was fueled by his anger. And his silly, stupid sketches were driven by one simple principle: "Stupid things are what irritate me the most."

He took a firm position about the guests he'd have on the show. He had the final word: "I can't go out there and fake that I'm in love with somebody when I'm not . . . people I disagree with completely just don't get on the show because if I've got hostility I'm gonna kill 'em—and I don't see the point in getting somebody up in public and start zinging them."

Johnny's staff whispered that there was a blacklist—guests Johnny would never invite back. Some had simply blabbered too much. Others had no rapport with him and made him work too hard at making them look good. Sometimes the guest deliberately deviated from the pre-chosen topics to outrageously plug a movie or pontificate on a boring favorite subject.

There were indeed guests Johnny did not want back, and they ranged from Elliott Gould to Milton Berle. They included guests who would have been "hot," but who were the kind of people Johnny had a personal aversion to. Johnny wouldn't have wanted them in his own home—and he didn't want to bring them into anyone else's: LSD advocate Timothy Leary, scandal celebrities like Elizabeth Ray, Linda Lovelace, and Fannie Foxe, or famous felons ranging from Manson clan members to slick con man Clifford Irving.

And there was frustration in having certain guests on that could only yield polite, vaguely interesting conversation. "So you have, say, Eydie Gormé on," Carson once remarked. "You ask her about her kids. What the hell else are you going to ask her about besides singing?"

One night, with Eva Gabor on the panel, Marlon Brando mumbled, "How long are we going to have to listen to this crap?"

There were many nights when Johnny had to ask himself the same question. Even now, when critics occasionally groan over repeat guests like boring Charles Grodin and ditsy Teri Garr, Carson finds it hard to mount much of a reply. Not every guest is a gem. Sometimes the silly soap stars and tabloid tootsies must be tolerated.

"I could not give a shit what Bianca Jagger is doing, or what Jackie O. is doing," Johnny once admitted to *Rolling Stone*, "but those are the people you constantly read about . . . without going into their names, some of them don't have anything except their manufactured celebrity status." Yet he had to have them on anyway. And critics demanded that every night be a great night, with sparkling satire and brilliant dialogue. Even as they wrote that the best thing about Johnny was that his show was low key and comfortable.

In September 1967 Johnny surprised some of his staff by flying, "on the spur of the moment," to Rochester, Minnesota. He entered the Mayo Clinic for a "routine checkup."

When he got back into town the following month, the vacation was definitely over.

It was raining heavily in New York on the night of October 25. As was the custom, Johnny's chauffeur, Clarence Leonard, arrived in front of Rockefeller Center to wait for Johnny. The rain was especially heavy and as it pelted the sidewalk little v's seemed to appear in the spray.

When Johnny came out, the chauffeur came to the curb, hoisted up an umbrella and stepped forward. Leonard waited patiently with the umbrella raised as the hiss of the driving rain grew louder and louder in his ears.

Slowly and carefully the two men made their way back to the car. There was a dirty black river of rainwater flowing along the gutter. They were about to step over it into the car when they noticed something.

There was no car. Johnny's Cadillac was gone.

With an Oliver Hardy–like look of chagrin, Johnny returned to the building while Clarence Leonard dashed forlornly into the night. It was too late.

Johnny called up Joanne.

"I'll be a little late," he said glumly.

Johnny was really bugged. Inside the Caddy were his eight brand-new "formal" white turtleneck sweaters!

"You can't find those in New York!" he exclaimed. "I don't mind losing the car," he told Joanne. "A new Cadillac you can always get. Anyway, it was last year's. But those turtleneck sweaters!"

Carson mentioned the story on the air—and received dozens of turtlenecks from fans. Ever since he's been careful about mentioning his needs on the air, realizing how his loyal fans will react. He has to be even more careful about non-needs. During the 1986 Christmas season, he described how much he loathed fruitcakes. Naturally, he received a bunch of brick-like cakes in the mail. When he appealed to the audience not to send any more, it was a big mistake. He had to admit, with mock chagrin, "Some fruitcake sent me another fruitcake!"

As for the turtlenecks, this was just another example of Carson's subtle effect on the culture. When Johnny began wearing them, it became a trend. Restaurants and offices began to allow men a choice between ties and turtlenecks.

Meanwhile, the trend on TV was talk shows. The competition was getting nasty. The staffs of the Griffin and Carson shows were at war. There wasn't enough room in town for both of them. Griffin's guests were told: "If you talk to Merv, then you'll never talk to Johnny again."

Variety investigated the charges, discovering that Jack E. Leonard, Myron Cohen, Hugh Downs, Lorne Greene, and singer Noel Harrison were among the stars intimidated by "Tonight Show" personnel. The trade paper intimated that "The Tonight Show" was raiding Griffin for new talent, like a major-league club grabbing promising rookies. After polishing their comedy on Griffin's show, John Byner, George Carlin, and Brother Theodore were now "Carson only" acts. A spokesman for Johnny's show said the stars were being given good advice. If someone went on Griffin's show, "we may or may not be able to use them if there is a risk of their playing opposite themselves." Just do "Tonight" and there's no overexposure.

Spinning the dial, Johnny could not only see a bunch of new talk show hosts—he could even see his wife.

In 1968 Joanne began turning up as a regular on the astrology game show "What's My Sign." She received $100 a week for her chores.

This wasn't a sign of unrest at home—it was just the "Total Woman." Joanne told Kay Gardella, "If anything, I think I'm helping my marriage by understanding better what Johnny goes through when he has to prepare for a show. Instead of telling him all my petty little troubles, now when he arrives home I let him unwind first."

At home the petty squabbles began to get louder and louder. Joanne still felt the opposites were attracting. "How men and women get along in the first place amazes me," she allowed. "They think so different. But no people get along perfectly all the time. I guess it's just that I think like a woman and Johnny thinks like a man. I'm emotional; he's logical."

Johnny's point of view on the differences between men and women was sometimes as cut and dried. He and his producer were once out shopping, wondering what to get the wives for Christmas. Johnny stopped and advised, "Women are like children, they want lots of packages. Don't just buy one gift—buy lots of little ones."

Residents of the UN Plaza didn't see much of Johnny and Joanne. Sometimes, when they did see Johnny, they were not amused. The building was very ritzy, and plain old John was irked by some tenants' nouveau riche pretensions. That explained why he liked to go downstairs for the mail wearing sloppy clothes and sneakers. He confided to Bob Williams: "I get these looks from certain people in the elevator . . . like this is not quite proper for this address, which always tickles me, and so I keep going down in my sneakers just so they'll get upset."

Several well-known people lived in Carson's building. Robert
F. Kennedy was one. Another, a close neighbor, was the writer
Truman Capote. Back in the late sixties Joanne admitted that few
people were entertained at the Carson house, but "Truman often
comes down . . . we cook and eat in the kitchen and sometimes
sit around talking until two or three in the morning."

Capote remarked of Johnny, "When I knew him, he really had
no friends at all. . . . The only time he comes alive, you know, is
on camera. The moment the camera goes, so does he."

Johnny and Joanne's relationship was getting rockier. They
tried to keep the problem quiet—as quiet as volatile emotions
would allow.

In the book *Conversations with Capote*, Truman Capote described the misery of the slow break-up: "I felt extremely sorry for
his wife. I feel even sorrier for her now . . . she was very good to
him. She did a tremendous amount for Johnny. I don't think
Johnny would have survived or have had remotely the career he's
had if it hadn't been for her. But he was mean as hell to her. And
they lived right next door. He would holler and get terribly angry
and she would take refuge in my apartment. She would hide and
Johnny would come pounding on my door, shouting, 'I know she's
there.' And I would just maintain a dead silence."

The wife of one "Tonight Show" staffer recalls that the battle
didn't come to a head, "there were many heads. It just took a long
time for the final head to be chopped off. She was very persistent,
obviously. She persisted for how many years before she got married? Others would've walked away from it, so why should she
walk away from it easily . . ."

Whatever the problems were with Joanne, nobody doubted her
true feelings for Johnny. One woman, who knew Joanne from the
day she married Johnny to the divorce, insists that despite the
occasionally strange behavior or silly sitcom histrionics, "She was
one who had his best interests at heart."

Impish Little Johnny. He loved to imitate Popeye the Sailor, hide under the front porch, and shoot off Christmas tree ornaments with his BB gun. (*Anthony Stark Collection*)

High School. Johnny wrote gags for his high school newspaper and yearbook. "Football season opened this month and I went out to make the team. I would have, too, if they hadn't found out where I hid my brass knuckles." (*Photo Archives*)

Johnny and Jody. She was the assistant to "The Great Carsoni" at the University of Nebraska. They married in 1949, moved from Omaha to California—but didn't survive the move to New York. (*Pictorial Parade*)

Bedtime Stories. Jody was the late-night entertainer as far as sons Kit (four) and Ricky (three) were concerned. She reads to them before bedtime in this rare home photo. (*Pictorial Parade*)

"Who Do You Trust?" It's slim, handsome Johnny as the housewife hearthrob of daytime TV. His risqué cracks titillated them but critics sniped at him for being dirty. (*Photo Archives*)

Backstage at "Tonight." Aside from Ed McMahon, Johnny needed his producer close by. Just out of camera range is producer Art Stark. Taped in the late evening, the clock's set to "Tonight Time," to help convince everyone it's night. Johnny's doing his "Aunt Blabby" routine. (*Anthony Stark Collection*)

On a Break. When the camera's off, the pressure is off and the smiles come on. Guest Richard Kiley, Johnny, and member of the staff. (*Anthony Stark Collection*)

Show Portrait. Johnny's admitted to feeling confident on his show, but shy off-stage "where I'm not in control." (*Ronald L. Smith*)

Posing at a Party. It's a rare photo where Johnny's the outgoing partier and Ed McMahon glowers in the background! Johnny is shaking hands with opera great Jan Peerce. (*Anthony Stark Collection*)

Johnny Signs In. In 1963 Johnny's handwriting was analyzed by Muriel Stafford of the *New York Mirror:* "He's more sensitive than you might realize. Those far-slanted letters reveal an ardent nature. Emotionalism is combined with cordiality and consideration according to the wide, U-shaped letter *n*." She saw fully closed *a*'s as a sign of tact, the "daggerlike" crossed *t*'s as a sign of sarcasm, and the triangular *t* in "out" as a sign of "super sensitivity." (*New York Public Library*)

Signing in — Johnny Carson SEP 29 1963

N. Y. MIRROR

Laughing at Trouble. Johnny and producer Art Stark go over the cluttered list of guests for future shows, circa December 1964. (*Anthony Stark Collection*)

On vacation. Ed was Johnny's drinking buddy, sidekick, and best friend through the sixties—even after Johnny nearly fired him for getting too many laughs. (*Anthony Stark Collection*)

"I get restless if I'm not working at something," says Johnny, who was smoking too much, worrying too much, and had little appetite, sometimes dining on some popcorn and milk. (*Anthony Stark Collection*)

A private moment in the dressing room, October 1963. Pictures of Johnny's three sons adorn the walls along with a portrait of second wife Joanne. (*Anthony Stark Collection*)

The Second Mrs. Carson. Ex-cheerleader and fashion model Joanne Copeland. (*Frank Edwards/ Fotos International*)

Looking for Love. Johnny's lone movie role was in the 1963 *Looking for Love*. He gets a kiss from Connie Francis. In '87 he was still cringing: when someone handed him the soundtrack album, he threw it across the stage. (*Movie Star News*)

Carson Collectibles. Johnny issued books and records in the mid-sixties. Carson's show was "X-rated" before there was even a term for it: nobody under eighteen allowed into the audience. The author kept this ticket from 1968—after he learned he was too young to get in and use it. (*Ronald L. Smith*)

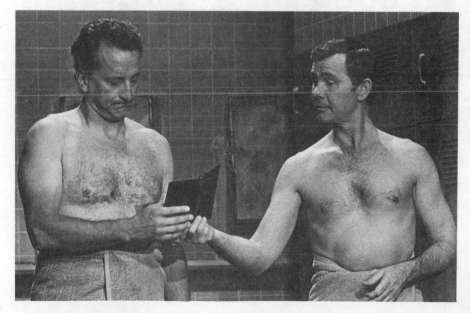

George C. Scott was part of the "Johnny Carson Repertory Company" for a disappointing 1969 TV special. It had Johnny wondering if he was a "not-ready-for-prime-time player." Aside from "Tonight" anniversary shows, he's rarely been seen on TV earlier than 11:30 P.M.

Triple Threat. "Tonight Show" writer Pat McCormick (left) and Don Rickles take turns breaking Johnny up. (*Countrywide Publications*)

Brother Dick. Dick started as a director on "Tonight" and ended up spending fifteen years working on "The Merv Griffin Show." The brothers, circa 1973, attending a screening of *Oklahoma Crude*. (*Photo Trends*)

Monkeying Around. Johnny's funny animal segments showed that he could be a warm, tender man. (*NBC-TV*)

Of course . . . the Carson charm doesn't work on every guest! (*Shooting Star/Photo Trends*)

The Carson Cast of Characters. (Top left and right) the failed magician El Moldo, the borderline mystic Carnak the Magnificent; (bottom left and right) feisty old Aunt Blabby, and Tea-Time Movie pitchman Art Fern. (*Movie Star News*)

Out with the Wives. It's Ed and Victoria McMahon, and Johnny with third wife Joanna Holland in 1981. Before long Johnny was dating Morgan Fairchild and Sally Field, and Joanna was dating Julio Iglesias. (*Robert Deutsch/LGI*)

An enduring lineup. Doc, Johnny, and Ed. Johnny was part of a different lineup in 1980. John Lennon's killer had him on his hit list along with George C. Scott and Jackie Onassis. "The only reason," Chapman explained, "is because he's popular . . . actually I kind of like Johnny Carson." (*Movie Star News*)

Johnny and Alexis. When they first met, Alexis Maas was the unpretentious, tousle-haired companion for tennis matches and fun on the beach. (*Stills/LGI*)

After her years with Johnny, she can also display a star luster of her own. (*Michael Jacobs/LGI*)

ABC loved having Johnny do their Academy Awards telecast—but they also wanted him full time doing "The Tonight Show" for them. They nearly got their wish during the Carson vs. Silverman feud. (*ABC-TV*)

Michael Landon had surprise advice for Johnny: "Up Rivers!" The Rivers-Carson feud proved to be the wildest brawl since his verbal slugfest with Jack Paar. (*Shooting Star*)

13 THE TONIGHT SHOW

Johnny faces "The Talk Show Wars," and
Merv and Dick and Joey and David

In 1969, Johnny Carson's hold on late-night TV led CBS to one conclusion: Fight fire with fire. Instead of movies, CBS vowed to hunt up a Carson-killer. They went to Jack Paar. He told them to go someplace else.

Who had a pleasant personality? Who had been around just as long as Johnny? Who had the experience?

CBS went to Merv Griffin.

Merv's syndicated evening show was doing well. In his heart, Griffin knew he could sneak into the dark of late night and bump off Joey Bishop. He wasn't sure about trying his hand against the fastest wit in America, Johnny Carson.

CBS begged Merv to come and kill Carson. Merv was flattered but frightened. Like a bounty hunter asked to track down a fast gun, he feigned nonchalance. He simply said: "You can't afford me . . . I know Johnny's salary. You'd have to double it."

CBS called Merv's bluff and handed over the cash.

"Suddenly I felt sick," Griffin recalls.

Griffin was not only sick, but feverishly sweating.

Through the blistering heat of a New York summer, Griffin practiced his sharpest questioning and quickest grin. He took over the empty Cort Theater and it became a fort where he, his new staff, and CBS huddled and strategized.

Meanwhile Johnny was huddling with his lawyers. Before the shoot-out with Merv, he wanted a new contract.

NBC tried to anticipate Johnny this time. Knowing that CBS was readying "The Merv Griffin Show," they sank two million dollars in renovating Johnny's studio—new carpeting, better dressing rooms, and comfortable new seats for the audience; in fact, more seats, increasing the number from 234 to 264 guests. NBC bought Johnny four new cameras, 23 monitors for the control room, 36 more speakers to boost the sound system, and added 600 square feet of stage space.

On July 2, 1969, George Gent of the *New York Times* reported that Carson's new contract, lasting through April 1972, was worth "probably between $75,000 and $85,000 a week," making him "the highest paid television performer in history."

The next day Carson blasted Gent. On the air he fumed, "I think it is damn unfair to me and damn unfair to performers. I want to disclaim it once and for all."

He told Jack Gould, the ranking TV reporter at the *Times*, that his salary was closer to $20,000, and insisted, "I am not the highest paid performer in television. As I said on the air, I think how much somebody makes is your own business. I don't like being evasive but I just don't want to discuss the matter."

On July 4, the *Times* ran a headline: "Report on Income of Carson Erred." And underneath: "$75,000 Figure Found to Be Unlikely—Data Are Secret."

"Investigation yesterday left no doubt that even with all the emoluments, Mr. Carson's revenue from the 'Tonight' show would not reach the $75,000 weekly sum."

But the *Times* wondered that, if Carson was denying that he, of all people, was not the highest paid TV performer, "that naturally invites the question of who is."

Carson's answer: Go ask the IRS. The *Times* claimed Carson had upped his income to between $50,000 and $60,000 a week. By contrast, Joey Bishop was getting $25,000 a week.

There would be three men fighting it out in the midnight hours: Griffin, Carson, and Bishop. And now riding into town following Griffin's move to CBS was yet another player.

David Frost had guest-hosted for Griffin, and, over the July 4 holiday in 1968, guest-hosted for Carson. He was brought back again on September 30 and made headlines with a controversial show that included a discussion of birth control and the Pope.

Actor Robert Shaw said, "As far as I'm concerned all of that business about infallibility is nonsense."

Frost recalled a nineteenth-century pope who said one afternoon, "I'm not infallible." And then at seven o'clock that same night he said, "I'm sorry. I made a mistake. I am infallible."

NBC received over a hundred phone calls. Johnny, vacationing in Florida, offered no comment. He may have thought, if Frost wants to be controversial, he should get his own show.

When Merv left Westinghouse for CBS, Frost took his place for a half a million dollars a year. After saying yes, he literally prayed for strength. He had his chauffeur drive him to the nearest church.

The "Talk Show Wars" began. The fighting got dirty. Staffers were lured from show to show. "Tonight Show" comedy writer Walter Kempley had been getting $1,000 a week from Carson. Frost bought him for $1,300. Dick Carson turned up as the director on Merv Griffin's show.

On July 7, 1969, the first "David Frost Show" was aired, featuring Prince Charles and The Rolling Stones. Frost vowed to be different from the other talking headliners. He picked guests like Dr. Spock and Tennessee Williams, Adam Clayton Powell and John Lennon. It was Frost who gave radical folksinger Phil Ochs his only national exposure.

Frost's show was so "relevant" that when Raquel Welch came

on, even she became profound. She told David: "The mind is an erogenous zone."

When Adam Clayton Powell appeared, claiming a conspiracy in the slaying of Dr. Martin Luther King, Frost was not awed. He demanded facts.

"When we leave here I'll tell you," Powell said mysteriously.

"No, no, no, don't let's have private chats. Let's talk to the people." Frost shot back, "Tell them!" Powell backed off. Frost cried, "That's the most irresponsible thing you have ever done."

That kind of point-blank accusation was absent from the talk show scene.

Johnny didn't want to hear about Frost's relevance. "Bullshit. That's my answer . . . controversy just isn't what this show is for. I'm an entertainer, not a commentator. If you're a comedian your job is to make people laugh . . . I get irked when the press says my show doesn't do enough relevant things. Neither does Dean Martin or Flip Wilson. That's up to Bill Buckley. That's my idea of what a talk show is."

Johnny was not inflexible. He'd tried controversy and it always seemed to backfire in his face. Atheist Madalyn Murray O'Hair was on the show and the audience booed her, which disgusted the always gentlemanly Carson.

He had politicians on, hoping for a big story, but was rewarded by devious tricks. "They'll tell you what they want to tell you and no more. They always have an image or a set point of view. . . . I had Agnew on, and he bored the shit out of everybody and moralized." When he had Ronald Reagan on, Reagan played coy—and announced he was running for President two days later.

In 1968, Mort Sahl asked Johnny to give some airtime to Jim Garrison. Garrison had some new theories on the Kennedy assassination. Johnny decided to go ahead with it, but quickly the lawyers jumped in and Carson was under pressure to navigate through potentially libelous terrain. The show got good ratings, but it was a critical disaster. The *Village Voice* reported: "Carson interrupted his guest about every minute and a half to have him qualify what he was saying or repeat that it was only his opinion.

tising, were now standing by their man. On February 21, 1968, they ran a two-page fold-out ad in the trade paper *Variety*. A huge picture of Carson was on one side, on the other, praise for their general in the "talk show wars":

"He used to bill himself as 'The Great Carsoni' . . . Johnny doesn't do much sleight-of-hand anymore. But no magician in all the world is so adept at making an audience appear. In the millions. We at NBC aren't precisely sure how Johnny does it, but we're glad he's on our side . . ."

In September 1969 the ratings confirmed once again that Johnny was tops. He got a 34 share of the viewing audience, Griffin just an 18 share, and Bishop a 13 share. More local stations went with Carson and NBC. They had 206 affiliates as opposed to CBS with 151 and ABC with 135.

Business was booming for NBC, and for Johnny, who was now represented by Sonny Werblin. Joanne was friendly with Werblin's wife and that's how Sonny got into Carson's intimate circle. Werblin began to reorganize Johnny's business ventures. Werblin was a stockholder in Monmouth Park Racetrack, owned the New York Jets, guided the splashy career of Joe Namath, and got movie roles for football player Jim Brown.

Johnny certainly needed someone to plow through all the business offers coming his way. "I can't tell you how many thousands of nutty schemes that people suggest. They always want money as well as my name—generally $200,000 or $300,000, a mere bagatelle . . . there was a guy who wanted to manufacture 'Johnny Carson Rubber Ducks' for adults to play with in the bathtub . . . somebody wanted to manufacture a rubber dummy to protect ladies who have to drive automobiles at night without a gentleman escort—the 'Johnny Carson Lady Protector.'"

The Carson-Werblin company was named "Raritan," after the river running near Werblin's alma mater, Rutgers University. Among the ventures undertaken in 1969 was a chain of "Here's Johnny" restaurants. One reason the idea appealed to Johnny was that he could never find a good hamburger place in New York— and longed for hamburgers served like they were years ago at "The Hamburger Hut" in Norfolk.

"The restaurants are going to be good because if people get cruddy service, I'm the guy who'll get the flak," Johnny told Earl Wilson. "One of the first things I said was, 'How you going to make French fries?' You usually get a potato that's been boiled then dipped in grease. I don't like them that way."

On late-night television, viewers didn't like things Joey Bishop's way. Merv Griffin began to overtake him in the ratings and in December 1969 Bishop was replaced by Dick Cavett. Griffin still maintained his number two rating. And CBS wanted number one.

The strain of Griffin's attempt to catch Carson was plainly evident: he was nervously overeating and had ballooned up thirty pounds. He was stoking his tobacco habit, going through three packs of cigarettes a day. Griffin knew he was out-gunned by Carson. He had to blow town.

Over the objections of CBS, Merv brought his show to Hollywood. Griffin's sidekick, Arthur Treacher, didn't make the move with him. Griffin's wife barely did. On the West Coast, Merv's marriage was on the rocks. CBS's Christmas present to Griffin in December 1971 was to cancel his show. Not only that, they canceled all his old shows, too: They destroyed every single "Merv Griffin Show" they had, reusing the tape to get some of their money back.

The "Talk Show Wars" had also taken their toll on David Frost. His long-standing relationship with Jenny Logan was scuttled soon after he began the grind. In the midst of the dizzying turbulence, Frost made headlines romancing Diahann Carroll. This couldn't last either.

Willi Frischauer, Frost's biographer, saw Frost's temperament change during the show's run. He "seemed nervous, giving his colleagues the impression that he was wrestling with problems. He obviously realized the magnitude of his undertaking . . . gregarious at most times, David now preferred to keep his own company. He did not seem overeager to go down to the studio. . . ."

The casualties mounted in "The Talk Show Wars." David Frost's show ended and Griffin came back to his humble syndicated desk job. He also went into therapy to heal the bruises of combat.

Johnny's tried-and-true methods had brought him through a tumultuous decade. He told *Newsweek:* "The idea of television, as I understand it, is to reach as many people as possible. That's one measure of success. Or is it to reach a manner of critical success, to do prison reform and other relevant things? If you do that, you're not going to reach the people. David Frost did that and for some reason he doesn't seem to be on any more.

"Look, I could do a 'controversial' show on capital punishment tonight," he told Digby Diehl. "What new [things] are you going to say? One guy says he's for capital punishment as a deterrent to crime. And then the next guy gets up with his figures showing that people give no mind to being caught, and that it degrades society and so forth. Everybody does their number, and then they say, 'Thank you, and good night.' Wow. Wasn't that a wonderful show? Well, were it? Was it a wonderful show? I don't know. I'd rather go out and entertain."

Johnny did veer from his format when the news of the day demanded it. After the death of Martin Luther King, Jr., Johnny scrapped his monologue for the first time, and instead ran an interview King had done on "The Tonight Show" with guest host Harry Belafonte. King had said: "It isn't important how long you live. It's important how well you live."

Despite the differences in style, Carson's relationships with the other talk show hosts were always professional. Carson did a ninety-minute show with Frost, and also appeared on Dick Cavett's show. Johnny admitted that he was uncomfortable— mostly because someone else was controlling things and asking the questions.

When reporters asked Cavett about his years with Johnny, the fellow Nebraskan reported that Johnny was always "cordial and businesslike . . . he is not a man who seems to seek close buddies, and, if he were, the staff of his own television show would not be the ideal place to seek them."

Like Johnny, Cavett was a reserved personality who resented it when an interviewer became too presumptuously personal. Once when a female reporter demanded to know "how cold . . . is . . . Johnny," Cavett had the answer: "He is so cold . . . one day he was napping in the nude in his dressing room and I shoved a thermometer up his ass and the mercury froze!"

That ended the interview.

In 1969, Carson ended the year with one of the most successful single talk show broadcasts of all time. It beat out that year's Super Bowl and Academy Awards and every first-run network movie. It was the December marriage of Tiny Tim to Miss Vickie (Victoria May Budinger).

The only program that topped the marriage's ratings was the televised moon walk. "That shows you the priority we have in this country," Johnny remarked.

When Tiny Tim first appeared with Johnny, Carson snickered and said, "That's the damnedest act I've ever seen." Then he turned to the falsetto-voiced, stringy-haired, fluttery-fingered singer and deadpanned, "Are you married?" Tiny shut his eyes like an embarrassed coquette.

But when he did plan to get married, an alert talent coordinator on the show asked if Tiny would like to do it on the show. The result was perhaps the second "damndest" sight Johnny had ever seen. "We did it fairly tastefully," he recalls. And it was true. Bride and groom were dressed beautifully, and the cameras were at a respectful distance. The actual wedding vows were exchanged with their backs to the camera. Then they turned gracefully to kiss, as man and wife, for the nation. Of course, Tiny and his "Miss Vickie" would soon be divorced.

Johnny and Joanne's love nest was slightly more peaceful, but it seemed that an entire city was interfering. Johnny's tensions required relaxation at home. New Yorkers have always been proud that one can "get anything" in New York at any time of the day or night. There's an exception. New Yorkers can't get peace and quiet.

Johnny had no defense against a window washer who dragged his clanking scaffold past Johnny's bedroom window every morning at 8 A.M. Outraged by the simple lack of consideration, angered that the nuisance was taken for granted by most everyone else, Carson had to sue the landlord to get satisfaction, reporting that the noise was "destructive of the health, comfort, and property of those exposed to it." And he asked that the noisy work begin not at 8 A.M. but at 10 A.M. For good measure, he demanded $25,000 compensation.

Johnny often attacked Con Edison, the power company, in his monologues. There was good reason. They too often had disturbed Johnny's rest, drilling early in the morning. "And nobody knows what for. But I do. They're using it for a training ground . . . a guy comes to work and Con Ed says, 'You don't know how to dig? Well, go over to our practice area. . . .' What they're really doing is taking Manhattan away little by little. I think they're moving it to New Jersey."

At work Carson had to monitor a variety of problems that would heighten anyone's paranoia. There was the time that the American Forces Network dropped "The Tonight Show," claiming there were too many commercials for the soldiers to bear! The show had been broadcast over radio for years.

After a Carson protest and some investigation, the real reason for the move surfaced: The radio network was getting heat from the Administration over Johnny's many jokes about Nixon and Agnew.

Nobody was looking out for Johnny's best interests as much as Johnny himself. He was his own defender. In September 1968, NBC experimented with "Monday Night Football." Housewives didn't like it. But Johnny hated it.

"My contract with NBC says that my show will begin at 11:30 P.M. and end at 1 A.M. Any changes are subject to mutual agreement . . . just this week I found out that somebody at NBC sold a football game for Monday night and they want me to cut down on my show. I won't do the show any night any more unless it starts at 11:30."

Again, Carson was outraged at the indignity of the treatment of his show by NBC: "It is not fair to treat my show like a late-night filler. This show is about the biggest moneymaker that NBC has, grossing about $27 million or $28 million a year. This is a tough show to do and if they start moving it around they are jeopardizing my career and also a contractual obligation."

Johnny knew then a valuable point that networks still don't know today. When ABC went with Dick Cavett and Jimmy Breslin late nights in the fall of 1986, viewers never knew when they'd be on. The shows were often pushed back by football games and specials—until they disappeared off the air entirely.

"Unless my program starts at 11:30, I do not plan to do a show. It is the only recourse I have to protect my show. Anything is habit. If the show does not go on at the scheduled time . . . pretty soon people won't know if we're there or not."

Johnny won, but there were plenty of other cases to fight. If it was major or minor, he was ready to take action. He became known as a "suer" not to be played with. Nobody takes advantage of J.C. Even in the smallest town, you could run but you couldn't hide.

Out in Clayton, Missouri, one David A. Drake promoted his "Drake Institute of Hypnosis," using a brochure with Johnny's picture on it. The last time Johnny played St. Louis, Drake was one of the many fans who asked to have a picture taken with him. Drake's brochure showed the two men together and the caption, "David Drake and Johnny Carson at an NBC party."

Only five thousand of these brochures were printed up by Drake for his little "Institute," but Carson found out about it anyway and demanded $300,000 in damages. Very quickly, Carson got what he really wanted: a restraining order effectively preventing Drake from using the brochures.

If "The Talk Show Wars" were now going in his favor, there was still sniping from his own side by NBC and the censors. He couldn't believe it when a "Tea Time Movie" sketch with busty blonde Carol Wayne was snipped to pieces, so badly that he refused to do it.

Carson took his case directly to his viewers, angrily insisting, "You can find obscenity in anything." Using the sound of a censor's "bleep" he recited nursery rhymes that were filled with innuendo:

"Jack and Jill went up the hill to BLEEP . . ." "Little Miss

Muffet sat on her BLEEP . . ." "'Mary, Mary, quite contrary, how does your BLEEP grow?'"

The audience broke up. "I think that gives you an idea," Carson added.

One of the running gags Johnny used around this time was the mention of the "Fakawi Indians." It was just a sly joke played on the censors, who for months didn't catch on to the tribe's significance.

It was an old joke: a Cavalry troop were out hunting the fearsome Fakawi Indians. They hunted over forests and deserts but could never find them. They used an Indian guide who led them deeper and deeper into nowhere. Finally, the exasperated Sergeant asked the guide, "Where the Fakawi!"

Over the years, Johnny found running gags about many unlikely topics and people. He did weather jokes about the "crack meteorologist" on local New York TV, Frank Field. He talked about his real-life attorney, whom he jokingly referred to as Henry "The Bombastic" Bushkin. He mentioned names like "Leopold Fechtner," who was a joke-file keeper and gag writer from Queens.

The show itself was running smoothly. Though he hadn't the reputation of emotionalism that Jack Paar did, he had just as much anger when crossed. On Monday, March 1, he was going to open the week with Muhammad Ali as a guest. Just before showtime, a member of the boxer's entourage phoned and calmly announced that the champ wasn't going to make the show.

Carson's monologue turned into a lecture. "This is the second time it has happened and I think [twice] is enough. I think if you can't make this show, you ought to have a little better explanation than 'I'm not going to be there' forty-five minutes before the show!"

Four days later, Carson checked into the New York Cornell Medical Center.

The hospital reported him in "fair" condition, suffering from hepatitis.

Gossip columnists weren't buying the story. Wasn't it convenient that Joan Rivers was already scheduled to "guest-host" the Friday night show? And that Joey Bishop was in town for Monday's show and available to host the entire week? And that Tony Randall had been contacted for some guest-hosting?

The rumor was plastic surgery for the bags under his eyes. Insiders on "The Tonight Show" at the time say that Johnny was always sensitive about his eyes. Though he was sometimes characterized in the press as "skinny" and more than one person found him "snub-nosed," Carson was more concerned that his eyes were too small. With the age wrinkles, his eyes seemed smaller and his appearance may have struck him as too wizzened.

Robin Sloan Adams in the *Daily News* was one of the reporters who said he'd had the surgery done. There was never any denial that Johnny did have plastic surgery, though no one ever went on record as to the exact date.

The new, improved Johnny Carson was still tops—on talk shows only. When Dick Cavett was a staffer on "The Tonight Show" he'd asked Johnny, "Where do you go from here?" Johnny had no answer. He was king of the talk shows—why go anywhere else. But . . . there was still that nagging notion that he couldn't make it anywhere else. Was it good sense or fear that kept him from making movies? And what would happen if he ever decided to leave "The Tonight Show"? Would it spell obscure oblivion like it did for Jack Paar?

In December 1969, Johnny tried a variety TV special. Unfortunately, the results uncomfortably confirmed that he was no better than he was in 1955 at this "standard" form of video entertainment.

The *Village Voice* hated Johnny: "The Carson time-waster was an insult not only to the viewers but to the performers, with the possible exception of the star. Talented actors and actresses like Maureen Stapleton, George C. Scott and Marian Mercer were . . . humiliated by a format that offered nothing more than standard Carson skits, which, at their best, might appeal to a sixth-grade audience of low achievers, and which are always the lowest point of 'The Tonight Show.'"

There were moments of satire on the show that Carson never

got credit for. At one point there was a commercial for a new, expensive toy. Then the camera pulled back to reveal three black kids in a tenement watching the commercial in misery. Carson had gone so far as to hire three actual Harlem residents for the spot.

The *New York Times* felt that most of the show was not satire, and not funny: "Everyone involved . . . should feel contrite this morning. . . . Two of the sketches—one purporting to spoof contemporary sexual morality, the other a spoof of the pornography in our movie houses—were witless and tasteless. A parody of Tennessee Williams' *Cat on a Hot Tin Roof* was downright dull. A fourth sketch, on children's television, was simply silly. It all added up to wasted talent in a wasted hour."

And it brought Johnny into the seventies, wiser, grayer, saddled with the same show and the same wife he had through most of the tumultuous sixties. Viewers weren't tiring of it all. But could the same be said for Johnny Carson?

14 The TONIGHT SHOW

Johnny confronts Joanne with a divorce. Gun-wielding terrorists confront Johnny with an extortion plot of kidnap and murder.

After seven years of marriage, Johnny had had enough. On June 6, 1970, he confronted Joanne. "He told me he no longer wanted to live with me, and no longer wanted to cohabit with me," Joanne said in court. "He said he wanted a divorce." Of course, she admitted: "He told me that on other occasions."

To say that the marriage was strained would be an understatement. Carson was under pressure. As for Joanne, she was in worse shape: "I could be sitting in the back of a chauffeured limousine—a sable lap robe over my legs—surrounded with packages from Fifth Avenue shops, and suddenly I'd burst out crying."

She told *People* magazine that she went through lithium treatments and sessions of holistic medical therapy, and claimed she had low blood sugar and low thyroid function. "Had it been diag-

JOHNNY CARSON															165

nosed earlier, I more than likely would still be married to
Johnny."

"Finally," Joanne said, "on June 8, 1970, he changed the
locks on our home, and I no longer had access."

The separation was tense. A few months after the lock-out,
Joanne was announced as a guest on David Frost's show. Then
suddenly Joanne canceled, due to "family problems."

In January 1971, Joanne herself filed papers, asking for
$7,000 a week. Carson's attorney, Henry Bushkin, who had be-
come one of Johnny's closest friends, told curious reporters:
"There is no reason for this to be in the newspapers. It makes
everybody's job more difficult having these problems aired in the
press as a forum rather than in private or, as a last resort, in court
if need be."

Three months later, an agreement was finally worked out. Carson, still living at 860 United Nations Plaza, retained control of
most of the property. Joanne got more than enough cash to keep
her alive and well at 112 Central Park South.

The separation was handled far away from reporters, in the
obscure courtroom of Bronx Supreme Court Justice Wilfred A.
Waltemade. News leaked out anyway—this was not a low-key
hearing. Not when it was interrupted by Joanne's almost uncon-
trolled sobbing. Grounds for the separation included the charge
by Joanne of "abandonment and adultery."

"Abandonment and adultery" was as good a phrase as any to
wrap up the anguish of the marriage gone wrong. All that was left
was to bury the package in the divorce files and let Johnny and
Joanne go about the rest of their lives.

During the actual divorce proceedings, more than a year later,
Joanne was still in tears. She told the judge, "I was a good wife."

"Try to compose yourself," he said. "It is not unique. Thousands wind up here."

Joanne gave the court all the official legal language it needed
to hear when she asserted that Carson was "abusive . . . I feared
for my health."

Ten minutes later, Joanne, wiping her eyes, emerged from the courthouse. She had her divorce, pleading "cruel and inhuman treatment."

"Johnny is a genius," Joanne said. "I'm still his number one fan but I wasn't cut out to be married to such a high achiever. For ten years, I was living on the ragged edge of his genius."

An observer through "The Tonight Show" years says: "I'm sure she would've liked to stay married for the rest of her life. I think she probably genuinely loved him. But just as he outgrew his manager and producer, he outgrew his wife."

The actual terms of the settlement had been reached on March 19, 1971. Joanne received $200,000 in cash and got a President's yearly salary: $100,000 a year.

"He was my first and only love," Joanne told Earl Wilson, "and I'm still in love with the guy." She wept as she brought up the name of an ex-model named Joanna. This was Joanna Holland, a young divorcee once married to Tim Holland, whose main claim to fame was as a backgammon player.

Wilson listened sympathetically as Joanne told him about the house Johnny bought—a half-million-dollar estate that once belonged to Mervyn LeRoy. She'd hoped they'd have a new start in California. "I had hoped that we would get back together. All I can do now is pick up the pieces. . . ." Now it looked like the rival Joanna would be moving in instead.

"I don't know what she's assuming," Carson answered. "I have no plans to get married."

Joanna said she had no plans to get married either. In interviews, she would later claim that she wasn't bowled over completely by her new boyfriend Johnny. A well-traveled, sophisticated, and beautiful woman, Joanna was enjoying a jet-set lifestyle before she met him and he was still under scrutiny to come up to her standards.

Ex-model Joanna and fashion designer Mollie Parnis were dining at New York's posh 21 restaurant. Johnny was there and, in the recollection of those who were with him, his eyes were riveted to the beautiful brunette across the room. Jack O'Brian recalled: "He was like a stud with that laser-beam stare." He got in touch with Joanna's friend Mollie and, after four days of constant calling, finally got her to fork over Joanna's phone number.

Joanna, already in great demand, also played it coy. She turned down the millionaire "Tonight Show" superstar when he asked her out. She was already involved with men like Geneva-based businessman Max Kettner, who once gave her $160,000 "as a gift."

Joanna turned Johnny down again and again. Once she claimed she was sick. The smitten talk show host said, "May I call you tomorrow to see how you are?"

For weeks Joanna toyed with the ardent Johnny. Johnny pleaded with her: his birthday was coming up. As a kind of birthday present, would she go out with him on his birthday?

She said yes—but she decided to be as old-world courtly as her Nebraskan suitor. She wanted a chaperone. It turned out to be Ed McMahon.

They continued to date. Joanna recognized that the introverted comedian needed her badly. She was willing to overlook some of his gaucheness. The man had not, after all, ever been to Paris!

Joanna later recalled to Marilyn Funt (the ex-wife of "Candid Camera" host Allen Funt) that Johnny "was coming out of a bad marriage and he needed to relax—have no pressure—be with someone who was not dependent on him financially. We went together for about two years. We did not live together. I lived with my son and couldn't have lived with Johnny in that way."

Johnny was making big changes, both in his personal life and in his show. "The Tonight Show" was going to move to Hollywood. Gossip columnists rubbed their hands in glee, ready to dive into the juicy reason for the move. Johnny was getting 3,000 miles away from cheerleader-gone-wrong Joanne—to share a love nest with gorgeous, woman-of-the-world Joanna. That was interesting news. But it was embellished. *The National Insider* wrote that Joanna was responsible for Johnny's breakup with Joanne and that California-based Joanna instigated Carson's move West. The blatant lies fueled Johnny's longstanding hatred of the tabloids. He sued the paper over their April 9, 1972, story and persisted with the battle until he won. Unfortunately, by that time the tabloid had been out of business for two years.

Actually, the move to California did not concern a sexy brunette. It had more to do with a pudgy, graying man named Merv Griffin. Merv was getting more than his share of Hollywood stars after moving his show to the Coast. New York was slumping and few big stars lived there anymore. Few TV shows were shot there anymore. Johnny's pals were all West Coast based. The ratings were always better on the weeks when Johnny brought his show to California. The "Talk Show Wars" were still on and the move would protect his number one position.

When Johnny announced the move, Joanna was aghast. She told Funt: "We'd gone together for a year and a half. . . . I felt I had just wasted a year and a half of my life because there was no way I would live there. New York, Paris, London, but never California. He asked me to come out just to see where he worked and how it was. I did and saw he was treated like a king."

She agreed to become his queen.

John and Joanne's divorce, granted on June 21, 1972, became final on September 5.

On September 30, in honor of his tenth anniversary with "The Tonight Show," Johnny was toasted in the Crystal Room of the Beverly Hills Hotel. The centerpiece was an eleven-tier cake nearly eleven feet tall.

Flip Wilson, dressed in drag and wearing a Playboy Bunny outfit, said, "I got my start on your show. I wanted to give you my best salute." Jack Benny stepped up to the microphone and announced, "I'd like to say I also got my start on the Johnny Carson Show." And Carl Reiner rose to announce "Johnny is a phenomenon: a Gentile star who has the wit of a Jew."

Johnny, handsome in formal black tie, was with his young, dark-haired companion, Joanna. She was wearing a tight sheath of a dress that seemed to sparkle with a thousand rhinestones.

After the salutes, Johnny and Joanna held up their champagne glasses. Johnny said something simple:

"A lot of columnists have been asking me why me and my gal

haven't set a date for the wedding, so I think I will tell you that we were married at 1:30 this afternoon."

Lucille Ball spoke for all the guests. She said to Johnny, "You really surprised the hell out of all of us. We all love you."

The guests, including friends like Bob Newhart, Don Rickles, and Ed McMahon gathered around him. Rosalind Russell echoed, "I'd like to wish you half the joy you've given others."

Johnny was forty-six, and Joanna twenty-six. "It's difficult to hide things in this town," Johnny added. "We'll celebrate two anniversaries at once."

By this time, some of the guests had recovered, especially Don Adams: "Would you believe it's going to last ten years? Would you believe . . . five? Would you believe . . . it's over tomorrow!"

Carson fired back wisecracks of his own, but he was genuinely touched. "I hope I never become so sophisticated and involved that I don't appreciate something like this."

But no one, not even Ed McMahon, had known about the marriage. It was that much of a shock.

Johnny's ex-wives were unavailable for comment. Jody, whose wedding anniversary was the day after Johnny and Joanna's, always kept a low profile. She even withdrew her name and address from the University of Nebraska alumni files so that reporters couldn't track her down to her Connecticut home.

Joanne was sticking to a recent agreement not to comment on Johnny. Some months earlier she had sued Johnny for making ex-wife alimony jokes on the show. She wanted $125,000 to ease the "public disrepute . . . and/or public ridicule."

The pretty ex-Mrs. Carson was highly visible, though. She had beaten Johnny to California, moved into a home uncomfortably close to his, and started her own local TV show in Los Angeles. Her feelings for Johnny were highly visible, too. Reportedly she had her wedding ring melted down into a teardrop, and she wore it around her neck.

Johnny's domestic problems were treated sympathetically by Ed McMahon and Doc Severinsen. They knew what he was going through.

Ed's wife, Alice, charged Ed with desertion after "The Tonight Show" moved West, and she demanded $60,000 a year as part of the divorce settlement. Doc and his wife, Evonne, also got divorced, and by the time she was through, she'd gotten $75,000 a year plus cars and a ranch.

Others seemed to be caught up in the turmoil, too. In the fall of 1971, Johnny's nineteen-year-old son Ricky seemed the model of the clean-cut kid. While many teenagers were wearing beards and long hair, he was a petty officer third class at the Quonset Point Naval Air Station at Cranston, Rhode Island.

But somehow, he and a friend caught the attention of two narcotics officers as they went out for a noonday drive. The car was pulled over and searched. Marijuana was found in the glove compartment.

Now, a little more than a year later, in New Haven, State Trooper John Niezelski found thirty-seven Quaaludes in Ricky's car. That may have accounted for Ricky's somewhat suspicious behavior: driving his car into the guard rails along the Connecticut Turnpike.

These were minor scrapes at best, and Johnny's reaction to the press was controlled. On the pot bust, for example, Carson issued a terse statement: "I have heard that my son was apparently involved in a marijuana smoking incident in Rhode Island. I have no other information at this time."

The very low-key nature of Johnny Carson, so obvious in such family matters, may have set him up for what would be the most harrowing brush he would ever have with the law.

An extortionist plotting a crime that could include kidnap or even murder would need the right target. Johnny seemed the type who would shun publicity and keep things quiet. Perfect. He had just spent a half a million bucks on his new California home and had plenty more where that came from. Perfect. And, he had three sons and a newlywed bride to protect. Perfect.

Not long after his son's problems with pot and drugs, Johnny faced the spectre of kidnap—even murder.

At 7:15 on the morning of October 8, 1972, workers at Johnny's new home discovered a hand grenade. Careful investiga-

tion showed that it wasn't a real one. But what about the typed
sheet of paper next to it? Someone wrote out a threat. It sounded
real.

The wording was garbled, the spelling poor. It seemed like the
work of foreigners:

"We have just presented you with this," the mad letter next to
the grenade began, "at the cost of $250,000. We believe it is
senseless to tell you not to inform any inforcement agency or to
discuss this matter with anyone. It will make matters worse for
you and anyone else concerned.

"We want the bills in twenty- and fifty-dollar denominations.
The serial numbers cannot be in a consecutive order of more than
eight. If the money is not paid or the bills run in consequtive
order of more than eight, or the bills are marked in any way, we
will reply with more conviction.

"Do not insult your intelligence by dismissing this matter; it
will only denote a lack of cooperation. This will only place your
family, your parents and other relatives in a very poor position.

"You have exactly three days from today. We will contact you
again with further instructions."

Johnny had security as tight as a clenched fist: almost nobody
knew about the secret meetings between Johnny Carson and the
police department. The grim evidence was examined, but the
highest paid performer in all of television and one of the most
sophisticated police forces in America knew that the next move
was not theirs. It belonged to the extortionists. Identity unknown.
Method unknown.

The comedian glumly hoped that it was a joke. But to reach the
porch of the Bel Air fortress and leave a warning was not the act
of jokers. It looked more like the work of well-organized comman-
dos.

It was quiet around the house.

It stayed quiet.

Wednesday afternoon, Johnny got a phone call.

"Did you get the note?"

"It's a joke . . ." Johnny offered, still in character, the reason-
ably nice and indulgent host.

No joke. A hang-up instead.

An hour later, the man called back, and the instructions were explicit. A quarter of a million dollars. In cash. And if not? Let's just say that Johnny Carson and his family would be in serious, serious trouble.

It was cool vs. cool. The felon calmly told Carson that he didn't want the money right away. He gave Johnny time to think about it. He said he would call again within forty-eight hours.

Once more, Johnny Carson was left to wonder if this was a joke, or the celebrity nightmare that he always felt was lurking somewhere in the adoring crowd. The police were on guard through the tense days and nights. Everything was on ice till Friday.

By a strange quirk of fate, it had been arranged a month earlier for Joey Bishop to be the guest host that night. Viewers asking "Where's Johnny tonight?" could never have guessed that he was participating in something closer to "Dragnet" than "The Tonight Show."

On Friday evening, October 13, Johnny Carson drove to Lankershim Boulevard. He pulled up slowly to a parking lot and walked mechanically to the three phones near the parking lot of the Shopping Bag market. The time was 7:30 P.M. The phone rang at 7:30 exactly.

The instructions: Do a little more driving. This time, to the corner of Fulton Avenue and Oxnard Street near the campus of Los Angeles Valley College.

Johnny carefully wrote down the new address. Using his skills as a card-manipulating magician, he managed to slip a carbon copy sheet under his paper and duplicate the address. A little more sleight-of-hand and it was hidden in the coin-return slot.

Johnny drove off. The police retrieved the paper, confident that if they lost Johnny somehow, they could reconnoiter at the new location.

As the cops pulled out to follow Johnny, they noticed that another car was following him, too. From a laundromat conveniently close to the market, a man and a woman, both of college age, had watched Johnny leave the phone booth and get into his Lincoln Continental.

Now, for block after block, Johnny kept driving, and the couple were tailing him in a red Camaro. The police, weaving up close and then ducking out of sight, kept up the surveillance as the cars moved through the dark, warm night.

Johnny was close to his destination. He slowed down.

The car that was following him slowed down too, and in a matter of seconds, the cop cars were right there.

The cars stopped dead. The cops had shotguns. They rushed toward the car and dragged the man from behind the wheel. His female partner watched in horror as he was hauled out of the car, thumped onto the ground and dragged to his feet, blood streaming from his face.

Thoroughly beaten, he confessed that he had been following Carson.

But just then, another man appeared, racing out from a garage near the drop site. He was making a dash for the suitcase with the money in it.

The cops pounced on him too, and in the wild melee, three suspects were now in custody; two bruised and bloodied men, one frightened woman.

The cops brought in the couple, and the man who had made the pickup.

The man who grabbed the suitcase was the foreigner police expected, the man who wrote the garbled threats. He was an illegal alien who had arrived in America by way of Germany; twenty-six-year-old Richard Dziabacinski.

The other two were identified as Richard and Linda Culkin. And they kept saying they were just "fans" of Johnny Carson.

Horribly enough, they were telling the truth.

Like anyone else, they were shocked and delighted when they happened to see their favorite star pull into the parking lot. They had been doing their Friday-night laundry when they noticed him at the bank of pay phones. Excited, shy, they recognized him but didn't know what to do. When he began to drive away, they realized they'd blown their big chance!

They couldn't let Johnny get away!

The two well-meaning fans followed Johnny, hoping that maybe he'd stop someplace else and they could merely get his autograph. At least maybe at a traffic light they could pull up and get another look at him.

But the cops got them first. Richard Culkin told columnist Marilyn Beck that he barely knew what happened. But he knew what hit him: "I was hit about thirty times in my body and face. And once [the cops] threatened they'd throw me out on the highway and I wouldn't live through the night if I didn't tell the truth. They opened the car door part way open so I could hear the road pass . . . they kept saying obscene things about my wife, called me a fag and kept hitting me during most of the ride."

Mr. Culkin spent the evening at the County–USC Medical Center. His wife was treated to accommodations at the Sybil Brand Institute for Women.

The following day, Lieutenant Charles Higby explained that the extortion plot was "not amateur." When they searched the Sun Valley home of Dziabacinski, who claimed to be a writer, they found a sawed-off rifle and a .38 pistol. Impressed, they treated him like a pro: he was jailed, and after a two-hour hearing that guest-starred Johnny Carson, Dziabacinski was indicted on charges of extortion.

15 THE TONIGHT SHOW

Johnny goes to California with wife number 3. He goes "into the dumper" as critics and comics jeer his ten-year-old formula and his approaching middle-age.

Johnny seemed to be thriving with his beautiful new wife and his beautiful Bel Air mansion. Getting close to fifty, the rejuvenated Johnny announced, "I feel better physically now than I did when I was twenty-five. I'm more active physically now. I have a gym in the basement and I work out—when I was twenty-five, I didn't have time. I was too busy trying to make a living."

Joanna was seeing to it that the living was easy. She encouraged him to enjoy the star-studded parties thrown by the Hollywood elite. She advised him to build an adjunct office to the mansion so that work and play would be separate. On his office couch he had a cushion with the embroidered axiom, IT'S ALL IN THE TIMING. Joanna offered some cosmetic tips, too. She suggested that Johnny let his hair go naturally gray, giving him a look closer to a Silver Fox than a Clairol Kid.

Johnny's producer, Fred DeCordova was enthusiastic, "He's

got one of the most beautiful homes in the world with a built-in gym, a tennis court, and, of course, a pool. He's a real health and diet freak. I don't think he's ever been in better spirits or shape."

Johnny adopted the California lifestyle completely. To Richard Warren Lewis he said, "New York has changed . . . the city is increasingly rude, hostile, and unfriendly. People on the streets are unsure and insecure. They're uptight about everything. If a stranger says hello, your first reaction is that he's attacking. I don't like people coming up and grabbing at my clothes . . . or when I'm having dinner being confronted with somebody saying, 'Will you sign this?' That's irritating. Things are much more open in California . . . people have a different attitude towards you. They're not as curt. There's a greater feeling of peace."

He told Cecil Smith that the show wasn't really "New York" or "Hollywood." "You know where 'Tonight' is located for most of the people who watch it? Right at the end of the bed, slightly to the left of the wife's big toe. That's where I want people to believe it is."

He exulted that, after living in Nebraska and New York, "I've had it with cold and snowstorms. . . . If you really want to see snow and ski all you have to do is drive up to the mountains here in one hour. But you can also get to the desert in one hour, or San Francisco. That's what I like about California." He once said, "I like the idea, as corny as it sounds, of a yard and a house."

On "The Tonight Show" over the next few years Johnny strove for a more laidback work schedule.

In 1974, Johnny began taping the shows a day ahead of schedule. This would remove some of the pressure of taping a "do or die" show just a few hours away from its airtime.

This turned out to be a bit too laidback, though. In May of that year Johnny went back to the same-day taping schedule. Critics were quick to point out that it didn't matter much—because Johnny himself wasn't around every day.

In 1975, the New York *Daily News* reported that: "For the first eight months of this year, Carson had at least a week's vacation every month except May. He was off for two weeks in April, two more in June and the entire month of August."

It seemed that Johnny was gone more often than he was on. Audiences coming to the show couldn't even get a good look at him. During commercial breaks the lights would go off so he and the guests could take a break from the glare and the heat. Perhaps it was a sign of the times—following the sixties and Watergate, the last half of the seventies was indeed a torpid, fairly aimless time. "The Tonight Show" was just marking time.

Writer Tom Shales noted that the show looked "sad and worn." "Severinsen suggests an aging urban cracker who buys embroidered jeans at E. J. Korvette's and should have changed to gabardine about a decade ago. Ed's jaw trembles slightly, like a grandpa's, and during interviews, he sits silent on the couch . . . like a still-life from the Hollywood Wax Museum."

And Johnny? Well, the popular gag wasn't "Heeerre's Johnny" but "Wheeerre's Johnny?"

Johnny wasn't around much, and when he was it seemed like he was operating on automatic pilot. Critics began to resent the formula jokes. They could see through Johnny's cast of comic characters and see the originals underneath. "Aunt Blabby," the feisty old crone, was just Jonathan Winters's "Maude Frickert." "Art Fern," the Late Night Movie maven, had Jackie Gleason's voice matched with pitchman Sid Stone's oversell style. "Carnak" was just Steve Allen's "Question Man" with a turban on, and "The Mighty Carson Art Players" could be traced back to Fred Allen's "Mighty Allen Art Players."

And Johnny was still tossing in imitations of Dean Martin, Don Adams, Don Rickles, Bob Hope, Henny Youngman, and Jack Benny in his stand-up routines.

One of Carson's comedy writers, Bill Majeski, remembers all the formulas. In California, lines would be written around "Taco Bell restaurants, massage parlors, Sunset Strip crazies," as well as the foibles of Burbank, Doc and Ed and Tommy Newsom, the dull member of the band. Carson had "savers" already scripted in case a joke bombed: "This is the type of crowd that would send an Arrow shirt to General Custer." After a while cynics wrongly assumed that Johnny deliberately picked a few jokes that were bad just so he could comically bomb. According to Majeski, the writers had to deliver "twelve to fifteen jokes each day to the head writer to give to Carson." Johnny picked out the best from the fifty submitted.

But cynics were quick to point out that many "ad-libbed" lines spouted by guests had been scripted in advance by the writers. And that such staples as "Stump the Band" were far from spontaneous either. It was reported that talent coordinators would audition possible contestants beforehand and then sit them in strategic locations near to Johnny. Johnny had no idea what songs these people would sing, but he was told whom to call on. It was pretty easy for him to choose, too. The coordinators somehow managed to pick jovial, silly housewives or pretty, ditsy girls from out of town.

Ex-talent coordinator Craig Tennis even revealed how a "funny animal" segment could be prepared in advance. Johnny "learned very early on that if he put a handful of peanuts in his pants pockets, the elephant would smell them and keep going for Johnny's crotch with his trunk."

Johnny's act on TV was predictable, and so was his Vegas set. In April 1972 *Variety* monitored Johnny, noting that he was still doing his old "Deputy John" (hungover kiddie show host) routine, and telling worn-out Vegas jokes: "Where but in Vegas can you see a lady in a mink coat in an air-conditioned Cadillac counting nickels?" *Variety* wrote: "When Johnny Carson indulges in the oldest Las Vegas joke and gets the loudest laugh of the show and scarcely departs from his tried and true routines of many past week-only trips, then the die is definitely cast. . . ."

A new generation was getting definitely tired. In 1972, comedy began to change. "Straight" comics who had once appeared on "The Tonight Show" changed radically. George Carlin was now a wacky hippie, and Richard Pryor a militant satirist. A new humor magazine, *The National Lampoon*, signaled a "new wave" in comedy. In their September 1972 "Boredom" issue, they roasted Johnny and his formulas.

Writer Michael O'Donoghue catalogued every cliché in the Carson monologue. These included using funny names (Sonny Tufts and Maria Ouspenskaya were sure laugh-getters), funny professions (Avon ladies and hairdressers topped the list), funny animals (yaks, wombats, Gentle Ben, and beavers), and funny foods sure to amuse (prune juice and kumquats).

There were lists of Carson's sure-fire subjects, like Jockey shorts and Living Bras, traffic on Mulholland Drive and the Slauson Cutoff, 5-Day Deodorant Pads, the San Andreas Fault and "Let's Make a Deal," the Man from Glad, Ralph Williams, and the Jolly Green Giant. They even catalogued his ejaculations ("Weird!" "Crazy!" "Yah-hah!" "Whoopie!") and his catch-phrases: "Can you imagine some drunk watching the show who just tuned in?" "It's a biggee." "If I said what I'm thinking right now this place would be a parking lot tomorrow. . . ."

They illustrated the piece with a switch on the over-used Ed Ames video clip. There was Johnny Carson, naked, the Ed Ames tomahawk embedded in his groin.

The young comedians satirized Johnny on record, too. The Credibility Gap performed a ten-minute "Tonight Show," complete with rimshots, Ed McMahon laughing and crying out "Yesss!" and guest star Don Rickles. It sounded exactly like material from "Magic Moments from The Tonight Show," a double album set based on a 10th Anniversary broadcast. That album was a bomb that soon was a $1.98 bargain-bin item. It was a fine album but released at the wrong time.

In the movie houses, the time was right for Mel Brooks and *Blazing Saddles*. Mel had offered the Gene Wilder part to Johnny, but the conservative Carson turned it down. When Johnny vacationed in Mexico, Mel sent the script down, figuring that the Western atmosphere might help. Johnny wrote back, "I read it in L.A. and it wasn't funny, and it's even less funny in Mexico."

Some believed that Johnny was worried about bombing in a movie, or being out of touch in a "youth market" film. Later he had a better excuse—he claimed that there was no way he could make this or any movie—he was only off "The Tonight Show" for a few weeks at a time.

"Anybody could make a movie," Carson said recently, "but I'm on every night playing myself, so it would be hard to make the transition."

Blazing Saddles could've done for Johnny what *Cat Ballou* did for Lee Marvin, but Johnny wasn't taking any chances. It didn't feel right to him, and to his credit, during those turbulent days of the late sixties and early seventies, he remained true to himself. Other stars his age were sporting beards and long sideburns—anything to appear hip. They only looked older and more ridiculous. Johnny kept his dignity.

He kept control over late-night TV, too. There simply was no competition. Dick Cavett on ABC was floundering so badly the network cut him down to one week a month, with two weeks taken over by made-for-TV specials and one week for Jack Paar. "I'm funnier now," Jack insisted. He wasn't. He was woefully out of touch with his bowties and home movies. He embarrassed himself with his tirades against rock music and long hair. His sidekick was Peggy Cass, and together they looked like someone's parents who had accidentally gotten their own show.

Johnny might have been perceived as more "hep" now than "hip," but he was light-years ahead of Paar. Jack's show was given a quick burial, and Dick Cavett was gone too.

"I let them all down," Paar said. "I had lost interest in television. I couldn't seem to adjust to the new music . . . and to a studio audience made up of mostly street people in T-shirts. The big laugh subjects were mostly pot, dope, and deviant sex. I was underwhelmed!"

Paar later went on "The Merv Griffin Show" and announced: "I guess the next event in my life will be my death."

Johnny continued to live very well, despite all the criticism. He even put in some "deviant sex" that Jack Paar would have considered underwhelming. Carson brought out guests like Dr. David Reuben for semi-serious discussions of sex. Carson remembers, "I had an edict from upstairs that we couldn't discuss masturbation . . . I couldn't understand why. On the program I asked the doctor why people had such a strange reaction to the word . . . a few titters were heard. I then said, 'Now that you've got it out of your system, the subject tonight is masturbation.' We discussed it intelligently and in no sense was it titillating."

Except when David Steinberg turned around and said, "The reason I feel guilty about masturbation is—I'm so bad at it!"

Offstage, Carson elaborated on some of his ideas on sex in an interview with Alex Haley for *Playboy*.

"I recognize there are all kinds of sexual deviations in this world," he said. "They are real needs for a lot of people . . . as long as it's this way, I think we ought to come to grips with the fact that there never can be any successful legislation against private, non-exploitive sex. I don't want to start sounding like some boy philosopher, but our sex laws seem to be predicated on the puritanical assumption that all sex—especially any variations from the marital norm—is dirty and should be suppressed. At the same time, our national obsession with sex seems to be predicated on the belief that sex constitutes the entire substance of the relationship between man and woman—and that's just as sick as feeling that it should have no part in human relationships. It's a damn healthy part of a good relationship, that's for sure. But it's just a part, and we seem bound and determined to make it unhealthy."

Sometimes on the air, Johnny's staff had their own ideas. Once after a monologue a beautiful girl strutted out to hand Johnny a sponsor's product to plug. As he held up the product and did a lead-in for the commercial, she turned away from the audience and smiled broadly.

The letters "F-U-C-K" were printed on her front teeth.

The audience had no idea why Johnny was laughing so hard he could barely finish the spot.

Sometimes the spontaneity of others was not appreciated at all. One night Dick Shawn was a guest host and during one high-flying moment, tipped over Johnny's desk. Johnny was furious when he heard about it, and Shawn's days as a guest host were over. "It was mine!" Johnny thundered. "He had no right to do that." It was a simple matter of manners.

Many of Johnny's quirks were just such reactions to questions of taste and manners. His strict Nebraska upbringing chafed against any show of disrespect, whether it was a fan cutting in on him during dinner in a restaurant or a guest repeatedly talking out of turn on the couch.

He had the lowest "walk-out" ratio of any talk show host, in part a reflection of his manners and taste. Guests had no reason to walk out. Once, when Eddie Fisher was on, and gossip about his love life was ripe, Carson refused to ask a pointed question: "I wouldn't embarrass him by asking him about his divorce any more than I'd want him to ask me about mine."

Though he had a reputation for uninhibited ad-libbing, Johnny always held himself in strict control. He wouldn't go "over the top" like the late Dick Shawn. Ed McMahon recalled the time the two of them got into a spontaneous, Laurel-and-Hardy–type bit of slapstick on the air. They began snipping at each other's ties and shirts. "At the precise moment that we were destroying very expensive clothing, it crossed both our minds that this was a very bad thing to do at a time when there were a lot of people out of work who couldn't afford to buy clothes . . . just how Johnny communicated to me the thought he had about the bad taste of what we were doing, I can't for the life of me say." But, somehow, the silliness ended before they began cutting up their jackets and pants.

Johnny's favorite practical jokes were always in good taste. There was the time producer Fred DeCordova vacationed in Africa. While he was away, Johnny had the prop department completely re-do Fred's office with African plants, masks, and hut furnishings. When Fred walked in, jungle drums were playing, birds were chirping, and several natives in full costume sat in his office, waiting.

In the seventies, tastes were changing. "Saturday Night Live" was something new in late-night entertainment, and loaded with sketches often deliberately designed to offend. The humor was hard and hip. Asked for his appraisal of the show, Johnny didn't gloss his opinion: "I've seen some very clever things on the show . . . but basically they do a lot of drug jokes, a lot of what I would consider sophomoric humor, and a lot of stuff I find exceptionally cruel, under the guise of being hip."

One night the "Saturday Night Live" gang did a parody of the Ed Ames tomahawk routine, insanely milking laughs by hacking a statue to bits.

There was talk of Chevy Chase taking over "The Tonight Show." Chase hiply denied any interest, claiming he wasn't about to bore himself talking to brainless starlets like Johnny did. The rumors about Chevy Chase replacing Carson irked Johnny. When pressed, he said that he doubted if Chase had what it took to stay in the hot seat night after night. He added, "Chevy Chase couldn't ad-lib a fart after a baked bean dinner."

Carson still got flak for running an "adult party" where sex was always the preoccupation. Typical of the style back then is this bit of conversation between Dean Martin and Johnny:

> JOHNNY: "Can I—"
> DEAN: "That's MAY I!"
> JOHNNY: "Excuse me—"
> DEAN: "You were dangling a participle!"
> JOHNNY: "Well, I'll wear a long coat and nobody'll no-
> tice! Ever thought of having a partner again? No?"
> DEAN: "I tried Linda Lovelace but she said she had it
> up to here."

Some thought this kind of thing was juvenile, especially the ogling of sexy actresses on the panel. "These actresses come on hanging out of their dresses and then act offended at jokes about breasts," Johnny fumed. "Now come on, who's kidding whom? If you ever look at the women's magazines, all you see are ads for breast development. So there you are."

Carson has never departed from these gags. He's right when he says that some starlets deliberately exploit their assets.

One night the chesty actress/comedienne Elvira was on the show. She was talking about a horror film called *The Thing With Two Heads*, but, giving a little jiggle, she began describing "The Head with Two Things."

The audience roared. Johnny grinned and cut away for a commercial. Elvira recalls that during the break, "I turned to Johnny and said, 'Oh, I'm so sorry, I didn't mean that . . .' He said, 'Don't con a con artist, baby,' but he said it in a very nice way."

Sometimes Johnny also got fed up with the game. One night, when a starlet came mincing out in a skintight and low-cut blouse, breathing heavily, Johnny simply stared right down her dress. "That's the biggest set of jugs I ever saw!" he said. "Now that we've got that out of the way, let's talk."

As the seventies rolled on, some of the "old time" comedians faded away. One of them was Jack Benny.

Jack had been extremely important in Johnny's life. So many of Johnny's basic comedy techniques came from Benny. On "The Jack Benny Program" Jack always strove to make his guest star look good. If a Bogart, a Karloff, or a Hope got big laughs, people would say "The Jack Benny Program" was great last night. Johnny always tried to make his guests comfortable enough to shine, for the same reason. As Johnny said, "You should try to help the guests be as good as they can be, because the better the guest is, the better I'll be."

Johnny wrote jokes for Benny over the years, just to help out Jack during personal appearances. When Benny was scheduled to appear for a Texas concert, the big news down there was the closing of Edna's Chicken Ranch, one of the best little whorehouses in Texas, an institution for nearly a hundred years.

Johnny gave Jack a gag to use during the show: "I'm down here because they're closing Edna's Chicken Ranch. The reason I came . . . is because I was here for the opening and I'd like to be here for the closing."

Jack had gags for Johnny, too. At a dinner for Carson in 1970, Jack rose at the dais to proclaim: "Tonight we are paying tribute to a man whose talent is exceeded only by his salary . . . a million three hundred thousand dollars a year. . . . Now, Johnny Carson's brother, Dick, is the director of the show. . . . His salary is a thousand dollars a week . . . and Johnny, who acts as his agent, collects eleven percent." Then Jack mentioned that a guest star on "The Tonight Show" goes on for "approximately three hundred dollars . . . meaning . . . he's a schmuck!"

Johnny's laughter was the loudest in the house.

When Jack died, Joanna couldn't console Johnny. He was in tears. Joanna couldn't remember a time she had seen her husband cry.

Johnny rarely mentioned the deaths of celebrities on the show, or any tragedy. He did once, ending a show by acknowledging the passing of Stan Laurel. He did again for Jack Benny.

Once someone asked what Johnny wanted to have written on his tombstone. He answered, "I'll be right back." But in private, he told friends that he didn't want to have a tombstone. He didn't want a funeral. He wanted to be cremated, with his ashes scattered into the sea. He wanted his friends to go out that night and have a party.

He confided that he'd given Chasen's money for just such a party in the event of his death.

For his fans, such thoughts were beyond comprehension. There was Johnny, night after night, a calming influence in a changing age. He could not be replaced. His influence with the public was unquestioned. Johnny never really put it to a test, but one December night in 1973, he inadvertently gave all of America an idea of just how influential he was.

During his monologue, Carson confided to viewers, "We've got all sorts of shortages these days, but have you heard the latest? I'm not kidding . . . there's a shortage of toilet paper!"

Once America heard it from Johnny, they went rushing out into the night to purchase and hoard precious supplies. People who'd missed "The Tonight Show" were surprised to see their neighbors stockpiling their shopping carts with the precious cargo. They became spooked and started stocking up, too.

Before long, the chain was pulled and stores all across the country had a tremendous toilet paper shortage! When the stores frantically called manufacturers for more, the startled companies couldn't meet the demand.

Johnny's panic in the john led to a full-scale investigation. The real culprit was not Carson, but a Wisconsin Republican named Harold Froehlich. Representative Froehlich, worried about the paper industry (a mainstay of his state), had been upset to discover that the government no longer had the customary four-month storehouse of toilet paper. He'd issued a warning that Johnny's writers soaked up: "I hope we don't have to ration toilet tissue," the politician said. "A toilet paper shortage . . . is a problem that will touch every American."

Johnny couldn't improve on Representative Froehlich for comedy. But he proved that night in December that what Carson had to say to America each night was taken far more seriously than anything government officials put in the newspapers.

Through the late seventies Johnny became more political than ever before. Though he was no Richard Pryor or "Saturday Night Live," he became the closest thing to a Will Rogers or Mort Sahl that mid-America could watch. He regularly reported on bureaucratic bumbling in the news and the foibles of both local and national politicians.

Even the most apathetic Americans began to know about "flaky" Jerry Brown, or nasty James Watt, or power-obsessed Alexander Haig. They heard President Ford described as looking like "the guy at the Safeway who okays your checks." Carson's monologues, while never put to any finite test, have probably done much to shape public opinion for millions of people. When he makes fun of someone, like Geraldo Rivera (the "newsbreaking" reporter who rarely was), it can be devastating. When he decided, in the sixties, to use the name "Bruce" as a code word for gays in jokes, the impact remained for decades (much to the discomfort of men named Bruce).

Johnny even dared satirize commercials, not only in his "Mighty Carson Art Players" black-out sketches, but in pointed putdowns. There was the time he smashed a Corning "break-resistant" cup during a demonstration—and kept shattering them on the floor in disbelief.

During an ad Ed McMahon was doing for Smucker's Butterscotch Topping, Johnny noticed something funny about the vanilla ice cream. It was a prop, made out of lard. "There ought to be a certain amount of honesty!" Johnny said.

Sponsors weren't too pleased. As a lead-in for a Sara Lee ad, Johnny ad-libbed, "Who is this Sara Lee person? I'll bet she's some drunken old bat in a kitchen somewhere in Des

Moines . . ." Sara Lee was actually the daughter of the company president. "The Tonight Show" lost the account.

It didn't stop Johnny from sounding off about sponsors. During the Christmas season in 1986, he was disgusted by a fast-food chain's ad announcing, "This season give Chicken McNuggets." He stared into the camera: "All I want for Christmas are some dried lumps of processed chicken."

Offstage, Johnny has never hesitated to put his money where his anger is. In 1975, he filed a $38 million civil suit against Paramount Pictures over the failure of his Carson–Paramount Productions company. In 1977, he filed suit for $3 million against the real estate company, claiming that it had circulated rumors about Carson moving from Bel Air to a development site they owned in San Fernando Valley.

Johnny sometimes went public with his cases. Viewers were well aware of his "slant board" accident in August 1974. Carson was exercising at home on the board when it gave way, injuring his back and neck. He was off the show temporarily and did a number of jokes that were as stiff as his aching body. He pursued the case against the company, L&R Industries, for two years, finally arriving at an out-of-court settlement in November 1976.

As the laidback seventies progressed, some of the California sunshine seemed to wear off. The grind of doing the show was still a grind. Psychotherapy hadn't worked for Johnny, and neither had drinking. And the anger was still there, waiting to come out.

"He explodes!" Joanna told Marilyn Funt. "He is always sorry afterward, but I do get frightened and very quiet. Often his anger has nothing to do with me—which is why I won't yell back. . . . I often have felt like responding with anger—yelling back—that was the pattern of his first wife. I never have."

There was no question that Carson could be a match for anyone. A young man wanted, for reasons unknown, to get a closer look at Johnny and his Bel Air mansion. He climbed the fence and just dropped in. Johnny met him almost immediately. Carson put him up against the wall, barking orders like a cop. When the

police came, there was the intruder, arms flat against the side of
the house, almost white with fear.

One of the funniest incidents on "The Tonight Show" during
the mid-seventies was fueled by anger. It was the time Don
Rickles damaged the cigarette box Johnny kept on his desk—and
Carson went out after him. It happened during the middle of the
monologue—Carson suddenly discovered the damage and brought
the camera across the hall to where Rickles was taping "C.P.O.
Sharkey." And there, in front of both Rickles' audience and "The
Tonight Show" audience, Carson gave Don a nonstop barrage of
put-downs that, for once, left the sharp-tongued comic speechless.

Still, no comedian, not even monologue master Johnny could
control the process that turned hostility and angry observation
into slapstick comedy and ironic satire.

Johnny played tennis and still pounded on his drum set. He
craved calming, solitary pursuits like astronomy. At one point he
bought a CB radio, but trashed it in disgust. "I just couldn't bear
it, all those sick anonymous maniacs shooting off their mouths."

There was more noise from Johnny's Bel-Air neighbors. Sonny
Bono's yelping, mewling miniature poodles were driving him
crazy. When Johnny filed suit against the noisy nuisance, the
newspapers laughed. They couldn't sympathize with a millionaire
in a mansion who only worked a few hours a day.

Johnny's contract with NBC was going to be up soon. He
wasn't sure if he wanted anymore. "People say, 'Jeez, Carson's off
the show a lot.' Well, I'd be in a rubber room and fed by paid
attendants if I wasn't." At least a rubber room is soundproof.

16 THE TONIGHT SHOW

Johnny battles with his NBC boss, Fred Silverman. And then with wife, Joanna.

J oanna told Johnny, "You're only happy when you're
performing." Johnny didn't deny it. "I don't think that's
completely true. But it is a great high. If I quit tomorrow, I don't
know what the hell I would do."

In December 1977, Johnny and NBC reached a new salary
agreement. The contract was valued at $2.5 million a year, ex-
tending through 1981.

Carson's other financial ventures were bringing him a small
fortune. While the American Inn Here's Johnny restaurants never
cooked (not even with such items as the "How Big Is It?" Cheese-
burger), the Johnny Carson Apparel line was a big hit.

Back in 1972 the *New York Times* reported that "no performer
in the modern era has had as much impact on style trends as
Johnny Carson." Johnny's clothing line became "one of the fastest
growing concerns in the history of the men's wear business," gen-

erating millions for him. It didn't hurt that Johnny not only wore
his line of clothes every night, but pointedly joked about how
Doc's outfits looked by comparison.

Carson expanded his portfolio into a wealth of products and
companies, trying to get into TV stations and casinos as well as
real estate. His Carson Productions controlled "The Tonight
Show" and other properties, including David Letterman's show.
By January 1979 he was literally "laughing all the way to the
bank." Already a co-chairman of the Commercial Bank of California, he and his attorney, "The Bombastic Bushkin," as Carson
liked to call him, joined with three other investors to buy a 94
percent interest in the Garden State Bank, located in Hawaiian
Gardens, California. The price for the takeover was $1.75 mil-
lion. Someone suggested they rename the bank after Johnny to
assure business. They didn't have to go that far. After all, the
bank happened to be on Carson Street.

For his Vegas gigs, Johnny mentioned a little bit about bank-
ing. "Early withdrawals—that's what got me in trouble with one
of my ex-wives. Of course, I didn't leave it in the full six years."

People magazine estimated he was making between $12 and
$15 million from his real estate, clothing, and similar outside
enterprises, in addition to his salary and his $225,000-a-week
Vegas price. Producer Fred DeCordova put it this way: "In the
time it takes me to pee, Johnny has made $5,000."

Johnny was unquestionably the big star at NBC, the prince
who had quelled every uprising (from Griffin to Cavett and back
to Paar) and stood like a rock while mortality claimed some of
TV's enduring greats (Jack Benny and Ed Sullivan), and ratings
and demographics took care of the rest (Red Skelton, James Ar-
ness, Lucille Ball). Who had a winning streak to rival Johnny
Carson? Nobody.

Who made more money at NBC?

Well, there was another guy who had a superstar salary. One
Fred Silverman. He'd been wooed away from ABC to become
NBC's president at $1 million a year.

Flashy Freddie was going to bring NBC back to number one,
and he was going to make sure his number one star led the way.

It was "The Boss" vs. "The Franchise." It wasn't enough that Johnny's show was raking in millions for NBC. Silverman wanted Johnny to become a team player. The rookie manager was going to make the superstar sweat.

Silverman didn't like Johnny's four-for-five workweek. Johnny's contract said he could take Mondays off twelve weeks a year.

Silverman liked Johnny's three for five workweek even less. Johnny only had to show up Wednesday through Friday for twenty-five weeks of the year.

Silverman hated Johnny's zero for five workweeks: the fifteen weeks of vacation time scattered through the year.

Even a George Steinbrenner would've thought twice about criticizing a moneymaking superstar who went three for five and four for five consistently, whose hot streaks saved many a ratings week, who had absolutely no competition and no replacement.

Coach Silverman used shaming tactics. He went to the press and openly blasted his star player.

After complaining that Carson's pinch hitters couldn't score as well as Johnny, Fred urged Johnny to come to bat more for the team: "I only hope that there will come a moment in time when he will say to himself: 'I love "The Tonight Show" and I'm going to do a little bit more.'"

Coach Silverman intimated that "The Tonight Show" was getting a little flabby in the ratings. He gave Johnny a playful sock to the jaw: "He's a very competitive and professional guy. I don't think he must enjoy reading that the thing is slipping."

Coach Silverman, according to a reporter on the *New York Post*, then began "leaking stories to reporters relating Carson's sweetheart contract . . ."

It was the old Steinbrenner trick: Shame your employee by telling the world that he makes millions and should be loyal and grateful.

Those who didn't know Johnny figured all hell would boil over. Insiders knew that all hell would freeze over instead. Johnny's choice was always the cold war.

Johnny confronted Silverman on March 18, 1979, and announced that he was benching himself. Permanently.

"You have a contract and we expect you to honor it," Freddie said.

Carson walked.

If it had been Lou Gehrig calling it quits after 2,130 games it wouldn't have had more impact. Gehrig had been a Yankee regular for fourteen consecutive years. Carson was in his seventeenth consecutive season with NBC.

When Carson quit cold, it made the front page of the usually staid *New York Times*. The paper reported that Carson was ready to broadcast his last show on September 30, which would mark the exact end of his seventeen years (which began October 1, 1962). Johnny, master of timing, would be leaving NBC at the start of the fall classic—the fall schedule of premiere programming. Without Carson anchoring the late-night schedule, NBC wouldn't have a chance of being the number one network in the crucial fall ratings.

Don Rickles one night joked with Johnny and said, "Who cares if you don't do 'The Tonight Show!' It's not important! You think you're a big star and you're not!"

The *Times* differed. They reported that Carson's bombshell even shook Wall Street: "The shares of the RCA Corporation, the parent of NBC, eased 3/8, to 27, yesterday on the New York Stock Exchange after trading as low as 26 3/4. Wall Street analysts attributed the decline to reports of Mr. Carson's plans."

Wall Streeters knew that Carson's show was generating $23 million for the network. Seventeen percent of NBC's profits were tied to one man: Johnny Carson.

Concerned viewers wondered what they'd do without Johnny. He had been taken for granted for so long.

One of the more unlikely celebrities to pay tribute to Johnny was Andy Warhol. In his words: "'The Tonight Show' is always good simply because you never have to get embarrassed for Johnny Carson: he has TV magic, is always cool, clever and American . . . he wants to make things easy by entertaining, and he does that night after night. When you look at him you never have to worry that he has a problem—you know he won't fall apart . . ."

If Johnny is there, whether it's the crisis in Iran or the war in Vietnam, whether it's an assassination or nuclear disaster, then it's all right. For many viewers, Carson is more than just some kind of video tranquilizer. His smile, his jokes, his easy and assured manner gives them their only light moment of the day, and a good feeling to face the night. A hyper Joan Rivers or a sourly hip David Letterman can't do it. No more Carson and there is a void.

Carson and Silverman's feud was front-page news. Some ardent Carson fans prayed for Johnny to stay on. The *Christian Science Monitor* prayed for him to go. They decried the way he continued to deal in "sophomoric double meanings." They were disgusted by the "hours wasted" with "the trivia and innuendo purveyed during those midnight hours."

NBC's "Nightly News" sought out Johnny for some encouraging news. "I'm unhappy, obviously, for the network. I've been with them for a long time and obviously this does not come at a very good time for them. But as I told Mr. Silverman, I don't want to feel like Benedict Arnold and I think that after seventeen years you can hardly be called a deserter."

Johnny pointed out that his $2.5 million a year wasn't all that much considering that Marlon Brando got more for a few weeks' work in *Superman* and that ballplayers got that for five months' work. He was taking fourteen weeks vacation, but insisted, "If I stayed on the show and did five shows a week . . . it might contribute to an audience getting tired of me." And, he added, he might get awfully tired of the show, too.

Mike Douglas felt a host should be on more often. "I feel that if people tune in 'The Mike Douglas Show' they're entitled to see Mike Douglas." Perhaps he'd been on too long. His show was bumped off the air and he took a very long vacation.

Johnny had two years left on his contract, which would take him through 1981. The Boss was trying to hold him to it. The now white-haired Carson insisted he was feeling "mentally and emotionally tired."

He told NBC all about his feelings—on a news show broadcast by ABC: "No one can force a performer to work if he doesn't feel

he should. It isn't as if I'm threatening to walk across the street
and do the same thing at another network."

NBC didn't have to read that one between the lines. ABC loved
Johnny's work when he hosted the Academy Awards show for them
and it was no secret they wanted him permanently. They gave him an
ostrich-skin attaché case as an added gift for hosting the Oscars and
brought him to the French Riviera as an added bonus. In an
interview for "60 Minutes" Carson admitted that "they had made no
direct overtures, but I would assume that when somebody has you
socially for dinner and—I'm not that naïve—that they might say,
'Hey, it would be nice if Johnny Carson worked over here . . .,' it
seemed like a bit of an invitation."

"Would you go?"

"I can't answer that."

Johnny was then asked if he had any comment for Fred Silverman, should Silverman be tuning in.

"I hope when this show is seen you're still with NBC," said
Johnny.

It was ironic that back in July 1977, Kay Gardella had broken
the story about ABC's initial efforts to swipe Johnny from NBC.
At the time, Fred Silverman was at ABC. Fred had told Johnny,
"There's only two stumbling blocks. The NBC contract and you."
He was referring to Johnny's loyalty to NBC.

Johnny knew NBC was quaking. The offices at the suddenly
crumbly "30 Rock" in Rockefeller Plaza were in turmoil. NBC
was having a tough, tough time. Their new shows were disasters.
In an untimely federal investigation into expense-account embez-
zlement, company bigshots were fired in a scandal about nearly
$1 million in expense-account spendings. RCA had recently
dumped $200 million worth of businesses that were not making
enough profits. Now NBC was no longer number one.

Did Johnny realize that NBC was having trouble? "That's like
saying the *Titanic* had a small leak," he said.

Ratings points confirmed that Johnny couldn't be replaced.
When Johnny was on, he grabbed nearly 40 percent of the available audience.

By comparison, the bright young comics of the day, Steve Martin, Gabe Kaplan, and David Brenner barely reached 30 percent. Bill Cosby and Joan Rivers were not hot stars in 1979, and averaged 27 percent and 25 percent, respectively. Carson's pals, Don Rickles and Bob Newhart, couldn't break 30 percent and the past master of the talk show, Steve Allen, netted 25 percent.

NBC raised a white flag. Johnny had won again.

Like Grant and Lee, Carson and Silverman held a summit of sorts. It was Sunday night, May 6, 1979, in front of more than 1,500 people—a packed house at the Waldorf-Astoria Grand Ballroom. It was the banquet held by the Friars' Club in honor of Johnny Carson, "Entertainer of the Year."

The two men were not smiling as they sat on the dais, with only Johnny's wife Joanna between them. But, if this momentous event could bring out such disparate guests as Ambassador Evron of Israel and Ambassador Ghorbal of Egypt, anything was possible.

Called upon to toast the guest of honor, Silverman expressed relief that Johnny was staying: "I was so relieved that I got down off the chair and put the rope back in the closet."

The audience roared. Then Freddie completed his penance, admitting that his new shows like "Supertrain" and "Hello Larry" were instrumental in "bringing the network from third place to where it is now." Third place, of course.

The network president could only manage a quick swipe at Carson's lawyer, thirty-eight-year-old Henry Bushkin. Alluding to NBC's bid for the Olympic games, he said, "I'm happy to announce that in Moscow 1980 Henry will be a javelin catcher. It's the least I can do for Bushkin after all he's done for me."

Silverman said to Johnny, "You're more than the entertainer of the year. You're the entertainer of your time, you're the best friend TV ever had."

Bob Hope interrupted, "He said the same thing to me last year!"

The guests on the dais came to praise Johnny, not to roast him. There were Lucille Ball and Kirk Douglas, Ruth Gordon and Garson Kanin, David Brinkley and Howard K. Smith. The speakers included Mike Wallace and Barbara Walters. Walters turned her sensitive eyes toward Johnny and recalled the days when she was still at NBC, working on the same floor with "The Tonight Show" star. "You were too shy to say hello to me then, Johnny, but I was grateful for that. Because if you had, I'd have been too shy to answer."

Host Bob Hope toasted John and roasted Freddie, saying he was "the only man in America who knows what it feels like to rearrange the deck chairs on the *Titanic*." As for Carson, Hope mildly acknowledged, "It is not often that I find somebody who has stolen more from NBC than I have . . . he never dreamt that he'd some day be the busiest John in America."

With a sardonic smile he added: "I admire a man who can do what John has done to his network—as many times, as many ways and in as many positions."

When the dinner of Filet Mignon Périgourdine and the dessert of frozen praline soufflé was over, Carson rose to acknowledge his applause. Amid "Tonight Show" regulars Fred DeCordova, Ed McMahon, and Doc Severinsen, there was no need to stick any more needles into the deflated carcass of The Coach. But in explaining why it took so many weeks to decide whether to continue or not, Carson did note, "I was waiting for the Marvin decision." At the time Lee Marvin was battling a palimony lawsuit that threatened to take away half his earnings.

"I thought I might get half of what NBC has earned in the last seventeen years," he deadpanned. As for what had been a long, long evening, Johnny said: "When Ruth Gordon arrived here tonight, she was jailbait."

Included in Johnny's new deal was a radical change in format. "The Tonight Show" streamlined from ninety minutes to sixty, with Carson taking Mondays off plus vacations.

Monetarily, Johnny got what he wanted professionally.

On the show, it was a different story. According to Ed McMahon, their relationship had changed. "I only see Johnny for maybe a minute before we start taping."

Life on St. Cloud Road in Bel Air was not going smoothly. In November 1979 Sonny Bono and his noisy dogs moved out. But *Hustler* magazine publisher Larry Flynt moved in, with bigger dogs. And the yapping dogs of other neighbors, like the rich

Daryoush Mahboubi-Farbi, created a symphony of yaps. Once again, newspapers had a big laugh while Johnny made up in frustration what he was losing in sleep.

Sometimes Johnny's serious pursuit of happiness and his strict perfectionism were laughable. Ex-talent coordinator Craig Tennis told about the time Carson quite rightly flew into a rage when he discovered two of his servants completely drunk. He made them pack and leave immediately.

Then he haplessly realized the house was a mess. When Joanna came in later, she found the servants gone—and a stoical Johnny Carson mopping the floor. He was stark naked except for an Aunt Jemima–type kerchief around his head.

There were evidently less and less laughs of any kind. It was only a matter of time before Johnny once more made headlines with a very messy divorce.

17 THE TONIGHT SHOW

It's Johnny vs. Joanna in the divorce battle of the century.

Joanna and Johnny were opposites in many ways. One was in expressing affection. When Johnny would come home from work he was tense and distracted. Into his solitude would come Joanna, nuzzling and kissing. Johnny's reaction according to Joanna: "He would get very angry."

She told Marilyn Funt, and a national audience in *Good Housekeeping* magazine that life with Johnny was not all laughs: "He is very serious. Of course, he can be very funny, but all the pressures and problems tend to make him serious. Johnny is the fastest-thinking person I know—either in humor or seriousness. If you are having an argument with him, you can't outthink him on your feet. If you know this, you won't try."

Joanna was conspicuously finding another life for herself. In 1971 she joined Michael Vollbracht's fashion company. Like Johnny's second wife, she immersed herself in charity work, be-

coming president of SHARE ("Share Happily and Reap Endlessly"), a charity for the mentally retarded. She also was a
committee member of the Santa Monica Rape Treatment Center
and the Women's Guild of Cedars-Sinai Medical Center.

Some seemed to get the idea that the Carson marriage was on
the rocks. Joanna seemed to drop hints in interviews, but there
was nothing subtle when the big bombshell dropped. The draw
was dollars. Joanna was seeking one of the biggest paydays in the
annals of the American divorce court. According to Joanna's lawyer, Johnny was pulling down $18 million a year and she was
going to get her share. The battle between Johnny and Joanna
became front-page news.

The complexities of Johnny's personality came out as reporters
dug up quotes from co-workers. "His character points to a thousand little fears in a whole symphony of different ways," ex-talent
coordinator Craig Tennis wrote. "This is a man, after all, who
sleeps with his baby pillow—who, in fact, won't travel without it
and carries it everywhere in his suitcase."

Yet Johnny, who had worn his mismatched "lucky" cuff links
for a decade, had chosen to travel without them after his divorce
from Joanne.

Whatever his quirks, he was still Johnny, the man doing his
damnedest every night to relax everybody else for a good night's
sleep.

The pages turned on Joanna. The attractive jet-setter was an
unsympathetic figure, especially next to the hapless Johnny. It
seemed that whether it was a bombed joke or a failed marriage,
audiences always were on his side as he twitched his eyes,
dabbed his nose, shoved his hands in his empty pockets, and
squirmed.

The lifestyle of the rich and famous Joanna became the preoccupation of the tabloids. Joanna had seemingly been running
Johnny for years. Johnny, supposedly no fool, had bought the
Bel-Air mansion before the marriage. It would be in his name
should there be a divorce. But Joanna had "convinced" him to
stick her name on the deed and he'd agreed. And Joanna had
been the one pushing for a duplex in New York at the obscenely

posh Trump Towers. As if that wasn't enough, Joanna also
wanted—and got—a $2 million apartment at the Pierre Hotel.

Johnny was looking slightly pathetic—and everyone was sympathetic. Except Joanna. She continued to make splashy headlines that left her drowning in negative public opinion.

While a nation watched Johnny's losing game of "Who Do You
Trust?" Joanna was playing "Queen for a Day."

Carson's second wife, Joanne, had copped $100,000 a year,
but Joanna was asking for $220,000—a month.

Joanna pleaded for the bare necessities of life. Why, she
needed at least $40,000 a year just for new furs and jewelry. And
she insisted that she needed over a quarter of a million dollars
just to continue living in the style to which she had become accustomed. She wanted the Bel-Air mansion and the New York
apartments, too, of course.

The queen of the house was spending $1,400 a month on food,
$2,060 a month on "repairs and maintenance" around the house,
and $1,125 on utilities. And let's not forget minor details like
$120 for the cable TV and $75 for water. Joanna also reported on
how much money it took to maintain Johnny's fortress of security:
nearly $5,000 a month to pay the help, nearly $6,000 for guards,
$500 in payroll tax, and another $1,500 each month in insurance.

And it took $690 a month for "general supplies" and another
$690 to keep "household cash" around the household. And, fi-
nally, chalk up $245 a month to "miscellaneous."

Joanna was coming off more and more like a beautiful, aging
siren with a rich-bitch attitude. Newspapers loved running pictures of her in slinky, expensive garb, showing a provocative
amount of cleavage and generous portions of leg exposed by slit
skirts.

The Los Angeles Herald Examiner reported that "she's a very
shrewd businesswoman," evidently not entitled to much sympa-
thy. Many misinterpreted her cash demands—by law, she was
simply listing the cash necessary to keep her in the condition to
which she'd become accustomed. Instead, it sounded like she was

simply making demands based on some bizarre, unreasonable new calculations.

But Joanna's demands still seemed excessive, and her personality worked against her.

The wit and wisdom of Joanna Carson: "Anyone who says money doesn't buy happiness doesn't know where to shop."

By contrast, there was Johnny in his off-the-rack items of Carson Apparel. Joanna probably didn't deserve the rather cruel treatment she was getting in the press, but for a paper to side with her was as unlikely as saying that the Ayatollah had his problems too during the crisis in Iran.

Joanna reported that she and Johnny separated in March 1982. Johnny's lawyers insisted it was November 1982. Johnny's lawyer, "Bombastic Bushkin," had his own problems—he and his wife had separated, too. He was seen squiring Joyce DeWitt, of "Three's Company."

During the rocky proceedings, Joanna was awarded a temporary settlement of $44,600 a month. There was a howl in the press when her lawyer begged Superior Court Judge Frances Rothschild to increase it an extra $6,000. "It's really a drop in the bucket," the lawyer sniffed.

The New York *Daily News* editorialized: "Joanna sure has a large bucket." They slammed out snide remarks that Johnny could only have dreamed of using in his monologue. The *News* reported that the money "Johnny has been sending her is simply not sufficient to keep her smiling. It's enough to make her frown, and that only produces wrinkles. What will bring back that smile? Another $6,000?"

Judge Rothschild, who was making $72,000 a year, felt that Joanna could do pretty well with her $44,600 per month.

Joanna claimed that Johnny earned $15,600,000 before taxes in 1982.

The actual divorce proceedings were filed in March 1983. Both Johnny and Joanne cited "irreconcilable differences." By this time, Johnny knew where he stood with his viewers. They were feeling sorry for the poor sap who was kicked out of his own house

and left to stand in front of millions of people smiling sheepishly
and cracking shivery, lame jokes about his dwindling money and
failed marriage.

Johnny slowly injected a few lines into the monologue about
how he felt. One night he reported on an item in the papers: Tip
O'Neill speculated that when Nancy Reagan had to leave the
White House, she could always become "the Queen of Beverly
Hills." Johnny shook his head. "Nancy would NOT be the Queen
of Beverly Hills—I have the royal tab to prove it."

Johnny's jokes about his losses were feeble: "I heard from my
cat's lawyer. My cat wants $12,000 a month for Tender Vittles."
Others were haplessly silly: "I resolve if I ever get hit in the face
again with rice, it will be because I insulted a Chinese person."

Johnny moved down to a house in Malibu. When asked how
much this one cost, he answered, "None of your damn business!"
Gossip columnists linked his name with Sally Field, and later
bandied about a bevy of aging beauties from Dyan Cannon to
Angie Dickinson. Joanna, antagonizing the press with her showy
bicoastal lifestyle, was the subject of "new beau" rumors, too. In
her case it was supposedly the gurgling, syrup-voiced heartthrob
Julio Iglesias.

In the media it was Carson vs. Carson. Actually, it was Rubin
versus Crowley, as Johnny's lawyer Miles Rubin tried to stem the
high-powered charge of Joanna's Arthur Crowley.

It was reported that Joanna kept a bulletin board covered not
only with clippings about how the divorce was going in the press,
but with paparazzi "spy" pictures of Johnny on dates with other
women.

Johnny was seen in January of 1983 with Sally Field. In May,
he was squiring Morgan Fairchild. A photographer tried to get
pictures of Johnny and Morgan in a car together. Johnny shouted,
"If you stand in front of my car again, I'm going to kick your ass
to the sky!"

Johnny's problems only got worse. In April 1983 he canceled a
"Tonight Show" to fly to Scottsdale, Arizona, where his parents
were now living. It was one of the rare times when Johnny asked
that a re-run be put in place of a scheduled show.

His father died on April 8, at the age of eighty-three. His mother died two years later, on October 13, 1985 at the age of eighty-four.

Legal problems plagued Johnny constantly. By February 1984, part of the divorce proceedings was settled. Joanna received $2 million in stocks and bonds and $41,000 in interim support. Three months later, Johnny was named by the FDIC, along with twenty-two others associated with the Commercial Bank of California, in a lawsuit arising from the demise of the bank. Carson's lawyer spoke up for Johnny, claiming that Johnny was just a "passive director" in the bank and that his name was being used to give the case added notoriety.

The very same month, on May 25, Carson was hit by a bombshell thrown during the DeLorean cocaine trial. James Hoffman, testifying about DeLorean during the grand jury proceedings, had mentioned that "celebrity people and people that invested with him, were all heavy into cocaine usage, and he stated at one point that he had done some type of cocaine trafficking deal." When asked at the trial for the name of a celebrity that DeLorean had known, Hoffman mentioned Johnny Carson. He hastened to add that he thought DeLorean was just boasting, "puffing" about a famous name. Even so, Carson's name was splashed into the newspapers and Johnny had to tell his faithful on "The Tonight Show" that night, "I've been trying to contain my anger most of the day." He vigorously denied the charges, insisting that his half-million-dollar investment in DeLorean's car company was the only dealing he really had with the man.

When the smoke finally settled in Johnny's divorce case, Joanna was glittering with riches. She got $5 million in cash. She was awarded alimony of $35,000 every month for five years. She was given Johnny's Bel Air mansion estimated in worth at over $5 million.

When the *National Enquirer* reported that Joanna was getting $32 million, Johnny sued them—for $51 million.

Joanna's take included not only the Bel Air mansion, but everything in it, including a Picasso. She took possession of several real estate holdings in New York plus the Pierre Hotel apartment.

She won herself three cars including a Rolls-Royce and a Mercedes-Benz.

Johnny's business deals were now partly hers, too. She got half the profits from a dozen of Carson's ventures ranging from Vollbracht Design on the coast to the Albuquerque Broadcasting Company to the Astoria Film Studios in Queens, New York.

Since she lived with Johnny from 1972 to 1982, she was entitled to half the residuals he would collect from material rerun from programs over that fiscal decade. In other words, she would always have a chunk of "The Best of Carson."

When Johnny retires and is on a pension, Joanna takes half of that, too.

Of course, Joanna didn't get half of everything. The Carson holdings included one hundred gold Krugerrands. Joanna got seventy-five of them and Johnny got twenty-five.

Johnny and Joanna were members of the Beverly Hills Tennis Club. Johnny paid Joanna over $6,000 for her share of the membership.

Though Johnny was taking a bath, it wasn't a total loss. He had his Malibu beach house, a pair of condos in town, an apartment at the Beverly Hills Hotel, and his Trump Tower duplex in New York.

The Carsons had fought long and hard over the split, and now it was all over. Except for one item. Nobody wanted custody of the DeLorean.

There would be no comment from Joanna on the divorce, but there was always wife number two, Joanne. When Joanne's friend Truman Capote died in her Bel-Air mansion, she told reporters, "Ours was the greatest of friendships, but strictly platonic." That was no surprise. But then she added, "Yes, I'm still in love with Johnny." She told the *New York Post*, "You can't simply walk away after ten years and not care. We had some marvelous times. He is probably one of the greatest talents this country has ever had. But he doesn't enjoy the lifestyle, the pressure, the demands that go along with his celebrity. He desperately needs his privacy."

She knew he had to have another desperate need. "Will he marry again? I surely hope so. To me."

Joanne went back to her Bel-Air mansion to wait. Joanna wasn't hanging around in her own Bel-Air mansion, she went back to her jet-set lifestyle, including the party circuit in New York. Johnny was alive and well in Malibu, and on "The Tonight Show" it was business as usual. Johnny had nothing else, really. He seemed to have decided that movies were too risky and a TV series either comic or dramatic would be a danger too. He was, in one frustrated sense, "stuck" with being "The Tonight Show" host, even though it would be the pinnacle of almost anyone else's career. As Swifty Lazar once said, "Like a lot of people in our business, he's a mixture of extreme ego and extreme cowardice."

"The Tonight Show" kept going, right down the middle:

Johnny's tireless Carnak was still divining the questions to answers kept "hermetically sealed in a mayonnaise jar on Funk and Wagnall's porch." Sis Boom Bah. "Describe the sound made when a sheep explodes."

Johnny's ageless Art Fern continued his "Tea Time Movies," even after the death of chesty matinee lady Carol Wayne. There was some other dummy to stand there listening to references to "Squirt the Wonder Eel" and "Screamer the Wonder Beaver."

Johnny's physician, "Dr. Al Bendova" continued his dehumanizing practices: "Instead of a rubber glove he used a Kermit the Frog hand puppet."

Johnny's newest character, Floyd R. Turbo, American, continued to give his Pat Paulsen–styled editorial rebuttals: "If we have birth control, where are all the people gonna come from to fight the population explosion?"

Johnny fielded letters from the audience with the predictable ad-libs: "Susan? Where are you, Susan? Susan writes—would I like to go out for ice cream after the show. That all depends, Susan. Do you have two big scoops?" Pause and disclaimer: "Once in awhile you throw a teeny tacky one in . . ."

And there were the old standbys, like the auditions of new products, "Stump the Band," and the animal segments. Johnny still did jokes about Doc and Ed ("Stay away from Ed's breath, especially if you wear soft contact lenses!") and loaded up on gags involving dull Tommy Newsom ("He had a sad childhood. His imaginary friend dumped him for another kid").

The classic moments on the show still involved sex. In a kind of spoken version of Ed Ames' tomahawk, Johnny caused pandemonium with an innocent slip of tongue, not wrist.

Dolly Parton was the guest, cheerfully talking about being "healthy" and "bosomy" and "blessed." She told a joke about herself: "What's worse than a giraffe with a sore throat? Dolly Parton with a chest cold."

She said, "People are always askin' if they're real."

Johnny broke in, "I would never—"

Dolly said, "You don't have to ask. I tell you what, these are mine."

"I have certain guidelines on the show," Johnny said, smiling as the audience giggled. "But I would give about a year's pay to peek under there!"

It was vintage Johnny, and it seemed like he was still on a roll. But rolling in right after Johnny was David Letterman.

Tom Snyder used to follow Johnny with "The Tomorrow Show." Single-mindedly arrogant, abrasive, and obnoxious, Snyder's style irked many viewers, and Carson seemed to be one of them. He and Snyder had a cold war going on with a few eruptions now and then. Sometimes Johnny would get off a one-liner about Snyder's hyena chuckle or junior-exec hairstyle, but that was as far as it really got publicly.

NBC wanted Steve Allen to replace Snyder, but Johnny didn't like the idea. Steve wasn't happy with the snub but, always a man of quiet class and good nature, he refused to be drawn into a feud by eager, sympathetic reporters.

Johnny's choice was David Letterman, a hands-in-the-pockets stand-up who had many of Carson's mannerisms. Also a wiseguy from Middle America, Letterman had appeared on Johnny's show almost relentlessly. Gradually, viewers caught on to his own particular brand of low-key humor.

Often called the ultimate Carson imitator, Letterman had first

watched Johnny during the "Who Do You Trust?" days. Or, as
David put it: "Here was a guy in a suit who made fun of morons
and did it without hurting the feelings of morons."

David just took it a step further. He became a moron in a suit
making fun of the morons on his show while morons at home
watched. His classic contribution to late night TV was "Stupid
Pet Tricks," where David was stupid for having the animals on,
the trainers were stupid for training them, and the audience stupid for watching such dopey non-entertainment.

Letterman, who looked much like *Mad* magazine's Alfred E.
Neuman, seemed to have the same philosophy—that he and his
gang of "clods and idiots" were just knocking out dumb stuff for
other "clods and idiots."

If Johnny sometimes looked nervous or self-conscious (clench-
ing his teeth and jaw, jamming his hands in his pockets, his back
foot trying to pull the rest of him back from center stage), Letterman seemed as if he was really unhappy to be on stage. With his
facial grimaces, cynical asides, and bored preoccupation with
gimmicks like a desk with a decorative fountain spurting water,
his attitude suggested that it was all just a job and nothing to be
excited over or proud of.

Letterman's "anti-tainment" fit right in with such eighties' fads
as "trash chic" (watching deliberately bad splatter films, soap operas or pro wrestling) and "backward culture" (Keith Haring kid-
die-drawing art, proud "Couch Potato" T-shirts, and grousing
slogans like "Are We Having Fun Yet?").

It worked. Letterman could strap a camera to a monkey and
give viewers a careening picture impossible to watch. They
watched anyway. He could order the camera to turn upside down
during an interview with Peter Ustinov and leave it that way.
People still watched. His idea of a good time was putting various
household items into a hydraulic press and watching them get
crushed. People loved it.

It worked because Letterman was not only appealing to the
lesser traits of humanity, but also satirizing it at the same time.

He adapted age-old talk show devices to his personality and
made them seem new. Jack Paar liked to invite bizarre guests like

neurotic Oscar Levant. Letterman brought out Sandra Bernhard. Steve Allen covered himself in tea bags and dunked himself in a huge cup. David wore a Velcro suit and hurled himself at a wall. Merv Griffin baffled viewers with regular guest Brother Theodore. David "re-discovered" him. Johnny had a "light in the loafers" band leader who wore oh-so-trendy clothes. David went for over-kill with Paul Shaffer.

As Johnny turned sixty, it looked like a new generation was turning to David Letterman. The real partying was 12:30 these days, not 11:30 when some on-the-town Yuppies were still having dinner.

Demographics were in Letterman's favor. Though David was reaching about four million viewers to Johnny's steady ten million, David was reaching the young crowd with money. Johnny was getting the fifty-year-olds with prune juice.

Sometimes Johnny's show looked pale and corny compared to the stinging anti-tainment Letterman was dishing out. But as it turned out, Letterman's success, added to the praise heaped on "Saturday Night Live," seemed to signal to Johnny that it was okay to be more outrageous. Johnny, who had always wanted to perform stronger satire on his show, was finally getting the chance he craved.

Johnny did some borderline sick material, like his joke about getting a free lunch: "If you sit next to a blind man at Sizzler, you can sometimes steal his onion rings."

Some accused Johnny of deliberately trying to match Letterman's level of iconoclasm, but Johnny had it all along. After all, it was not David Letterman in 1986, but Johnny Carson in 1970 who said, "Talking to Miss America is like talking to a redwood tree. Sometimes I'd like to see the other girls tear off her crown and beat her savagely with it."

Back in 1970, Johnny would only say that off-camera. But now, in his monologue, he felt he could say a lot more of what was on his mind.

Johnny went after targets that he could not have touched before. He regularly shot darts at the followers of Lyndon LaRouche and had running gags on 7-Eleven when the company buckled to

Fundamentalists and stopped carrying *Playboy*. Sometimes he almost dropped the jokes entirely for a slick put-down. When
Geraldo Rivera broke into Al Capone's vault for an all-hype and
no-payoff special, Johnny said: "Geraldo should break into a good
school of journalism. Soon!"

One of his favorite targets continued to be the McDonald's
hamburger chain. Clowning around with McDonald's was dan-
gerous. He nearly got into a lawsuit with the company over one
joke: "McDonald's: twenty million hamburgers sold. That must be
over fifty pounds of meat!"

He didn't stop. Instead, he'd win the audience to his side by
mentioning the company's legal threat and lack of humor, and
then zing 'em with another one. Related to the country's growing
problem with illegal aliens: "I saw a sign over McDonald's. Over
seven million employees given amnesty!"

Only once in a while would he half-heartedly defend commercials: "If it wasn't for commercials I'd be standing in a grain
elevator in Nebraska saying 'Third floor—corn!'"

When anti-porn Ed Meese began dictating censorship changes
to the nation, Johnny described his next duty—hiring "construction workers to sandblast the boobs off the statue of Justice."

After Jimmy Carter's "I'll whip his ass" quote about Ted Kennedy, Johnny found another taboo word freed for use. Censors,
spinning in circles trying to keep up with the words used fre-
quently on soap operas, talk shows, and in the print media, sometimes let "The Tonight Show" do as it pleased. Steve Martin
actually was allowed to use the term "scum bags" on the show. As
it turned out, a censor monitoring the show thought that Martin
was referring to some kind of filter used for cleaning swimming
pools.

The hot young comics of the eighties were more than welcome
on Johnny's show. They all found John hiply attuned to their
styles—and warmly supportive. Richard Lewis shakes his head
recalling the time he nervously did "The Tonight Show" and ignored the stage manager's "get off" sign. He ran over by about
five minutes, a suicidal move for any new comic. Feeling miserable, sure his career was over, he retreated to a restaurant, alone.

"Lo and behold, Carson was in the booth across from me! And I still had my stage makeup on, I was a wreck, and he was sitting there with his lawyer, and I raced over there. I mean, he got startled! I looked like an assassin! I started apologizing and he said, 'Hey, you were into your thing, Richard, it's cool, I loved it.'

Older guests on Johnny's show reiterated that there was no other host like him. Bob Uecker wrote that "what makes it all work is his wit, discipline and generosity." He was relieved and happy to find Carson supportive between the commercial breaks and an obviously caring, interested host during the interviews. "There is a kind of art to the way he puts you at ease . . . you can sense the empathy he has."

For the young comics, the "average folk" often booked, or the nervous personalities awed by Johnny, Carson never failed to provide all the courtesy, calm support, and friendly encouragement needed for them to shine. Staffers over the years recall hundreds of examples of Carson's empathy. Some cases even made the papers—like the time a jet-lagged Peter O'Toole woozily went numb during a show and Johnny led him off-stage, returning to emphatically explain that it was not drunkenness but fatigue that had felled the guest. And there were the many times Johnny tossed away suggested interview questions about a star's divorce or other scandal, choosing manners over a splashy ratings boost.

"I have a theory about Carson," Uecker added. "I believe one reason he has survived so long, and so well, is that he has less ego than his critics think. He isn't always drawn to the center of the stage. He doesn't have to be 'on' all the time."

Billy Wilder had a similar view, which he told to Kenneth Tynan: "He has no conceit. He does his work and he comes prepared . . . even his rehearsed routines sound improvised. He's the cream of middle-class elegance, yet he's not a mannequin. He has captivated the American bourgeoisie without ever offending the highbrows, and he has never said anything that wasn't liberal or progressive. Every night, in front of millions of people . . . he does it without a net."

Johnny can be scathing in his monologue—then turn around

and do the warmest, most joyful segment with baby animals. He can do a sexy "Tea Time Movie" with a jiggling blonde one night, and then open the next one by interviewing a hundred-year-old lady and then, celebrating her spry stamina, invite her for a slow waltz on center stage. He can read off sly Carnak one-liners, or he can supply the sweet narration of "The World of Stuart Little," an NBC special for children.

Johnny did not exclude anyone from his audience.

Johnny's show and David's show were a contrast, but they worked well back-to-back. Letterman's mannerisms for the eighties were pretty similar to Carson's attitude in the sixties when he was the hip New Yorker and the rest of the nation "Timmies." When someone asked, "What made you a star?" Johnny shot back, "I started out in a gaseous state, and then I cooled."

Carson's monologue was still cooler than Letterman's. Together, Carson and Letterman locked up two best-selling hours for NBC. Both shows came from Carson Productions, so the success of Carson protégé Letterman was a double victory for Johnny.

David knew how to handle his good luck. When reporters asked "Johnny questions" of him, he kept his mouth shut. He also stayed at a comfortable distance from Johnny. In fact, the awed Letterman once admitted, "I'm terrified of actually spending time with him." His answer to "Would you want to take over 'The Tonight Show'?" was always "No."

There were others who were ready to say "Yes." In his sixties, Ernest Hemingway was ready to fight off any challenger to prove that, during his lifetime, he was America's greatest writer. In his sixties, Johnny Carson displayed his own brand of macho. Late night was still his undisputed domain until he chose to retire as talk show king. There was David Letterman behind him. And suddenly in front of him were two people speeding out of his control—one a former friend, the other a protégé of old rival Fred Silverman.

Alan Thicke's syndicated "Thicke of the Night" was the product of producer Fred Silverman. "Thicke of the Night" was going to be the big competition for Johnny. Taking a cue from Letter-

212 Ronald L. Smith

man's success, Alan Thicke was going to clobber the gray-haired Carson by taking away every viewer under forty.

For a new generation, it would be Alan Thicke followed by David Letterman. And Fred Silverman would have his revenge. But it didn't work out that way. Thicke was thin competition.

When Johnny celebrated his twentieth year on "The Tonight Show," Alan Thicke couldn't even celebrate his first. Johnny arrived in a tuxedo for the gala prime-time special, and mentioned passing a guard at the artists' entrance. It was a familiar face. "Pops Silverman."

The audience didn't get it, but the laughter off-camera from the staff more than made up for it.

Johnny won when he clashed against "The Thicke of the Night." In 1985 he won a Peabody Award. But up ahead would be a big battle for an old warrior. Many thought he would drown at the mouth of the mighty Rivers.

18 THE TONIGHT SHOW
THE LATE SHOW

The Tonight Show: Host, Johnny Carson

The Late Show: Host, Joan Rivers

Johnny may not have lasted long with Jody, Joanne, and Joanna, but there was always Joan. For two decades they had a solid, professional relationship.

Joan Rivers first appeared on "The Tonight Show" in 1965, a nervous and self-deprecating female Woody Allen. She did jokes about herself and weird Woody-like routines (like the story of how she turned her blonde wig into a household pet).

Joan wrote in her autobiography: "The empathy that . . . existed between Johnny Carson and me was there from the first second. He understood everything. He wanted it to work. He never cut off a punchline. When it came he broke up. It was like telling it to your father—and your father is leaning way back and laughing, and you know he is going to laugh at the next one. And he did. He made it fun and that spilled over to the audience."

Johnny said, "God you're funny. You're going to be a star." He

invited her back again and again over the nearly fifteen years it
took her to achieve superstardom. Along the way Joan had her
own daytime talk show that didn't make it, a TV movie that did,
and a theatrical film that was roasted by movie critics. Through it
all, Johnny was supportive and "The Tonight Show" was always
open to her.

Around the time Johnny and Joanna's relationship went sour,
Joan went sour, too—hilariously so. After so many years of turning her jokes inward, she began to tell savagely funny gags about
other celebrities. Her bitchy, biting one-liners on England's royalty, Liz Taylor, and Mick Jagger were hot—and Joan graduated
from occasional guest host to the "permanent" guest host, edging
out her friend David Brenner for the honor. In 1983, she signed a
deal to host nine weeks a year.

She never forgot Johnny. She always praised him lavishly, saying success, and even marriage to late husband, Edgar Rosen-
berg, all stemmed from her involvement with "The Tonight
Show." She wasn't being "show biz." She was sincere. Insiders
know that she is among the kindest and most considerate stars in
private life. Though she went overboard with insult humor, react-
ing to the enthusiasm of her audience, few could say that the
private woman was anything like her comic persona.

As the permanent guest host during Johnny's vacations, Rivers
sometimes had better ratings than Carson himself. Her celebrity
put-downs were new, her kibbitzing interview questions unpredictable. Her frantic personality and glitzy fashions were a good
contrast to Johnny. Some believed Johnny was jealous over Joan's
success, but Johnny knew her strength early on when she was
simply guest-hosting. If he wanted to wreck his show's ratings and
call attention to his indispensability, there were more than
enough bad hosts to choose from.

Some questioned Joan's humor—her jokes on physical traits of
the stars. She howled over Mick Jagger's "child-bearing lips."
She snickered that Elizabeth Taylor was so fat she got stuck between the arches at McDonald's—coaxed through by a Twinkie
waved in front of her face. She claimed that Bo Derek was so
dumb that when she saw a sign that said "Wet Floor" she did.

Joan, Johnny admitted, "gets a little tough sometimes. But it works for her. What some people think is funny, others find in abominable taste. I caught Eddie Murphy in concert. Wow! I've heard the language, but he gets away with it!"

Joan and John did bump heads now and then. In June 1985, there were reports that a secret memo listed possible permanent replacements for Johnny—and that Joan wasn't on the list. Would Joan really be the host of "The Tonight Show" when Johnny retired? She wanted to know, and so did the press.

John read the papers, and when columnist Kay Gardella called him for a reply, he said, "Joan's a pretty clever girl when it comes to publicity. I'm sure the whole thing started out as a joke and she got caught up in it." He added mildly, "NBC has never come to me and asked, 'Who do you think would be a likely candidate . . .' I wouldn't continue if I didn't enjoy it. The show is still fun."

Over the next year, Johnny's retirement remained a possibility. Many believed Joan Rivers would take over with his blessing. There was another possibility, though. What if a competitor got to her first?

Back in 1979, Johnny himself was being wooed by the competition. ABC wanted him badly and he was not shy about letting everyone—especially NBC—know about it.

Johnny felt a loyalty to NBC and stayed. Joan felt a loyalty to Johnny. But was the feeling mutual?

Fox Broadcasting, stoked by Rupert Murdoch, wanted to become "The Fourth Network." Fox owned six key independent stations in New York, Los Angeles, Washington, Houston, Dallas, and Chicago. Barry Diller, the man making $3 million a year as chairman of Fox Broadcasting Company, played poker often with Johnny Carson. Now he wanted to play with Joan Rivers.

Fox figured a blockbuster syndicated talk show with the nation's hottest new personality was the best way to build a network. To grab Joan, Fox offered a three-year contract—at $10 million. Johnny's yearly contract was worth $5 million.

Joan was still guest-hosting "The Tonight Show" in May 1986 and she was still making up her mind. Fox was hot for her. NBC

was cool. Joan claimed that they weren't offering her big bucks to
re-sign. She brought up the "secret memo" listing likely suc-
cessors to Johnny—and her name not even on the list.

She signed with Fox, evidently assuming that Johnny or
Johnny's people were willing to let her go without much of a protest.

She had two months left on her NBC contract when she made
the switch. Nothing wrong about that. When Johnny signed to
take over "The Tonight Show" in 1962 he had six months left on
his ABC contract.

Joan was elated about her good fortune. She knew that she had
Johnny to thank for all those years of support, for the "permanent
guest host" break. Joan asked her secretary to call Johnny.
Strangely, Johnny wasn't available. The second night, the secre-
tary was successful. She called Joan to the phone to speak with
Carson. When Joan picked up the phone she said, "Hello."

All she heard was a click.

Then came the explosion.

Front-page newspaper headlines blared out the story:
JOHNNY VS. JOAN.

Joan was shattered. When Johnny's snub became the hot story
all over the nation, all Joan could do was express teary bewilder-
ment. She was literally sick from worry. Some cynics figured it
was an act. It wasn't. Years earlier, in an interview with the author, Joan admitted that physical illness was sometimes her response to insecurity and crisis. She mentioned that, after
watching her critically acclaimed TV movie *The Girl Most Likely
To*, she threw up. "How's that for liking yourself?" she asked
grimly.

Joan was going to be a $10-million woman—but her crowning
achievement was tarnished by Johnny's disdain and trashed in a
media scandal. Was Johnny proud of her? No, he hated her!

Actually, for Johnny this was just one more betrayal. His
stoicism was just a bitter reaction from a man grown cold from
abuse. Joan didn't appreciate him after all. This was the proof he
should've expected all along.

Johnny certainly wasn't pleased about having competition from someone with proven success on "The Tonight Show." Even so, the white-hot anger in Johnny wasn't over her leaving but the way she did it.

She had been involved in secret dealings when she should have come right out and said, "John, can we talk? Fox offered me this package. What do you think?"

Johnny knew all about Joan's defection. Long before Joan had deigned to call, he'd met with NBC exec Brandon Tartikoff about the problem. It came down to those words embroidered on a pillow in Johnny's office: "It's all in the timing." When Joan told Johnny, it was too late.

Proof of that seemed to come from David Brenner, who broke the news that he was off on his own syndicated talk show, too. "Think of Johnny Carson as the father," he told the *Daily News*. "That's what he is, a television father-figure for Joan and me. I went up to him and said, 'Hey, Dad, they're talking about giving me a job out of town and I might be leaving home,' and he wishes me good luck . . . then the daughter calls up from 4,000 miles away and says, 'Dad, I'm living here now . . .' that is the difference. When I left home, Dad knew all about it from the beginning."

So Johnny would not forget and could not forgive. Doc Severinsen dared to wish her luck. Ed McMahon did too, giving her a public hug when they met in a restaurant.

Doc said, "Johnny would have been very supportive of Joan. He probably would have plugged her show or even done a walk-on for her. But he and others on 'The Tonight Show' were disappointed nothing was said to them until the last minute."

Joan was still under contract to Johnny—and so he made an emphatic point of ripping up her contract and canceling the two weeks of guest-hosting she was scheduled to complete. Again it was front-page news: "Carson Fires Rivers."

Ironically, just a week before Joan Rivers had guest-hosted "The Tonight Show." She had known even as she was appearing on NBC that her future would be with Fox. May 2 was her last night doing "The Tonight Show." Then came the feud, breaking wide open a few days later.

On May 7, 1986, the papers were filled with the stunning John vs. Joan news. Would Johnny make an acknowledgment on the show?

Ed called out "Heeerre's Johnny." The band pumped out the theme music, hard and brassy. Johnny came out through the curtains, smiling. The applause was deafening. "You know, I don't know what I'd ever do if the applause sign ever had a meltdown. Thanks for coming . . ."

Everyone was waiting. One of Johnny's stock lines was "Let's see, what was in the papers today." The front page was him.

And today he was going to treat the front-page story like any other front-page disaster. Ignore it. Take folks' minds off it. Everything's gonna be all right.

There was chaos at Carson Productions. Joan was practically in a state of shock. Carson himself was filled with anger. Yet he stood there grinning, telling jokes, going from one topic to the other—but never mentioned THE topic. The audience laughed. He finished a monologue of light gags when he probably was raging on the inside. Instead of a clenched fist, there was his easy golf swing . . . "We'll be right back."

When the commercial was over, there was Johnny, sitting at his desk. He picked up his coffee cup and quietly raised it. "To you," he told the audience.

After the applause, Johnny brought out his guests. There was a novelty acrobat who could balance tables, ladders, and a baton. And there were Bunnies from a local Playboy Club.

"What turns you on?" Johnny asked one of them.

"Big tips!" a blonde promptly shouted.

"As MacArthur said, these proceedings are closed!" Johnny cracked.

There was only one slight crack in the perfect hour. One of the Bunnies remarked that when the Playboy Club folded she thought she might like to take a stab at being a talk show host.

John quickly went on to something else. For Johnny, the modus operandi would be to maintain a dignified silence.

For Joan, there was hell to pay. During the week of May 12

Joan was booked for appearances promoting her book *Enter Talking*, the one with all the praise for Johnny.

Over and over she apologized for the misunderstanding. "If I walked out of this door right now and bumped into Johnny, I'd be delighted," she said. "I'd say, 'Isn't this funny and didn't we get a lot of press out of all this?'" She had to admit though that Johnny would not be the type to get emotional: "He's much inside of himself and controlled. He'd die of embarrassment if he saw me by surprise."

She insisted, "I've had a wonderful relationship with Johnny, twenty-three years . . . I wanted it to end nicely. I'm a lady, my mother brought me up right. I knew I owed him a call."

Looking stressed and tired, Joan brought her book promotion to "Live at Five," the news show on NBC's flagship New York station. She wearily confided to Liz Smith, "I've become a tabloid tootsie." As for her battle with Johnny, she groaned, "There's NO fight. All I did was defend myself against statements that NBC put out. Never him. Never him."

Over the next week, the Carson vs. Rivers feud continued to be the hot story across the country. Editorials examined the morality of Joan's move. On May 8, for example, *Daily News* columnist Bill Reel used his editorial space to give a succinct appraisal of the two talkers: "Johnny Carson is a comic; Joan Rivers is a buffoon." Some radio station DJs began polling their listeners with call-in voting. Carson was usually ahead. On the radio, call-in shows gave listeners a chance to "vote" for which host they were going to watch. "Entertainment Tonight" polled their viewers and the split was just about even, with Carson getting the slight edge.

Along the way, the story of the feud changed shape like a snowball rolling downhill through mud. First Joan and then John was given a black eye. Then one or the other took a lump. One story had it that Joan called Johnny the moment she signed, and he'd hung up in a jealous snit. Another put it completely in reverse. Sniping between the Fox publicists and both NBC and "The Tonight Show" spokesmen got uglier.

Joan pleaded innocence and practically made an open apology to Johnny.

When Marilyn Beck tracked down Carson on May 22, he broke his silence only to say, "I'd rather not comment." When asked about his future on "The Tonight Show," all he said was: "My contract runs, I think, until September 1987, and I have made no decision about the future. It's as simple as that."

With no letup in sight, and commitments to keep regarding both her book and her new show, Rivers grimly faced interviewers. And she began to fight back. She defended herself for taking a three-year deal when NBC was playing it cagey. On "The Today Show," Joan said, "The whole thing really comes down to one question people should be asking. If he was signed for two years in the last contract, why was I signed for only one? I think that tells you that you're not as secure as you think you are in your job, and if another job comes your way, just take it."

What about that memo that seemed to nix Joan as the next "Tonight Show" host? Rivers blamed NBC for that, not Johnny. "I'll probably write him a letter, tell him I love him. I do love him. All this has nothing to do with Johnny. What NBC was saying was 'We don't want you.' All I'm saying is 'I'm a fifty-one-year-old lady. Let me go off and be my own hostess because you don't want me.'"

The feud didn't get any better when it was discovered that Joan had been calling up her friends from "The Tonight Show"—and offering some of them jobs. Peter Lassally, one of the key men on Carson's show, was told to think of her if he was "unhappy." Once again there were furious charges and equally furious denials from both sides.

On "Good Morning America" Joan tried closing a wound but opened it instead. She said, "Johnny is a wonderful, terrific person. The only thing is you can't get to him anymore to tell him these things. He's wrapped in cotton. You're always being told, 'Leave Johnny alone. Don't tell this to Johnny. Keep away from Johnny. Don't upset Johnny.'"

That upset Johnny.

Joan tried to quiet things down by denying that she was compe-

tition at all. She pointed out that her show was scheduled a half
hour earlier than "Tonight."

"I've had secret meetings in hotel rooms, in limousines, and
I've had solid offers. But I didn't accept anything out of loyalty to
Johnny. I cannot begin to tell you the deals I've turned down. I
just didn't want to go up against him. But this time, it's five
stations against 200. What's everybody getting so upset about?"

Joan went into a recording studio to tape the audio cassette
version of her book. Suddenly she broke down and began sobbing. She couldn't stop. "What are you so upset about?" one of
the engineers wondered. Joan was about to begin reading the
chapter about her big break on "The Tonight Show." She just
couldn't go on.

Over and over, in case Johnny was ever listening, she said, "I
love you. I wouldn't do anything to hurt you. I still want to be
friends."

The sob story of Johnny hanging up on Joan got so much press
coverage that Carson couldn't keep still. He began to sneak in a
few non-jokes about it in the monologue.

On May 15 Johnny mentioned how NBC was canceling their
new "Alfred Hitchcock Presents" series. He mentioned that NBC
President Grant Tinker "tried to call Hitchcock, but Hitchcock
hung up on him."

A few nights later, John mentioned the ad campaign Burger
King was running featuring a spokesman named Herb. He noted
that the ads were being discontinued. "Herb was fired. He's
opening a restaurant opposite Burger King . . . they tried to call
him but he hung up on them."

The audience gave him a sympathetic laugh. Another night,
Carson described some bad news from the Soviet Union. He said
that Gorbachev was mad at America. "It's all my fault," Johnny
deadpanned. "He called me . . . but I hung up on him."

Johnny's disdain and disgust surfaced again and again, each
time getting applause and support from the audience.

Bob Hope came on the show May 23. Johnny, as usual, paused
to tell the ancient comedian how young he looked. Then he mar-
veled at Hope's busy schedule.

"Do you have your year planned out," Johnny remarked. "Do you know what you're going to do next?"

"I don't know." Bob shrugged. "I was supposed to be on NBC, but I don't know about it. I called Grant Tinker, but he hung up on me."

The audience snickered and Johnny's face reddened. He giggled out of a spasm of laughter, wiping his eye. "There's a lot of that going around," he said.

"You don't have to worry about it," Hope added drily. "She left, but there's one you don't have to pay alimony to!"

Sentiment in the press was swinging toward Johnny as he stood vulnerably in front of the American public, weathering yet another turmoil. Carson's discomfort showed under the cool veneer. There was the nervous wipe under the eye, the little blinking twitch, the hands-in-the-pockets awkwardness. These little signals were proof that he was human after all. And whenever Johnny was uncomfortable—the audience was on his side.

In May, Bette Davis made a rare appearance and enjoyed talking to Johnny so much she practically did a monologue of anecdotes and stories. During a pause she said, "I suppose right now you thought I'd let you say something." Johnny answered, "Don't tell me you got your own show, too."

On June 17: "Justice Warren Burger retired. He wants to take on a new challenging job—he's starting his own late night talk show."

A month later, July 25, and still obsessed: "I hope Reagan runs again. If he doesn't he'll probably start his own talk show."

All through the summer the big news was the fall battle between beleagured Everyman Johnnny and that new woman after his job, Joanie. Every now and then a powerful bomb dropped on one or the other.

Fox execs cheered loudly when WBFF in Baltimore dropped Johnny's show and signed up Rivers. The station had wanted both programs—Rivers from 11 to 12 and then Johnny afterward. NBC refused to change John's 11:30 time slot.

Fox cheered even louder when Brystol-Myers announced it was pouring $1.6 million worth of ads into the Rivers show.

Like a bar fight, once Rivers and Carson began slugging, everybody started tearing up the joint. If Fox thought a talk show was a great idea, and that Johnny was vulnerable, then they must have a great idea. ABC not only had David Brenner, they also signed up Dick Cavett and Jimmy Breslin to share a talk show time slot. A stand-up comic named Robert Klein took over the talk show Cavett had been doing on cable TV. The talk show fever spilled into the daytime hours. Someone got the idea to pit Oprah Winfrey against gray-haired Phil Donahue. There was Ted Koppel talking about political intrigue, Dr. Ruth talking about sexual intrigue, and Regis Philbin insisting everything held some intrigue.

David Letterman claimed to have a new deal, too: "I just signed a lucrative contract. I'm going to be the new, permanent guest host on the new Joan Rivers show."

As Joan's show hurtled toward its premiere date, the big question was what type of guests she would have. Who were the stars that would dare risk Carson's wrath? Who were the David Letterman–type hip acts that would dare be blacklisted from the Carson-owned Letterman show?

At a press conference, Joan took a poke at the "old show biz" world of "The Tonight Show." She said, "There were certain people I couldn't get as guests because they felt it was not the right image for the show. I had to fight to get David Lee Roth, Boy George, and Lily Tomlin." She vowed to have young rock favorites on, and some of the glitzy personalities that Johnny didn't want, for one reason or another.

A few celebrities rose to Joan's defense. Cher announced she would do the Rivers show and didn't care if she never got on "The Tonight Show" again.

Johnny ignored the controversy. A few nights later, during the September 5 monologue, he mentioned all the big stars who lived in Palm Springs. Guys like his pal Bob Hope actually had streets named after him. There was "Bob Hope Drive." And there was "Frank Sinatra Drive," too. Johnny added: "The speed bumps are all named after Cher."

David Brenner offered his own solution—those who were

afraid to go on with either Joan or Johnny were welcome to compromise and do his show!

Gary Shandling replaced Joan Rivers as Johnny's guest host on
the week of June 2. A stand-up comic who joked primarily about
his sorry lovelife (looking like a cross between David Letterman
and Jimmy Carter being quite a handicap), Shandling was in a
tough spot.

On his first night, he hushed the audience and said, "Before I
can continue I have to take the guest host's oath." Suddenly a
judge came through the curtain with a Bible saying, "Raise your
right hand and repeat after me. 'I, Gary Shandling, will never
host another show opposite "The Tonight Show." No matter how
much money they may offer me.'" Gary repeated it. The judge
added,"'And I will not make fun of the way Doc dresses.'" "Uh,
gee." Shandling grimaced. "I just can't do that one, that's where I
draw the line."

Through the hot summer and into the fall, there was a flurry of
activity at both Fox and NBC. Both staffs were tense and excited.
Both stars seemed to go through peaks and valleys of bravado and
insecurity.

Fox was confident in their young rookie. NBC placed all their
faith in their old veteran. NBC's Brandon Tartikoff said that he
wasn't panicking, and that NBC wasn't looking for relief, just in
case. "We're not considering replacements now . . . you always
try to be prepared, but there is no college in South Florida with
twenty eager would-be talk show hosts in training." Of Johnny's
retirement just a year away, Tartikoff said, "My hope is that he'll
want to continue. Johnny always said that as long as he's excited
to drive into work and do the show and the audience is still
watching, he'd want to continue doing it. I have the sense he's
enjoying it more now . . ."

As the deadline for the Carson vs. Rivers warfare approached,
few reporters were sure exactly what would happen. Even veterans of the "Talk Show Wars" weren't sure. Alan Thicke didn't
want to get involved in the debate, and for a good reason: "I'm the
wrong guy to ask. If I had anything brilliant to say on late night,
I'd still be on it."

Dick Cavett and Mike Douglas both had doubts about Joan Rivers' ability to sustain. Cavett noted that Rivers was "high energy" compared to the smooth Carson, and Douglas added: "I think she's going to have her hands full because Johnny wears very well. As good as Joan is, I don't know if she'll wear as well. Also, Johnny will have all that network muscle behind him. It's a tremendous thing to overcome."

It was still too close to call. As the ads for Joan's show said, her program was going to be "live, unpredictable, daring and funny . . . late night's early alternative . . . more than just talk."

19 THE TONIGHT SHOW

It's war and peace for Johnny—making news with two blondes named Joan and Alexis.

On October 9, 1986, the first night of the Rivers–Carson war, Johnny's soldiers included Richard Pryor and Sean Penn. Joan loaded up with the youth-oriented acts that were to be her secret weapon against the aging, "old show biz" "Tonight Show." Nobody over forty was going to tune in to see Spandex rocker David Lee Roth or Baby-Boomer favorite Pee Wee Herman. For added glitz, there was Elton John and Cher.

Joan didn't have balding men playing big-band tunes. Her bandleader, Mark Hudson, guided "The Party Boys and The Tramp." The "Tramp" was the group's lone female, a hapless blonde sax player.

The show opened with frenzied electricity as "Live" from California, Joan was announced to a standing audience of cheering, wildly applauding fans. Blazing lights lit up the roaring crowd and then the cameras pulled head-on for Joan Rivers.

"I have a whole monologue—which I won't do tonight," the emotional star began, simultaneously cheered and drained by the excitement of the moment.

"I am just—it's been five months and so much has been said and so much has been written—I'm just—so happy to be here!"

If she'd just escaped a year's imprisonment in Iran there couldn't have been a more explosive shower of warmth and love from the crowd, or a more sincere look of relief and joy on the face of Joan Rivers. The audience rose to its feet for another standing ovation. Joan couldn't control herself any longer. Impulsively she drew close to the front row of fans. She opened her arms and began to kiss some of the ringsiders.

The premiere show was a party, a glittery high that peaked when Joan stood beside the piano while Elton John belted out a ten-year-old tune in her honor—"The Bitch Is Back." Joan hoarsely joined in: "I can bitch, I can bitch . . . the bitch is back!" She stared into the camera, as if into the face of Johnny Carson as she shouted a worn but defiant "I can bitch, I can bitch . . . better than YOU!"

Over on "The Tonight Show," it was dignified business as usual. Johnny made only one remark in any way aimed at Rivers. He downplayed the competition. "There are a lot of big-time confrontations this week," he said. "Reagan versus Gorbachev, the Mets versus the Astros, and me versus 'The Honeymooners Lost Episodes.'"

Johnny was hoping that Joan would be no more of a threat than a sitcom rerun, but the overnight ratings proved him wrong. Joan was doing much better than local reruns. She even bested Johnny in a few cities, taking San Francisco easily and New York as well, where she got a 27 percent share to Johnny's 22 percent. She was edged out in several other cities, especially in Mid-America, and Johnny won the night 25 percent to 19 percent.

Reviewers around the country had a field day picking their own winner. Fred Rothenberg of the *New York Post* seemed to have the majority opinion: "Joan Rivers finally got her own talk show. The next step is to make it funny."

The New York *Daily News* actually printed a score sheet. Johnny won for "monologue, band and second banana," Joan won

for "set design" and they tied on "guest lineup." Joan lost the last
entry: "laughs." Winner: Johnny Carson.

Joan tried to keep up the energy. She continued to book rock-
ers, trendy soap opera stars, and even Nancy Reagan. But slowly,
as the weeks went by, the ratings leveled off and the critics began
to find faults with a day-in, day-out diet of Joan Rivers.

To some, she was "toothless," trading in her witch's broomstick
for a velvet glove, gushing shamelessly instead of shaming stars with
prickly questions. As Steve Daley of the *Chicago Tribune* wrote,
"Her show is typical talk show pap." To other reviewers, she was
just as abrasive as ever, crassly classless with her tramp and boobie
jokes. Ray Richmond of the *Los Angeles Herald-Examiner* complained, "Joan is trying to be a glitzier, younger version of 'The
Tonight Show.'" Her high-energy personality seemed overpowering.
Like Tom Snyder and Les Crane before her, Joan aggravated critics
with her driven personality. The laid-back approach was needed for
viewers laying back in bed. Here was Joan clapping back at the
audience when they were ready to go to sleep!

As early as the second night, Johnny was comfortably joking
about the new "Talk Show War." He mentioned that Reagan was
out of the country and Vice President Bush was in charge: "Bush
said this would be his last week as guest president, he was starring in his own presidency soon."

Ratings for the flurry of talk show competitors was anemic. The
New York Post relayed the news that "in the late-night combat
zone David Brenner's new 'Nightlife' is bombing, with an average
2.5 rating. . . . Johnny Carson is snaring a 6.8 rating."

Many of the big-name stars who had boldly announced their
defections to Joan Rivers were having second thoughts. Rich Little, irritated that Johnny was doing such a good Ronald Reagan
and hadn't had the impressionist on in three years, must have had
second thoughts after doing a Christmas commercial for Wrinkles,
a talking dog. He played a yocking Johnny Carson on the spot.
The talking dog yipped, "Can we talk?"

Johnny may have been worried initially when "blacklisted"
stars now had someplace else to go. He may have wondered how
many of the stars who came on his show regularly secretly longed

to talk to someone else. Now he could rest easy. He was lining up the same high-caliber guests as before.

On October 24, 1986, Michael Landon showed up for a visit. Johnny was envious of Landon's timeless Westerns—"Bonanza" and "Little House on the Prairie." He expressed the gnawing self-doubt that his own career was ephemeral. "Fifty years from now this show will be dated," he said, no doubt thinking of how quickly the public had forgotten such one-time greats as Arthur Godfrey, Fred Allen, and Jack Paar. TV westerns were history, always interesting in reruns. Landon disagreed: "I don't believe the humor of Johnny Carson will ever be dated."

Then Landon suggested that Carson get away from talk shows and try his hand at a Western. Johnny shrugged warily, but Landon persisted, claiming Carson had the makings of an adventure film hero. He said he even had a film clip to prove it. Carson seemed momentarily confused as Landon cued the director to run the clip.

It was footage of a man and a woman in a canoe, paddling along the river. Landon spoke over it, envisioning Johnny as a rugged outdoorsman. There were more shots of the river and the canoe, and then the opening credits for the proposed Michael Landon film starring Johnny Carson. It was "Johnny Carson in . . .

"'Up Rivers.'"

The audience roared its shock and approval. A sea of applause washed over Johnny as he put his hand to his chin in embarrassment. He had a full, toothy smile as he gasped, "I had nothing to do with this!"

"Catchy title," he added. "You spent some time on this?" Carson shook his head, still red-faced but delighted. "I'm gonna pass on that one . . .," he said.

Off the TV tube, Johnny continued to pass on questions about Joan, and Joan always reiterated her claim that their feud was just a miserable misunderstanding.

Johnny's show did change slightly during the uncertain weeks of Rivers' threat. Johnny was unmistakably warmer to Ed and Doc than ever before. Now and then he would drop the name of a staffer. Once he even brought the cameras backstage so he could do some quick interviews with the propmen and some of the secretaries hanging out watching the show. Perhaps, stung by the negative image of having coldly hung up on heartbroken Joan, plus the rumors of staffers ready to defect to her show, he was trying to display a little more humanity and camaraderie.

On the air, Joan was struggling to achieve some kind of balance between the frantic gossiper she'd been as a guest host and the more gentle, supportive interviewer that would wear well night after night. Meanwhile her guest list quickly degenerated to the mundane standard. She gave time to an "ugly dog contest," made "funny phone calls" to local department stores, and entertained faceless starlets, nameless young comics, and the kind of stars who didn't exactly grab a viewer's interest. Who would stay up just to watch Joan talk to Vic Damone and Diahann Carroll?

Johnny's competition began to get snarled up in amateur's mistakes. One night David Brenner mentioned that the author of *The Mystery of Edwin Drood* was Shakespeare. Most literates would have correctly identified Charles Dickens. "You have just succeeded in turning me into the national dunce of all time!" Brenner raged at his staff.

Rivers's mouth got her into trouble several times. She found herself on the receiving end of a $3-million "invasion of privacy" suit when she started making cutting jokes about Victoria Principal and then, allegedly, added insult to injury by leaking the star's private phone number. Not long after, Jane Russell announced that she was going to sue Joan, too, using Victoria Principal's lawyer, Gerald Epstein.

Russell had come on the show to discuss her new line of fashions, "Jane's Way." That was what had been agreed on. Instead, Rivers ignored the prepared questions and instead asked the star if she'd really had an abortion early in her career. Russell tried to ignore the subject, but Joan insisted she'd read about it in Russell's own autobiography.

As it turned out, the abortion rumor had been printed not in Russell's book, but in a magazine article about her. Russell didn't walk off the show, but as soon as it was over, she strode right past Joan and angrily shouted, "I wouldn't wish this show on my worst enemy."

In what has become a cliché in show business, the big star took a hard fall. The magazine and newspaper machinery that helped build Joan Rivers was now turning on her and breaking her down. She was no longer cover-story material. Squibs in columns and "people" pages were negative.

By the end of 1986, *TV Guide* sounded an obituary notice. Rivers was "nowhere near Carson. Her syndicated 'Late Show' is pulling a 3.0 rating . . . below the 4.0 promised to sponsors by Fox Broadcasting."

Joan's running gags about "The Tramp" in the band were more annoying than Johnny's running gags about dull Tommy Newsom. In fact, Joan's entire bag of tricks that worked so well in small doses was growing predictable.

In a December issue, *US* magazine declared "careful calculation and good manners can keep an image fresh forever. Just look at Johnny Carson." As for Rivers, "she'll be around but she'll be just another barking seal, out of control, the kind of celebrity the old Joan Rivers joked about."

Once again, Johnny had plowed the competition. Over at ABC, Jimmy Breslin didn't wait to be nailed into an oversized coffin. In his November 23 column he expressed his disgust with his network and announced, "ABC . . . your services, such as they are, will no longer be required as of December 20, 1986." He added grandly, "I thus become the first person in America to fire a network." Dick Cavett, probably wearing an Oliver Hardy look of chagrin, simply waited for the ABC ax to once more bop him on the head.

It turned out that Johnny's biggest competition was not Rivers, Brenner, Cavett, or any of the comics. It was newsman Ted Koppel, who was getting a 6.0 share to Johnny's 7.8. The worse the news was the higher his nightly rating for his topic-oriented "Nightline" would be. CBS's movies were in third place with a 5.2.

When Johnny's twenty-fourth anniversary show aired in October 1986, some were doubting Rivers would see one anniversary. People remembered that even the greatest names in the field had not lasted long. Steve Allen's legendary "Tonight!" show ran about two and a half years. Paar lasted four and a half. Worthy hosts like David Frost and Dick Cavett couldn't make a dent either.

David Letterman was asked why Johnny was so special. "Johnny has been a hit for twenty-four years because he's funny, he's charming, and he wears comfortable shoes." Jack Paar answered, "He succeeded like no one else . . . he did have one advantage going in, though. He had the good sense to follow a hit."

The only man to approach Johnny in longevity was Merv Griffin. Johnny once said, "Only three things in this world are certain. Death, taxes, and Merv Griffin going 'Ooooh!'"

Griffin's show sputtered in its last few years, bouncing locally between dull afternoon slots and Joe Franklin territory at 12 A.M. It flickered out quietly with a depressed hour-long "Best of" that didn't even get a prime-time booking. Merv, walking through his eerily empty studio, showed film clips of his favorite moments on the show with Richard Pryor, Sophia Loren, Orson Welles, and Gerald Ford, among others. Then he said good-bye to members of his staff.

Up in the control room he introduced his director: "Has it been fifteen years, Dick? Sixteen years. Best director I could ever steal from his brother." Dick Carson turned around for a quick smile into the camera. Merv introduced other staff members and then said, "It's tough to say good-bye . . . I guess, this is the first time on this last show I've ever said this. We will not be back after this message. Th-th-th-that's all folks."

After it was all over, Merv came on Johnny's show. He had two words for Johnny: "You win."

They did some friendly sparring. Noting Merv's long-standing relationship with Eva Gabor, John asked, "When are you and Eva Gabor gonna get married?"

Merv answered, "When are you and Alexis getting married?" It was Johnny's turn to go "Oooooh."

The two men recalled their days as game show hosts. "You did 'Who Do You Trust?'" Merv said. "It was originally called 'Do You Trust Your Wife?' but they changed it on account of you." The audience giggled as Johnny mock-grimaced.

Merv reminded Johnny that they began their talk shows on the same day and year. Merv's show was over now, but, he noted: "We would be even in years . . . if we count all your vacations."

"You're getting it all out of your system!" Johnny smiled.

Merv did have a consolation prize—according to *Forbes Magazine*, Merv was one of America's wealthiest men, worth $235 million.

Johnny was set for life, too. But who was there to share it with? And what could he do after "The Tonight Show"?

Johnny's favorite form of relaxation was playing tennis, often with guys his own age like Steve Lawrence. Though he still had a trim thirty-two-inch waist, and weighed about 170, it was quite a challenge when the sixty-year-old comedian went up against someone significantly younger.

At the La Quinta Tennis Resort, there was Johnny daring to play with a strong-bodied young lady. Reporter W. H. Bowart was there. "He moves like a person twenty years his junior," the reporter duly noted, but the outcome was not in doubt. "During the third set, you can see that the years under hot lights may have taken their toll . . . endurance leaves him." The woman was running him "ragged with ball control, winning the set and the game. He comes off the court sweating profusely."

Johnny gazed back at the woman. "This is a way to get old fast."

But Johnny was eager to play again. The woman on the tennis court was Brooke Trabert, the daughter of tennis pro Tony Trabert. After talking some tennis with Johnny, the reporter dropped a sly question: "What's something good that you never had and don't want?"

Johnny paused. "I hadn't thought of that . . . well, I don't think, another marriage. But, who knows. Never say never."

He wasn't referring to Brooke Trabert. He was referring to his steady girl friend of the past four years, Alexis Maas. She was the one who had stirred thoughts of marriage when he took her to Avoca, Iowa, in the midst of the Rivers miseries.

News of Alexis had surfaced during the last stages of the Johnny vs. Joanna divorce battle. *People* magazine had discovered that Johnny wasn't missing Joanna or his Bel-Air mansion—not with his Malibu digs and Alexis, the thirty-six-year-old stockbroker's secretary who was now his companion. She was described as "a very family oriented, private person from a world completely polar to the Hollywood scene."

She was delighted with Johnny's attentions, surprised by the spontaneous gifts he offered. "He needs a plaything right now," an anonymous staffer told *People*. "It's a lot of fun to play Pygmalion with someone like her."

Romantics loved the story of Johnny and the down-to-earth secretary. After so many years, at last, he'd found someone who wasn't a showbiz phony. Instead, she was a working girl from Pittsburgh.

Cynics laughed at the story. Johnny had picked three stock types before: the college sweetheart, the perky "Total Woman," and the sultry, full-figured jet-setter. Now it was time for that old favorite—the leggy blonde bombshell. And the whole thing was pure Nebraska corn: the aging star blindly falling for a Sweet Bird of Youth. After all, how exactly did they meet? The story was that it happened on the beach at Malibu. Alex came swiveling by with an empty wineglass in her hand and actually asked the star if he could fill it for her.

Or, as *Newsday* put it succinctly, "Maas slipped into a bikini, strolled by Johnny's house on nearby Carbon Beach and got invited in."

Cindy Adams was one of the gossip columnists to find fault. During the U. S. Open tennis championships, Johnny vacationed in New York with his girl friend. "You've heard how close Johnny Carson and his blonde Alexis Maas ladyfriend are?" Adams wrote. "Well, they're not. Not when they're walking down Lex from 76th at 8 P.M. anyhow. They didn't link arms, hands or pinkies. Didn't reach out even when crossing big, busy Lexington Avenue. They just propelled themselves forward rigidly, like soldiers. Carson is not user-friendly."

Actually, Carson was surprisingly friendly. Paparazzi had no trouble snapping pictures of Johnny out on dates with Alexis. They both stopped and posed, wearing big smiles. Shots of the two lovers appeared in the papers often.

In December 1986, the rumors about Johnny and Alex intensified. Finally, "Tonight Show" spokesman James Mahoney ad-

mitted a week before Christmas, "They became engaged quietly
. . . there will be no formal announcement."

"We are very much in love," Alex said. "Johnny exudes a very
special charm. We are very happy . . . he gave me a ring, but I
don't want to describe it. That's just too personal."

The tabloids went after her for more details. How did Johnny
propose? She told *The National Star* that "it's too personal to
make public. It's just too close to my heart and Johnny's."

Johnny was comfortable enough to raise the cone of silence on
Alexis during his monologues. Before Christmas he snuck in a
silly joke: "My girl friend asked for a mink coat. So I gave her
two minks and a Julio Iglesias album." Twenty-five years ago, the
joke was "two minks and a Frank Sinatra album," and fifty years
ago, "here's a trap and some bait." But at age thirty-six, Alexis
probably hadn't heard of either before.

Others began joking around with Johnny, too. Bob Hope talked
about the engagement on his Christmas special: "Johnny's gonna
take his fourth wife. The first three took him! He's entitled to get
married again. He still has a couple of houses left!"

Reports around "The Tonight Show" from old-time staffers
were that Johnny was in great spirits, mellow at the office and as
smitten as a teenager when he was with Alexis.

The pictures told the story. The couple were smiling like any
couple in love.

Johnny's life changed with Alexis. Many believed that he could
be happy leaving "The Tonight Show," that he could be content
with gigs in Vegas and some TV specials. For a full twenty-five
years, he was the undisputed champion—a perfect 25–0 record
against all challengers. He could retire undefeated. Others figured that Johnny was so happy at home that work would now be
more of a pleasure. He could stay with the show, or take some
kind of "sabbatical" where one of his regular guest hosts would
pinch-hit for six months.

Everyone around Johnny changed. His last wife, Joanna, had
also found a new love. Her long-standing romance was with glitz
writer Sidney Sheldon.

Dick Carson has completed a long run as director of Merv Griffin's show, and sister Catherine is still the obscure Mrs. Ralph Sotzing.

After decades of comparative calm, one of Johnny's sons suddenly made the papers. While Ricky remained behind the scenes, a stage manager once associated with "The Tomorrow Show," and Cory also worked in the TV industry and as a teacher of classical guitar, people wondered about Chris, now thirty-six, who had the dubious profession of "golf pro" at a Florida country club.

As it turned out, Chris wasn't even that. His work for the Plantation Golf Club reportedly ended around 1980—and ever since Johnny had supported him with $35,000 a year and a home in Fort Lauderdale that set him back over $119,000.

What was Chris doing for the past seven years?

Well, he was living with a black woman named Tanena Love Green. And she bore him a daughter, named "Crystal Love Carson."

The news got out in March 1987, when Chris and Tanena got into a battle over the child. Tanena claimed that once the baby was born, Chris lost interest in her. She even suggested that it was Johnny's fault—that Johnny encouraged him to break off with her.

The thirty-five-year-old woman told reporters, "I think if I had blond hair, maybe, and blue eyes, his family would accept me and their only grandchild."

Chris was forced to pay $125 a month in temporary support for the child. Tanena had been collecting $182 a month in welfare. In a rebuttal not unfamiliar in cases where a Carson and an ex meet in court, Chris's lawyer insisted the woman was just trying to get as much as she could get.

The lawyer for Tanena spread the word that she and the baby were living "in abject poverty. I have photos of this child with rodent bites."

While the details of the settlement were worked out, Tanena posed with her baby and described having received modeling invitations from *Penthouse* and *Playboy*, though these were not in writing. The pictures in the paper did little to suggest why the magazines would be that interested in the welfare mom, but there was no denying that little Crystal, Johnny's only grandchild, was adorable.

"Don't you think she looks like him?" Tanena beamed. "I would like nothing more than for Johnny Carson to see his grandchild."

In the spring of 1987 Johnny signed a new deal with NBC. He ended the suspense early, but reports indicated that the contract also had an escape clause that "calls for him to give six months notice if he intends to leave."

One agent, who booked comics on both Joan Rivers's show and "The Tonight Show" shook his head and said at the time, "Johnny isn't going to leave till Rivers does. He's not going to let them say that Joan forced him off the air."

He added that the two "camps" were completely different. "It's so relaxed at 'The Tonight Show.' It's a pleasure. But the Rivers people are in chaos! It's unbelievably tense."

He added that, of course, once a star opted for one show over the other, that was it. That person was persona non grata on the rival program.

But as Joan's ratings continued to scrape the bottom, the rumors buzzed that Rivers was going to get the ax. When Johnny signed his contract, it might have spelled the end for her, a sign that there was no hope of him retiring and her pulling her way out of the ratings basement.

The Fox people had promised their advertisers high ratings and Joan wasn't delivering. David Brenner said "she's getting desperate . . . it's the old drowning person theory . . . I guess she's getting scared . . . she's in a state of panic."

Since older viewers seemed to be turned off to her high-powered personality, she went increasingly for the yuppie and teen audience, surrounding herself with rock stars, wrestlers, and a smattering of glitzy starlets and hunky actors. But it was like having "Mom" sit in at the party—she was trying to be part of the in-crowd and she wasn't, though the woman was trying her damnedest.

On May 15, 1987, it was over.

Everybody knew that the ax had fallen—and when Joan faced her audience that night, she was like a tired politician conceding defeat on election night. The fans applauded with never-say-die enthusiasm. She shook her head, asking them to stop. She told them she couldn't talk about the situation (she and Fox had yet to work out the complications of settling her contract, and whether she might come back on a rotating basis).

"It's nobody's fault," she allowed. She said she'd been on TV for twenty-three years—"and I'll be on the air for another twenty-three years."

She continued her show, business as usual.

At 11:30, Johnny Carson began his show, business as usual. He did running gags about the Scandal of the Day, the continuing saga of deposed evangelists Jim and Tammy Bakker. Jim had lost his ministry after a sex tryst became known. "Don't worry about Tammy Bakker," Johnny said, trying to control a boyish grin. "She just got an offer from Fox Broadcasting . . ."

He stuffed his hands in his pockets and basked in twenty long seconds of laughs and applause.

As serene as a sunbather, he looked off at nothing in particular and added, "I've been saving that one for a long time . . ."

Softly, over the twelve seconds of applause and laughter, he murmured, "I'm sorry . . ."

Few were, and few were as controlled about it. Kay Gardella in her syndicated column reported that Joan's fall was "not surprising. Rivers's biggest fault is that she talks too much, says too little, and most of all doesn't listen to her guests . . . there is a lesson here. Johnny Carson, a real pro, makes it look so easy that people get the idea anyone can do it . . ."

Joan's show had begun with gassy effervescence, a non-stop helium high. Now the balloon had deflated. In fact it was such a pathetic sight, this damaged party balloon, that Johnny could only nudge it with his big toe.

A few days later, Johnny was once again joking around about the Bakker scandal. The TV evangelists were hoping to get a new show. "I can't be funnier than the Bakkers," he said. "I understand Tammy's already got a new catch phrase for her new show: 'Can we pray.'"

The audience giggled mildly.

"Jim and Tammy called Jerry Falwell to tell them they were starting their own talk show—and he hung up on them, so . . ."

Less giggles. Either nobody remembered that Joan had hung up on him, or nobody cared. Johnny let it lie.

Joan tried to let it lie, too, though she couldn't avoid the press. As usual, she was in the midst of concert commitments that wouldn't allow her the luxury of hiding.

She knew what was on the audience's mind when she strode out on stage at Caesars Palace in Vegas.

"First of all," she said, "you are looking at a woman who has finally been able to make Johnny Carson happy!"

She put on a smile for the *Las Vegas Review-Journal* and said, "After the last show I felt no depression. I was almost thrilled it was over."

But the smile didn't stay on for long. "I didn't ask to leave. I was fired . . . they raped me."

The men at Fox managed to grab back half of the money they'd promised her for the three-year contract. Of course, five million bucks wasn't bad for less than a year's work.

In the next months, with a succession of guest hosts, "The Late Show" ratings sagged lower. One of the forlorn Fox vice presidents, Kevin Wendle, waved a white flag: "It's crazy to try to compete with Johnny Carson in the talk area. He's the master. If Joan couldn't do it, no one can."

No one included David Brenner. When his year's contract with King World was over—it was over. "I put more into this show than I ever put into my own life," he moaned, "it was the hardest job I've ever done—just exhausting."

But Johnny Carson continued on—no sweat.

Johnny is in his sixties but plays tennis like a man half his age. Does stand-up with the enthusiasm of comics half his age. Tells gags that would be hip for someone half his age. Looks in better health and with a firmer body than guys half his age. Romances a woman half his age.

Rumors about Johnny's marriage plans intensified. Now that Carson had finished off Joan Rivers, he only had one woman on his mind. And, having signed a new contract that gave him more money ($7 million a year) and less work (three nights a week again, with fifteen weeks vacation), why not spend more time with that one woman—and make it legal?

The couple had been "engaged" since December of '86 and their relationship now had more than three years of mileage.

"Johnny wants to get married," insiders on the show insisted. "He may have been burned a few times, but he still believes in marriage. He just needs a little push."

Alexis Maas gave him a push.

"Marry me or we're finished," she told him. Johnny was momentarily stunned, but when she phoned her mother back in Pittsburgh, her parents supported her. They'd been waiting years to have Johnny for a son-in-law.

It all came together during a few heated weeks in June. Johnny and his lawyers huddled for a conference. This time, a prenuptial agreement would be worked out in advance, to make sure that Alexis would get money—but not scalp—should the marriage fail.

The next step was to get the ring. Worried that a visit to a jewelry shop might arouse the news hounds, Johnny asked a salesman from a Beverly Hills jewelry shop to come out to Malibu with gold rings to try on.

And finally, there was the wedding itself. Johnny was firm about one thing—he wasn't going to have a big, public ceremony with photographers buzzing around. Even if it meant that Alex's parents wouldn't be there. Even if it meant that "Tonight Show" pals like Ed and Doc wouldn't be there.

On the afternoon of June 20th, Johnny's brother Dick showed up at the Malibu house, along with Superior Court Judge William Hogaboom and Hogaboom's wife. They gathered out on the lawn, joined by a photographer hired for the occasion.

A slight breeze blew as Alexis Maas came out dressed in white, carrying a bouquet of roses and carnations. Johnny, wearing a dark blue suit, stood alongside her.

The Judge conducted the short ceremony, made even shorter when the couple advised him to cut a word out—they would promise to "love, honor," but not necessarily "obey" each other.

Alexis' father gave the bride away—by speaker phone set up on the lawn. "I'll take good care of your daughter," Johnny told him.

The couple flew to England for their now-annual visit to the tennis championships at Wimbledon. They saw Boris Becker, the two-time winner, upset in an early round—while distraught gossip columnists and reporters back home announced "Johnny is married"—nine days after the event. Johnny had successfully kept the news hushed up till he was out of the country. He had to keep the wedding secret from some of his closest friends, and risk some hurt feelings, but he hoped they would understand.

The news of Johnny's wedding did lead to some new speculation. Johnny was treated to a front page story in *The National Enquirer*, but this time the subject was kind of cute. The paper was wondering—would Johnny now decide to become a poppa again?

They quoted Alexis as saying, "I've been aching to have a child. I don't have many years to go before it will be too late for me to have a child, so this [marriage] is a dream come true."

The Carsons' dream honeymoon plans included a long stay at the Hotel du Cap in France, followed by a cruise of the Mediterranean on a private yacht. Then it would be time to settle down at Malibu. The house, once a lonely exile for a bachelor who had lost his Beverly Hills home in divorce, was a real home at last.

Everyone else around him seems to have settled down. Ed McMahon and his wife Victoria even have a child—a return to domesticity now that Ed's four children by his first wife are all grown. In taking care of adopted baby Katherine, Ed says, "I get home from taping 'The Tonight Show' at 7 P.M. and my wife tries to wait until I get home so that I can feed Katy. Now that's my joy in life—getting home to feed the baby."

The mellow McMahon is content with his starring duties on the syndicated "Star Search" series. He dines at Chasen's, a star, sitting at the table once kept in reserve for his idol, W. C. Fields.

Ed and Johnny have very different lives now, very different needs after twenty-five years on "The Tonight Show." They don't see each other that much after hours. Yet they'll pass twenty-five years on the show together—still wanting to do it for a nation still needing to watch. It's hard to imagine ever not wanting to watch Johnny.

Ed McMahon says, "The last time I say 'Heeeere's Johnny' it's going to be a traumatic moment for America."

Johnny means something special to everyone. Director Fred De Cordova put it this way: "He's somebody's son, somebody's husband, somebody's father. He combines them all."

Johnny always said that the millions he made really had nothing to do with his happiness. He told *Rolling Stone:* "Having not had it and then having had it all, I can say that . . . all that money gives you is the state of not having to worry about money. That's all it gives you. Nothing else. And along with money comes responsibility, you know, and how you handle it. . . .

"If you ask people what they want, they'll always say they want happiness . . . well, you know, it depends. Do you have a capacity for happiness? A lot of people don't have a capacity. I don't know how big my capacity is. It's not as big as a lot of people's, but I'm getting better at it all the time."

When Johnny came back to Norfolk High School, he offered some advice on working. "If you don't like it, stop doing it. Never continue in a job you don't enjoy." He talked about happiness and success. "I have very high ups and very low downs. I can all of a sudden be depressed, sometimes without knowing why. But on the whole I think I'm relatively happy."

He added: "If you're happy in what you're doing, you'll like yourself. And if you like yourself, you'll have inner peace. And if you have that, along with physical health, you will have had more success than you could possibly have imagined. I thank you all very much."

INDEX